THE CAT I NEVER NAMED

THE CAT
I NEVER
NAMED

A TRUE STORY OF LOVE, WAR, AND SURVIVAL

AMRA SABIC-EL-RAYESS

with LAURA L. SULLIVAN

BLOOMSBURY

NEW YORK   LONDON   OXFORD   NEW DELHI   SYDNEY

BLOOMSBURY YA
Bloomsbury Publishing Inc., part of Bloomsbury Publishing Plc
1385 Broadway, New York, NY 10018

BLOOMSBURY and the Diana logo are trademarks of Bloomsbury Publishing Plc

First published in the United States of America in September 2020
by Bloomsbury YA

This book is based on the author's personal experiences. In some cases, she has changed the
names and other identifying features of people, places, and events in order to protect the privacy
of individuals. This is because this is not a book about the individuals she has described,
but one about her own experiences and how they have shaped her life.

Bloomsbury books may be purchased for business or promotional use. For information on bulk purchases
please contact Macmillan Corporate and Premium Sales Department at specialmarkets@macmillan.com

Library of Congress Cataloging-in-Publication Data
available upon request
ISBN 978-1-5476-0453-1 (hardcover) • ISBN 978-1-5476-0455-5 (e-book)

Book design by Jeanette Levy
Typeset by Westchester Publishing Services
Printed and bound in the U.S.A. by Berryville Graphics Inc., Berryville, Virginia
6 8 10 9 7

All papers used by Bloomsbury Publishing Plc are natural, recyclable products
made from wood grown in well-managed forests. The manufacturing processes
conform to the environmental regulations of the country of origin.

To find out more about our authors and books visit
www.bloomsbury.com and sign up for our newsletters.

To my family, Dinah, Jannah, and Tamer,
who healed me with their love . . .

The war didn't spring on me all at once.
Instead, like a cat, it stalked me quietly.
There might have been a rustle of leaves, a glint of golden eye.
But like a mouse, I didn't believe it was there until it pounced.

CONTENTS

CROATIA

Bihać

BOSNIA AND
HERZEGOVINA

SERBIA

CROATIA

SARAJEVO

MONTENEGRO

Adriatic Sea

CROATIA

THE CAT I NEVER NAMED

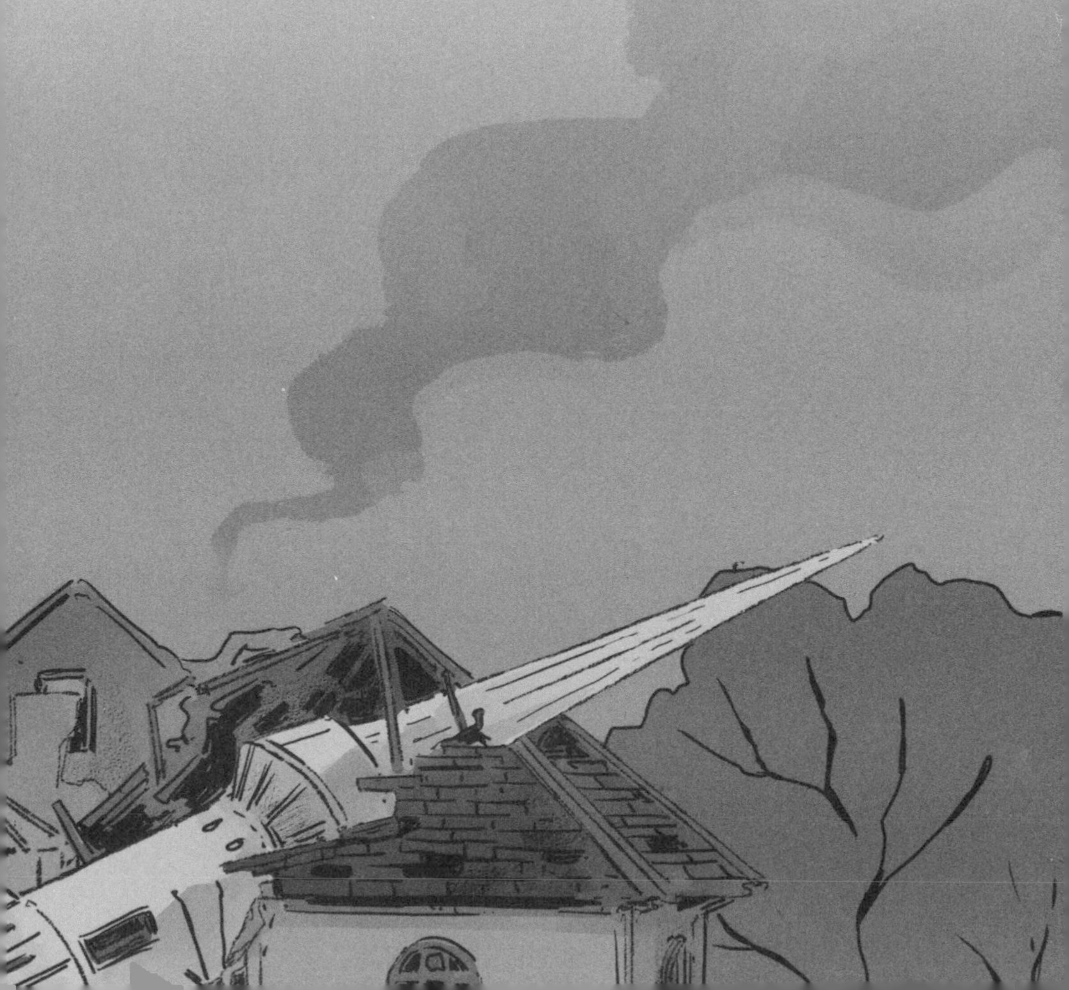

CHAPTER 1

Math, puzzles, logic, ciphers . . . my brain is still whirling from the battery of tests as I ride the train from Belgrade, Serbia, back home to Bihać, Bosnia. The tracks push westward, the setting sun gilding the hillsides. Families, mothers, children patter and laugh, scold and squeal, in a comfortable cacophony that lets me almost doze off. I'm sleepy from a long day of tests, and I'll be lucky to get home by one a.m.

A few stops later, the families get off, soldiers get on, and I realize with a sinking feeling that I'll be lucky to get home at all.

I lower my eyes at once as men stomp down the aisles. I don't have to look to know they are Četniks, the most vehement Serbian nationalists. They are dressed in black with weird tall hats. The men have beards, wild hair, and hate in their eyes for anyone who's not Serb.

I saw them all over the streets of Belgrade, sneering and shouting at anyone they thought might be Muslim, quoting Slobodan Milošević's hateful speeches. *Aren't you afraid?* I'd asked my cousin Žana. *It's not a big deal*, she replied with an indifferent shrug. *People feel like they can just say anything these days.*

But when these soldiers invade my train, I fear that they'll have far more than words for this lone teenage Muslim girl.

Within seconds the stench of them fills the train car. It is aggressively masculine and rank: sweat, liquor, grease, and gunpowder. They jangle like marchers in a macabre parade as their belts and bandoliers full of ammunition clang.

"Did you hear the way he begged for his life?" one barks.

"The Croatians, they are not real men," their commander says.

"But their women!" the first one leers. "Black-eyed angels . . ."

"Nothing to compare with Balije women, though," a soldier says. "Balije" is an insulting word for Muslims. "I've heard they are like rabbits, eager and soft."

The commander cuffs him on the head, and he reels drunkenly. "You don't fall in love with them, you idiot. You put Serb seed in their bellies." He grabs the soldier by the collar. "You wipe them out, generation by generation. You dilute their unclean blood. You honor them with half-Serb babies, and one day they will be gone from this earth, and only Serbs will remain."

Another Četnik chuckles menacingly. "I don't think they realize they're being honored. One I had screamed so loud . . ."

Their conversation is lost as they head to the back of the train.

I tuck up my knees, curling myself as small as possible as I fix my eyes out the window. I want to run off this train, but would that be any better? I'm still in a Serb-controlled region. At least now I'm heading home. I can't decide, and then it is too late. The train is moving again.

My parents are such fools, I rage inwardly. Anger feels better than the stark terror that is my only alternative. But I can't keep it up. My parents are naive—good, hopeful, innocent. They fervently believe that humankind is fundamentally good. To them, wars are mistakes, violence just a blip on the road to universal humanity. Sure, it has happened before, but they believe in their inmost hearts that any day now the world will come to its senses and be the peaceful, philosophical, intelligent place it was meant to be. They are sure the world can care for their children. They believe that education is the key to creating that utopia.

To that end, I recently took a bunch of tests in my hometown—math, logic, word puzzles, general knowledge. The results surprised

4

even me. I have a friend whose mother works in the Bureau of Statistics. *Who is this Amra girl?* the mother asked her. *She got one hundred percent on some of these tests. No one has done that in her generation!*

I was proud, but my parents were giddy. *You can do anything, Amra,* they told me. *Just follow through, never give up on your education, no matter what happens. It is the most important thing.*

That's why they put me on a train to Belgrade, in the heart of Serbia. It was the only place to take the next and highest level of tests.

It was also in a place where the majority of citizens would hate me if only they knew what I was.

Already the Serbs are in an outright war with the Croatians. Croatians want independence; Serbs want land and control. I don't know if the Serbs actually hate the Croatians. Soon the Serbs will be coming for Bosnia—and there is no doubt at all how the Serbs feel about Bosnian Muslims, Bosniaks. They hate us, they think we are subhuman. Months ago, their leader, Radovan Karadžić, already threatened we would be eradicated. In a speech in Parliament he said we were going to hell if Bosnia leaves Serb-dominated Yugoslavia. If these soldiers have done such horrific things in Croatia, what will they do in Bosnia?

Once, a dictator kept the country together. Now, Yugoslavia is falling apart.

My only protection today is that these Četniks don't know I'm Muslim. These men on the train are part of our army, the official Yugoslav National Army that was once supposed to protect all of our multi-ethnic nation—Muslims, Serbs, and Croats alike. But these men are all Serbs. Some still wear the official YNA uniform, though most of them have switched to Četnik dress and insignias. They have officially declared that they are the army of the Serbs, not the army of Yugoslavia. Henceforth, Yugoslavia will only be for their kind.

I stare too long, and one of them catches my eye. Instantly I spin frontward, looking hard at the seatback, hoping against hope that a train official or ticket taker will come into our car now. But even they don't want to deal with drunken soldiers. I'm utterly alone as one of the men rises unsteadily to his feet, takes a swig from an amber bottle, and staggers my way.

When he leans over my seat I smell the alcoholic, unwashed stench of him. His long beard is matted and greasy.

"Hello, young Srpkinjo," he says. *Young Serb woman*. A tiny part of me relaxes. He uses a friendly, familiar greeting. He thinks I'm Serb, like him.

And how could he tell? Muslim women here don't wear hijabs. We don't speak Arabic or recite the Qu'ran. We are Muslims of birth, of ethnicity, not religion, really. I have brown hair, fair skin, brown eyes. I probably do look like this Četnik's sister.

What if I pointed that out to him? If I said, if you can't tell the difference, maybe there is no difference. Maybe we're all just people. Would he change? Would he go home and preach that change to his family?

Of course I don't dare. Of course he would just say I am a sneaky, lying Muslim out to trick him and steal his country. And once he knew I wasn't one of his own people, he would consider my body his to do with as he chose.

I try to look polite and shy instead of quaking and terrified. A well-brought-up Serb girl wouldn't speak to a soldier alone on a train.

"Want a drink, sweetheart? It's a chilly night." He thrusts the bottle at me. Some of it splashes on my thigh. Its acrid smell curls in my nostrils.

I put on as much of a Belgrade accent as I can and say, "No thank you." I even try to smile.

"You shouldn't travel alone, you know," he says, looking honestly concerned. "The country is a mess. There are dangerous men around. But don't worry, you have the Četniks to protect you!"

He sways down the aisle back to his seat, and I hear them talking about how easy it will be to drive the Croats from their homes.

"Where there is one Serb, there it is Serbia!" they shout. "Srbija do Tokija!" *Serbia to Tokyo.* That phrase had innocent origins when the Serbs won a big soccer match in Tokyo. But they've come to use it as a nationalist slogan, proclaiming their desire to dominate the world.

They are traveling my route. They will pass through my hometown.

But they will not stop there. My home is near the Bosnian-Croatian border. If the stories I've heard are true, these soldiers or others like them will travel on, just across the border.

My city has been safe. So far. If I can just get to the Bihać station I'll be fine. My city is cosmopolitan, peaceful. Muslims, Croats, and Serbs have lived in harmony there for generations. Home is safe. That's what every child knows in their bones, right? Even a sixteen-year-old child like me.

Just get home, I chant to myself. Just get out at your stop and this will all be over.

If I miss my stop, the next one is in Croatia. If I miss my stop, I am in a war.

There are hours to go, and it is so late already. After a while, even the soldiers fall silent and still, lulled by the hypnotic motion of the train, the darkness, the drink. I force my eyes as wide-open as I can, making myself stay awake. But my eyes get glassy and dry, and I blink . . . and blink again, slowly, heavily . . .

Rough hands are on me, hands over my mouth, crushing me, blocking my air. They don't care if I die. If I'm dead, I'll stop struggling, which will make what they plan to do to me next easier for them. Easier, but less fun. They want me to cry. They want me to struggle and scream. I feel hands on my thighs, tugging at my pants. I can smell the rank sweat of them, feel their weight pinning me, forcing my legs open . . .

7

I wake, jolted as the train stops.

I'm on the train, unmolested. It was a dream.

A nightmare.

Did I miss my stop? Did I dream one hell only to wake to another one?

I grab my belongings and run down the aisle. Only when I see the friendly red sign welcoming me to Bihać do I feel relief. And then I start to cry.

I'm dry-eyed, though, when my father comes around the corner to pick me up. I can't tell him what could have happened to me. He'd blame himself for putting me in danger.

"Thanks for coming to get me, Tata," I say as he enfolds me in a hug.

"Did you do well on your tests?" he asks.

"I think so, Tata," I say as, hand in hand, we leave the station.

But I realize then that tests don't matter. No matter how well I did, those tests were ultimately meaningless.

Only one kind of test matters now. The test of survival.

CHAPTER 2

I don't know how, but I fall asleep the second my head touches my pillow.

I wake with a smile on my face. Today isn't a day for worry or fear. Today is my birthday.

Sort of.

In any case, today is my birthday party, my first grown-up party where I get to play hostess to my friends. My first slumber party, where we can giggle and gossip and stay up late.

A day I can forcibly forget last night, and tomorrow—known horrors and unknown horrors.

I roll out of bed and throw open the curtains, then the glass door leading to the balcony. The first pinkish glow of morning touches my city. A breeze pushes the curtain against my cheek as I step outside. All is hushed, waiting, perfect. I will it to stay that way, if only for a single day. I need this day to be special.

My bedroom door crashes open. Boot-clad feet stomp inside. I whirl to see a huge, strong-looking man in uniform. The morning light casts a giant shadow behind him, making him look even bigger. It's a Četnik from the train! The war against Muslims has begun! My mind jumps to gunfire, carnage. Where are my parents? Dead! Everyone is dead, and now the Serbs are coming for me!

The soldier steps toward me. I cringe away from his advance. I'm powerless. He could do anything to me . . .

"Oh, sorry," he says in a sheepish voice. "I thought this was the bathroom."

He introduces himself as Muhamed. I realize he is one of the young Muslim soldiers Mama and Tata bring home like lost puppies, hiding them from their terrible fate and trying to send them to safety. My father must have smuggled him in while I slept. He looked so terrifying in the half-light, but I know he is just a scared boy in a borrowed uniform, a young soldier now in more danger from his own army than from any external force.

"That's okay," I tell him, my voice shaky. "The bathroom is the next door to the left." He stands there awkwardly, looking so nervous and out of place. Though I'm standing before this stranger in my pajamas, I feel like I need to try to put him at ease. "Did you sleep well?"

He smiles, a goofy grin that makes him look about thirteen. How can any country send boys like this to war? He could be one of my schoolmates in high school.

"I don't think I'll sleep well until I'm home in Srebrenica. Until I hug my father and taste my mother's mohunje again."

"String beans help you sleep?" I ask, thinking of the flat, yellow bean pods freckled with purple spots.

"Mohunje tastes like home. You know how it is. You forget it when you're gone, yet the second you set foot in your home you know the smell, right?"

I think of my mom's mohunje, the beans cooked slowly with meat until they almost meld into the meat and fat. They cook until they are tender, almost creamy. Muhamed is right. Rich, seasoned mohunje is one of the smells of home.

He rubs his tired eyes, and I notice that his eyes seem much older than the rest of him. They've seen things. Terrible things.

"I never wanted to be a soldier," he says. "I only ever wanted to work in the spa. Have you been there?" Srebrenica is famous for its spa with supposedly healing waters. "It is in the mountains, and little streams trickle through the rocks, and the air smells like pines, and . . ." For a moment I think he's going to cry, and I want to hug him, but I just listen.

"When my mandatory year of service is over I was going to go straight back home. My mother said, just tell yourself that you're doing good deeds for your country. But they treated me like something you'd step on in the gutter. And then they sent me to . . . to . . ." He gulps hard. "It was a Croatian city. Sure, I'm Muslim, but we were all the same country just a few months ago. Why are we even fighting them? But they sent my unit to a little Croatian town I'd never heard of, and . . ."

He's crying now, but I don't think he realizes it. The tears just fall, one after the other, landing on the army jacket he still wears.

"They . . . we . . . the army dragged people out into the streets. The men were taken one place, the women to another. I had to do it! They would have shot me as a deserter! There was an old woman, she looked like my grandmother. She didn't fight. She just looked me in the eyes and asked, 'Why?' And I couldn't answer her. I had no answer. No one else was looking so I just let her go, and she ran into the forest. I went into her house, and I just stayed there until everything was quiet.

"I didn't help them." He looks at me like he's begging me, a teenage girl, a stranger, for forgiveness. "I just hid. When I rejoined my unit, they laughed at me, teased me, said I must have kept a house full of Croatian teenage girls to myself to have fun with, why didn't I share. Then my unit rode away in a convoy to the Željava air base. The next day they were sending us to another Croatian town."

His voice cracks as he goes on. "I couldn't do it. I couldn't face that again. It's inhuman! So I ran into the mountains. I didn't know where to go, what to do. I just had to get away."

"And you found Tetak Ale and Tetka Fatma," I say gently, finishing the story when he can no longer speak for the sorrow. "And my uncle and aunt saved you, as they saved other Muslim soldiers, and sent you to us."

Muhamed's voice drops to a whisper. "I heard the soldiers talking. They say the Muslims are next. One of them asked his commander, *What about the Muslim soldiers?* He said, *Don't worry, they'll be taken care of, like the rest of the Muslims, once we hit Bosnia.* It's coming. Something terrible is coming!"

I go up to him now and put a tentative hand on his shoulder. "Don't worry. My parents will help you. We'll get you civilian clothes, a train or bus ticket. You'll taste your mother's mohunje again."

My assurance feels like a lie. If he goes home, he'll be on the same train I rode last night, heading east. Right now Bosnia is a relatively safe pocket. War hasn't been declared . . . yet. But with Serb soldiers traveling back and forth through our land from Serbia to Croatia, how can a deserter travel the same route? But he's scared, and I have to give him some hope.

He wipes his eyes on the sleeve of his jacket and gives me a weak smile. "Thank you," he says. "You, and your parents, for being lights in the nightmare of my life."

Then he slips away, and a moment later I hear the shower running. To my surprise I hear him start to sing. He has a lovely voice, but the song is so sad, an old folk song about never seeing your true love again, about ripe fruit rotting on the tree, eaten by no one.

There is no good alternative for Muslims in the Yugoslav National Army now. Either they will be ordered to fight other Muslims or they will be killed themselves. We didn't realize it at first, but the army has been gradually weeding out Muslims for the past year.

I knew one of the men who had been killed. Roman was one of my mother's students, a young man so clever he became one of our country's top pilots. Not long ago, his plane crashed into a mountainside. Pilot error, they said. Maybe even suicide. But we all know better.

Several other young pilots—all Muslim—died the same way. No trained pilot would misread his instruments, make such a rookie mistake. We are sure his plane was tampered with. It wasn't an accident. It was murder.

My heartbeat has returned to normal, and I try to push the fear away for a little while longer. I make myself smile at the day to come, but the smile hurts my face. I can't help but think this might be the last day with any shred of real happiness. War is creeping closer every day. Hate is spreading. So far my city has been spared. But for how long?

Carpe diem, they say in Latin. *Seize the day.* I only want one. Just one day.

I close my door against further intrusion and get dressed. I don't have a lot of pretty, feminine clothes, but on my trip to Belgrade my cousin Žana gave me a green skirt with a little flip at the bottom, and tights that look like something an artist would wear—or create. They are brilliantly colored in red, yellow, and orange against a vivid green background. As I smooth them over my legs I think about the nice comments I'll receive later from my friends. I get a lot of compliments on my grades, but not many on my clothes. This will be a nice change, a birthday treat to myself. I smooth my hair and hurry downstairs.

Soon my mother and my brother Dino join me in the kitchen for breakfast. The radio on the counter drones the news in a tedious way that is easy to ignore, like the voice of an uncle who never stops talking but never says anything interesting. I don't want to hear the bad news it is conveying. Instead, I focus on the simple pleasure of breakfast and try to distract myself with a little silliness.

"Mama, look how sad my bread is." I angle the plate so she can see its bare surface. "It needs a comrade."

She just arches her eyebrows and pretends not to understand.

"It wants plum jam," I clarify.

"But it does not need plum jam," she answers. "Here, have some honey instead."

Honey, honey, always honey, thanks to Tetka Fatma and Tetak Ale. My aunt and uncle have a bee farm in the countryside near the city. I think half my friends like me because they get so much honey when they visit my house. As for me, I prefer the sweet-tart thrill of plum jam. It tastes like summer.

I let the honey drip onto the bread, and the sun streaming into the kitchen turns it into molten gold. I pretend I am King Midas, gilding everything I touch.

Tata comes into the kitchen, smoothing back his silvery hair. "Good morning, half-birthday girl!" He kisses me on the top of the head. "Zuhra will have finished your cake by midmorning. Shall we walk out together to pick it up? I just have to stop at the train station and do a few other errands first." He gives a significant glance toward the stairs, where Muhamed is still showering. "I have to buy a ticket for him, a late-night ticket when there won't be many people around to notice him. With luck, our friend will be home safe in Srebrenica within twenty-four hours." The sound of a folk tune drifts down the stairs. "I like his singing."

"Not as much as his family likes it," my mother says. "And every hour he stays increases the danger."

A deserter could be imprisoned or even shot. My parents are brave to help him and the other Muslim soldiers. We'd be in deep trouble for helping Muhamed. But thinking about how easily they let me venture into enemy territory alone, I wonder how much they understand the dangers. Sometimes I think they live in an old-fashioned world, only seeing the best in people. A world of kindness and hope. Last night my eyes were opened. Their world is not the real world. I think I see what is coming better than my parents do.

No, no, I'm not thinking about that. Not today. Please, let me just have today.

I'm always happy to get out in my city. I love the sights, the smells, the happy people. Quickly, I gulp down my sticky bread. Tata gathers his things, while Mama turns the radio knob. As the announcer fades to a whisper, I catch the words "refugees fleeing after a series of bo—" Then the radio clicks off entirely. The young soldier comes down the stairs, and I wonder how I was ever afraid of that gangling boy. He can't be more than nineteen. Like a puppy, his feet seem too big for his body. He moves self-consciously, as if he's afraid of tripping over them. Then I realize it's not his feet that are too big, but his shoes. He's wearing Tata's second-best pair.

Then I look up at the rest of what he is wearing.

I know those pants, honey-brown corduroy, baggy at one knee. I know that shirt, the cuffs unstitched to add an extra inch to accommodate long arms. With a sharp pang I realize these are my brother's clothes. I wear many of them myself, treasuring them despite their ill fit. Now these will leave today and I will never see them again. One more piece of him will be gone forever.

I tell myself Amar would be glad that his old clothes are being used to help save a Muslim soldier.

The young man isn't singing now. His lips are pressed in a thin line to keep them from quivering.

"Don't worry," my father says. "We will get you home to Srebrenica."

Unspoken was the common thought—will his home be safe? I don't know if any place in Bosnia will be safe much longer. At least he will be with people who love him.

Mama serves Muhamed breakfast, and Tata and I leave.

Like an old-fashioned gentleman, Tata offers me his arm, and we step out into the city of Bihać in the Republic of Bosnia and Herze-govina, which recently proclaimed its independence from the cobbled-together nation of Yugoslavia.

Soon we come to the Blue Bridge across the river Una. On each bank is a row of linden trees, very ancient with gnarled trunks, but strong and upright like proud old men. Soon these trees will be in flower, their delicate, buttery blossoms spreading such sweetness that bees will come from miles around. When I was younger, I thought they came all the way from Fatma and Ale's bee farm. Whenever I passed beneath the buzzing linden trees, I would whisper messages for them to deliver to my favorite aunt and uncle.

Sun filters through the boughs in stripes of dark and light, dancing on our skin, our clothes. My bright tights look like a garden, and I see some people look at them admiringly. As we walk in the dappled shade of the lindens, we say hello to our neighbors, known and unknown. Most faces are at least familiar. Everyone feels like a friend on this beautiful day. The fright of dawn seems far behind me.

Halfway across the bridge, though, I notice a change in the faces of the people we meet. They look anxious, tense, even sad. A woman I know vaguely from the market passes with a basket of onions, pressing a corner of her scarf to her eyes. I give Tata a questioning glance, but his eyes are fixed ahead. I am tall, but he is taller, and he can see over the pedestrians to the far bank.

"Tata, what is it?" I ask. The sky is still clear and blue, the Una still flows below us with its liquid song, little Communist cars chug by . . . but somehow the flavor of the day has changed.

A neighbor stops Tata, and they confer in hushed voices. "You should go home," the man says. "There's nothing you can do here."

"There is always something a person can do," Tata replies.

Our neighbor claps him on the shoulder, pats me on the head, urges us to be careful, and continues away from the city center. We press forward. It is a traditional shopping day, and I expect the city center to be crowded with people. The stores might hold less and less lately, but people still come looking. It is crowded, but as we go deeper into the city's heart I move closer to Tata's side. Because these aren't like the people I know.

We are at the Paviljon, the most famous restaurant in Bihać. As usual, people sit on the terrace in the shade of hundred-year-old trees, sipping coffee, enjoying the temperate weather. They look like they don't have a care in the world.

Near them, among them, mingling wherever there is space, is another crowd entirely. It looks like two completely different Hollywood sets got mixed up on the same sound stage.

One couple stands out for me first because they are wearing so many clothes. The heat is not yet merciless, but I am warm in my lightweight skirt and shirt. The man looks bulky in two shirts, one buttoned over the other. I can see a white collar peeking out from beneath a blue one. Over this he wears a suit jacket, with a heavier coat slung over his arm. The woman with him is also dressed in layers, two shirts and a sweater, the sleeves pushed past her elbows. They both wear boots that are much too heavy for their clothes: working boots. They are spattered with mud to the knees.

Strange, I think, and almost dismiss them as an oddity in the crowd. Then I see more like them.

Many, many more.

"Tata, who are they?"

This time he answers me. "They are refugees, fleeing from Serb violence against their towns. They are Bosniaks, Muslims. They are our people."

It has started, then. "Are we at war?"

"Some think we were at war the moment Bosnia declared its independence. Has there been a declaration now? I don't know. I thought . . .

I hoped there would be a solution. I hoped our leaders would find a compromise. After so many centuries, have we learned nothing?"

He takes my hand, and I see that there are tears in his eyes. My father weeps easily. Mama, practical and dry-eyed, teases him for it. But for Tata, every emotion is passionate and deep, and joy brings tears as easily as sorrow. Sometimes if he comes upon me walking with my friends he'll embarrass me by hugging me and shedding tears for no particular reason other than what he calls the miracle of our existence. He cries at weddings, and at family gatherings, and when a sparrow crashes into our window. His feelings are like clouds, and when they become too heavy for him, they rain down on the world.

There are so many refugees. They carry bags, and carts filled with a strange assortment of household goods. I see a woman in a lovely dress, wrinkled and mud-spattered, pulling a small handcart containing, of all things, an iron and a hair dryer.

"When the shelling started, they had to grab whatever they could and leave right away," Tata says when he sees where I'm looking.

They look so lost, these people. They search the buildings, the faces, for some sign of hope. The citizens of Bihać mostly continue with their shopping.

These people need help. "What can we do, Tata?" Because we always help people. Without question, without reward, we help.

"I don't know where to start," my father says, looking overwhelmed. "But we have to start somewhere."

He goes up to the closest refugees, a couple with two small children, and gives them the traditional Bosnian greeting, "Dobro jutro, kako ste?" *Good morning, how are you?* Then without saying anything else he presses some money into the mother's hands.

From person to person we go, Tata handing out bills from his meager stash until they are almost gone. To the last person he gives the handful of jangling coins from his pocket.

"A drop in the ocean," Tata says. "But many drops can turn a tide. I wish I could do more." I know that giving up that money means giving something up ourselves. I won't get a new pair of red Levi's I've been asking for. Dino won't get a new basketball.

Near us, I see a middle-aged woman stop in the middle of the sidewalk. Her legs are shaking slightly, and she has a peculiar unfocused stare that I recognize: she's about to faint. I catch her just in time, helping her gently to her knees. As she falls, the satchel she's carrying spills open and a framed photograph falls out, cracking on the pavement. With a cry she snatches up the photo and clutches it to her chest, hugging it like a person, rocking back and forth. Over her arms I can see a portrait of two men who look very much alike, with ruddy cheeks and cheerful smiles, obviously father and son.

Other refugees and locals gather around her, trying to help, not knowing what is wrong.

"Mehmed!" Someone in the crowd is calling my father's name. From my crouch beside the distraught woman I see a man about my father's age, smaller, with the demeanor of a suffering saint and piercing blue eyes.

"Omer!" my father bellows, and they are hugging.

One look at the mismatched clothes, the heavy bag he carries, and the careworn, dusty woman behind him tells their story, or some of it. These people, Tata's friends, are refugees too.

"We were traveling with this woman," Omer explains. "Her husband and son told her to run into the forest, and they would meet her later. But they never showed up. We made her come with us. She would have stayed there forever, waiting, but it was too dangerous. They were searching the forest."

"When did this happen?" my father asks.

"Two, no, three days ago," the woman behind Omer answers wearily, pushing her dark hair out of her eyes. "They came at dawn with tanks, guns. We had some warning and escaped, but other survivors said that they were . . ." She drops her voice so the woman on the ground can't hear. "They were shooting the men, and taking the women, the young women, away on buses, to . . ." She looks at me and falls silent.

"This is Omer and Erza. Omer and I were in school together." He looks at his friend and his wife. "They will be staying with us," he adds firmly. "For as long as they like. Amra, will you go now and pick up your cake? Then meet us back here, at the Paviljon."

I want to stay, to help, to hear what comes next, what happened to the young girls in the buses.

I want to know—and I don't want to know.

I tell Omer and Erza goodbye and head to Cousin Zuhra's bakery on the other side of town.

Like any teenager, I believed that I had suffered deeply. Jam deprivation, the cruel teasing of some of the Serb kids, the blatant unfairness of teachers . . . In my mind, these were profound tragedies that filled me with a poetic kind of melancholy for full minutes at a time. To have mountains of homework on a balmy evening when daylight stretched so late and I could hear my friends outside was the epitome of suffering. And the deepest sorrow, the one so profoundly etched on my soul it is almost buried, my older brother's death.

But when I look at these refugees, I know in my heart that my pains were mere splinters in the polished smoothness of my life. I never knew anything like this. Hollow despair shows in their faces. I pass a family: parents, a grandmother, four children. No, only three children, all younger than I am, clinging to their parents' clothes. The mother pushes a baby carriage, but I can see now that it is filled with a blanket, a tarp, jars of pickled vegetables. The mother's knuckles are white where she clutches the carriage handle.

I feel my eyes get hot, and I blink rapidly. No, Amra, I tell myself sternly. They took the carriage because it is the only thing with wheels. Nothing bad happened to the baby.

The news reports come back to me, things it was easy to overlook for so long because they were adult affairs, paling in comparison to my own concerns. There is always bad news, right? Announcers don't look into the camera and tell us cheerfully that many children are happy and healthy, that cities are safe and people well fed. No, they tell us that some city was bombed, some politician assassinated. And if by chance people are at peace, they speak of hurricanes and mudslides, of fires and famine. The news is never good news.

But this is home. Somehow, I never truly associated news of the breakup of Yugoslavia with my peaceful city.

Until today.

The press of people thins, and I walk lost in thought. I hear a low rumble and look up at the piercingly blue sky. Thunder? Is even the weather conspiring to take away my one good day?

Resolutely, I turn my thoughts to cake. A little bell tinkles as I push open the bakery door. Inside I smell all things delightful: chocolate, hazelnuts, burned sugar, vanilla. For just a moment, the day's troubles are gone, banished by delectable scents.

While I wait for my cousin I look at the treats behind the counter, cookies and fruit tarts, little fingers of sponge cake soaked in syrup, tall white cakes that look like they are made entirely of fluff. Children with their parents look smug as they buy pastries, cramming them greedily in their mouths even before they are paid for.

But they all stop dead when they see the magnificent creation my cousin brings out for me.

Seven layers of chocolate, each tier filed with a different cream or texture. The entire cake is enrobed in dark, glistening chocolate, sprinkled with ground pistachios and glittering edible silver balls.

"Mommy, I need that cake!" a chubby little boy cries as my smiling cousin presents me, and only me, with the most beautiful and delicious cake in the world. When the customers' eyes have had their fill she boxes it carefully and puts it in a sturdy bag with handles.

"You see it as a free cake," Zuhra whispers to me as she hands it to me. "But really, it is free advertising for me. I bet half the people in here will order one now."

I feel the eyes all on me as I walk proudly out, and she's right; even before the door closes behind me I hear at least three people put in orders for one for themselves.

Then I hear one of the women say, "I heard the deliveries have been getting stopped. This might be the last special chocolate cake any of us ever have."

Part of me wants to give up. Nothing can salvage this day, not even Zuhra's cake. Every moment is tainted by the coming storm.

But if this is the last treat of my life, I mean to enjoy it. I can almost taste the cake already as I walk down the street back toward the Paviljon. It is so bright and blue outside, birds are singing. A butterfly abandons the potted peonies it has been feeding on to flit past my colorful tights. It must think I'm a walking flower. The heavens have been kind to me. They have given me one last perfect day.

Then the thunder rumbles again, much closer than before.

I see a monster rolling toward me.

A row of monsters.

I've seen tanks before, but never so close. They are huge, dwarfing the cars that scramble to get out of their way. They never slow, not even when an old woman with a cane stumbles to one knee. Some people rush forward and pull her to safety. The line of tanks rumbles mercilessly on.

Even scarier are the men who ride them.

Dressed all in dark military green, they look bigger than normal men, and they're covered in weapons. Guns, knives, things I don't even recognize. Maybe they are grenades? The soldiers look like the huge shaggy Šarplaninac dogs that guard herds from wolves and bears.

It is the Yugoslav National Army. For weeks, after Bosnia's citizens voted in a referendum to leave Yugoslavia, the politicians on the radio have been reassuring us that YNA is here to protect all of Yugoslavia from its enemies until Bosnia transitions into independence.

Then why are they crushing our peaceful streets beneath their tank treads?

The tanks are a tight fit, and the treads veer up the curb and onto the sidewalk. I give a little scream when the lead tank crushes a flowerpot full of peonies just like the one my visiting butterfly came from. The streets here are narrow, and there is barely any room for people on each side of the grinding treads.

Hypnotized, I wait too long. I want to run, but some strange instinct that is both terror and pride keeps me from flight. I won't give these men the satisfaction of seeing me afraid.

The first tank comes close, and I shift my precious cake behind me. The day has grown dark somehow.

Those soldiers, those arrogant, confident, leering, loud soldiers tower above me. Armed with weapons and unshakable confidence, they rake me with their eyes in a way that makes my skin crawl. They are all shouting, and at first I can't pick out any of their words, just a deafening cacophony. Then I hear the whistles, the catcalls, and all their attention seems to focus on me. I realize everyone else has fled or ducked into a shop.

"Lift up your skirt for us! Give a soldier a treat!" Unlike the Četniks, these soldiers know I'm Muslim.

They make me feel naked, dirty. But I stand tall and keep my eyes fixed on some imaginary middle distance, not looking at them but refusing to look away. They are the dirty ones, I tell myself. They are the ones showing their naked souls for the pitiful, wretched, filthy things they are. Why should I feel ashamed?

They shout other things, much worse things. They tell me the things they want to do to me, tell me how much I'd like it. How many could I take at once, they ask with guffaws. Open your mouth, they tell me, let me see if it will fit.

They want a reaction from me—anything, anger or laughter will do. Tears would be even better. But my composure infuriates them, and they turn to insults.

"You should be flattered that we want to have you," one shouts.

Their words are like hands, groping me. I hear a ringing in my ears, a sure sign that my blood pressure is dropping. I won't let myself faint in front of these monsters. I won't give them the satisfaction.

Holding my head high (and the precious cake on the far side of the tanks) I march past them, tall and proud and aloof. You don't exist, I think to them. Not today. Today is my day. I'll be afraid of you tomorrow.

I try to think of the brightest, happiest thoughts: the taste of decadent Sacher torte. The sleepover tonight with my three closest friends. The cheerfulness of my tights.

But I can't hold on to it. The soldiers are angry now that they can't get any response from me.

"Hey, what are those things on your legs? She's wearing soccer socks! Look at those ugly Muslim soccer player legs! Long green man's legs. Hey, Sušić! Can you score a goal?" Safet Sušić is Bosnia's most famous soccer player—and a Muslim.

They are like bully schoolboys, saying anything they hope will be hurtful. This morning I was so proud of these colorful tights. I felt like a painting come to life, like a beautiful, creative soul expressing myself to the world. Now, with a few words, these men have made my tights

24

ugly. They have looked at my body—my female, Muslim body—and made it theirs to ridicule, to ravage with their words.

As the last tank thunders past I hear one more insult. "Is it a boy or a girl? Ha! Are you selling yourself? Who would want an ugly Muslim like you?" He holds up his hand, his thumb and first two fingers extended. The three-fingered salute, the symbol of Serb nationalism. Symbol of the hatred of anything not Serb. Such as me.

Then he spits in the road in my direction, and I am left in the dust and fumes the tanks belch in their wake. The street is cracked and crumbled where they passed.

I know how it feels. My heart feels the same.

I held myself together while they could see me, but now my strength flies away. My knees tremble. I need to sit down or I'll collapse. I stagger the rest of the way to the Paviljon and crumple onto a crate full of cabbages that were just delivered around the side of the restaurant. My father is nowhere to be seen.

I close my eyes. All I want to see now is darkness. The world has become too terrible to look at. But even with my eyes squeezed shut I see the tanks. I see the refugees, bleeding and frightened and hollow-eyed. I see things that haven't yet come to pass: planes, fire, rubble, wailing, death . . .

Where has all the beauty of the world gone?

I open my eyes, looking for answers, at first seeing only the brick walls and concrete ground. And then my eyes catch movement. A small shape, all symmetry and softness, appears in my view. A cat emerges from behind one of the crates and sits, watching me, her tail lashing against the cobblestones.

"Go away," I say absently.

She doesn't. Instead she gives me one long, slow blink, settles her body into a compact bread-loaf shape with tucked-in paws, and stares at me until I have to look away.

But a moment later, I look back again.

I don't like animals, especially dogs. When I was very young, an uncle's huge dog lunged at me and scratched my face badly. I think it would have bitten my throat next if my father hadn't pulled it off me. The scars have faded, but the memory hasn't. Now I don't trust anything with teeth.

Teeth plus claws? Forget it.

Still, this cat is a pretty little thing. Most of her body is creamy white, but there is a calico patch over exactly half of her face. Another patch of swirling color decorates her back—mostly black and brown, with touches of orange-red. It looks like glowing embers in black coals, on a bank of the purest snow.

Her soft and quiet beauty gives me something to focus on. As I look at her, my pulse begins to calm. It becomes easier to breathe.

I close my eyes again, willing the memory of tanks to go away, forcing my breath to return to normal. I still feel on the verge of passing out. Then I feel a brush of plush against my calf. For a second I am startled out of my panic. The kitty is rubbing my leg with her soft cheek, and her touch is so reassuring, so affectionate—so normal in this world gone awry—that I forget I don't like cats and reach down to stroke her head.

In that moment our eyes meet. Hers are the warm orange-gold of autumn bonfires. In the back of my mind I still hear those soldiers' mocking voices, but in that briefest instant a sense of peace washes over me.

The next time I look up, my father is walking toward me.

I feel strong enough to stand and meet him. "Thank you," I tell the kitty, though for what I'm not quite sure. I leave without looking back.

CHAPTER 3

I run up to Tata, hugging him like he's been gone for years. Omer and Erza are with him. I take one of Erza's bags in my free hand, and together we head home.

"You have met my friends," Tata says later as we cross the bridge. "Now, who is your friend?"

For a moment I'm confused. Then I see Tata looking down at my feet. To my astonishment, the kitty is strolling at our side. When we stop, she sits like a prim schoolgirl, her tail curled around her body.

"Oh, that's nothing," I say. "That's just a cat."

I see a frown dart across Tata's brow, swift as a flying barn swallow. He crouches in front of the kitty, holding out a hand for her to sniff. She rests her pink nose against his knuckles, then in one sinuous movement rubs against his hand.

Tata stands, a bit stiffly. "I believe she thinks she is more than just a cat," he says. Then to Omer and Erza he says, "Come, our house isn't too far. Can you make it? I know you've been walking a long way. We will plan for the future. You must be tired and hungry."

The couple says nothing, but the kitty gives a loud meow, as if he were talking to her too. Tata laughs, and we walk down our street. Sometimes when I'm with Tata, I feel like I can never be unhappy again.

When we are close to home I see that I am still being followed. A sneaky spy on velvet feet trails us silently.

"Tata, the cat . . ."

Omer laughs. "Do you see the trouble that kindness brings? Your father was kind to us, and now we are following him home. You were kind to that cat, and now she is following you home too. Be careful! If you feed her once, she is yours for life."

Tata seems delighted. He pats her from nose to tail. Her purr is like the low rumble of a tank engine.

"Go away," I whisper halfheartedly. "We don't need a cat in our life." With danger so near, we don't need one more thing to worry about.

Tata hears, and says, "Perhaps it is like the bread and plum jam. We do not need a cat. But it may be that a cat would make life better?"

"I don't see how," I say.

More quietly, he says, "Maybe it would make her life better."

"She must have a family," I argue. "She should go be with them."

"Look at her paws," is all Tata will say.

I do. Though the rest of her is scrupulously clean, I can see mud caked between her toes. Just like the shoes of the refugees. And she is limping, just a bit, too proud to let it show.

Suddenly her story is as clear as if her meows and purrs were words. She came with a refugee family. She walked all the way from some battered and terror-stricken town, following the people she loved.

But now she is alone.

Does she feel like I felt on the train? As if the whole world had turned against her and there was no chance of safety?

My heart melts, and I don't think so much of her teeth and claws. Only of her hopeful bonfire eyes.

"You can come if you like," I tell her. Then, because it is only fair to warn her, I add, "But I don't know what Mama will think!"

Mama takes one look at Omer and Erza and welcomes them in without question. I follow behind, but she bars the door with her foot when the cat tries to follow.

"I won't have a maci in the house," she says. "Maci" is the Bosnian word for cat.

"But she's lost. She's alone."

Mama doesn't weaken. "Animals belong in a barn, not a house. She would make messes, scratch the furniture, leave hair everywhere." Mama, a history and geography teacher, is deeply caring and compassionate. But she is also very practical. She likes neatness, order, routine, predictability.

"She needs us," I try again.

"We can't take on another responsibility, not with what is coming," she says, echoing exactly what I thought myself. But I changed my mind. Maybe she will too.

Omer and Erza are on the verge of collapse, however valiantly they're trying to stay strong, so Mama sweeps them up to the bedroom that will soon be officially vacated by Muhamed. I follow her to plead the cat's case, but she shoos me downstairs and tells me to put the water on for coffee. "Our guests are hungry."

At those words, my heart lights up. Mama has set a trap for herself. She simply can't help feeding people. Like a mother bird, she brings delicious food to any open mouth. If one of the poorer kids from her school starts to look a little skinny, she brings them home to fatten them up. She pretends all the while she only wants to talk about their grades, even as she feeds them bean stew or cabbage leaves stuffed with rice and beef. Dino's friends all know to drop by around dinnertime.

"The maci is very hungry too," I say. "Did you see her ribs?"

If her ribs are sticking out, her fluff hides it. But I see Mama's resolution falter. She gives a little huff and says, "There's some leftover ćevapi in the back of the refrigerator. It's probably gone bad by now, but you can give it to the maci if you want."

I hurry to make a little dish of the sausages, breaking them into tiny pieces. When I open the front door the maci is sitting patiently.

When I put the dish down in front of her, though, she only looks at it, then looks back at me.

"Aren't you hungry?" I ask. Maybe I was wrong. Maybe she's just a spoiled local cat. She followed us for reasons of her own, and she'll run away in a few minutes. "Or isn't Mama's ćevapi good enough for you?"

She just looks up at me, waiting. Then a thought strikes me. It seems so odd, but . . . is this little maci being polite?

"It's for you," I tell her as I push the dish nearer. "Go on."

She gives me one of her long, slow blinks and finally starts eating. The meat tidbits are gone in seconds.

"You were starving, you poor maci!" Since Mama is busy I don't even ask, I just get the cat some more, and a dish of water. I sit next to her, watching the way she gulps the food so neatly and quickly. When she is done she takes a sip of water, her pink tongue curling under cleverly to make a dipper. Then she settles down to wash her face and paws.

Only when she is clean does she rub against my hand. I caress the hollows in front of her alert ears, and she starts to purr.

Mama comes out a moment later to call me back inside.

"We do not own a cat," she reminds me.

"If you say so, Mama," I answer, but both Maci and I have our doubts about that.

While Mama talks to Omer and Erza, I make the coffee. The beans have already been ground to a fine powder. I heat the water to boiling in a long-necked copper pot called a džezva, then pour a little into a separate bowl. To the džezva I add the coffee and swirl it around, first counterclockwise, then clockwise, as I've seen Mama do countless times. Then I put it back on the stove and let it boil again until the concoction almost bubbles over the top. Three times I let it cool a bit and boil to a frenzied foam. Finally I add the reserved water, which miraculously makes the foam even thicker.

There, perfect Bosnian coffee!

I put the džezva on a round tray, along with glasses of cool water, a bowl of sugar cubes, and another bowl of sweets flavored with rosewater. Omer and Erza thank me, but the adults are talking too intently to pay me much attention. I snatch a piece of rosewater candy and occupy myself while I wait for my guests to arrive.

Ours is a house of sunlight. Roomy and bright, with two stories, it is my parents' dream home. For years, before and after the birth of their children, they scrimped and saved to build it. Now I don't know if we are rich or poor. We have one of the nicest houses of all my friends, but we never have enough money for new clothes or shoes. We always have food on the table—and for any neighbors who stop by—but we are the only family I know that still has an old black-and-white TV.

As I wait for my party, I feel like I'm living in a house of glass. There are windows everywhere. Every room, including my bedroom, has tall glass doors opening onto a balcony. No matter where I go, Maci is at a window, begging to come in.

No, I can't call what she does begging. She never makes a nuisance of herself. At most she will give one loud meow to attract my attention. Then she will put a paw on the glass and pat it as gently as a mother might pat her baby's cheek. When she is sure I'm aware of her, she'll watch me with her glowing eyes, waiting to be welcomed.

"Mama, please?" I ask over and over. The first few times she says no. The next dozen times she doesn't even bother to answer.

Dino goes to meet her and announces that she is "sweet, but a little boring." His friends' cats pounce on everything, or grab his hand with every tooth and claw, kicking their feet and rolling their eyes like demons. "Maci is too well behaved."

I study Mama's face as Dino says this. It is just about the best thing he could say about her.

"You better get ready," Mama says, putting an end to the conversation.

I look at the clock and realize she's right, so I run to my room to change my clothes and freshen up. I can't afford my own makeup, but today Mama let me borrow some of hers. I have the rainbow tower of makeup that Tetka Fatma brought her from Italy. There are two tiers of mini lipsticks in every color imaginable, even punk colors like yellow and green. I choose my favorite hue, a dark burgundy-red that looks nice with my dark hair, against my white teeth. I put on a little eyeliner, a touch of blush. Oh, there's the door. They're here! Flushed with excitement, all bad thoughts banished, I run downstairs. I'm sixteen. Life is about having fun, right?

What I see: three girls, my best friends, giggling as they dance around the dining table, setting out plates and napkins for my birthday lunch.

What someone else might see: A Muslim girl. A Serb girl. A half-Jewish girl.

Those distinctions have never mattered to me, or to my family. Bihać is a cosmopolitan city where everyone gets along.

"Not that I'd complain about any excuse for a party," my best friend, Olivera, says as she folds a napkin into a floppy swan shape. Our little radio plays a love song in the background. "But isn't your birthday in November?"

"I thought spring would be better for a party," I tell her casually.

That isn't quite the truth. Really, we couldn't afford a party in the autumn, but I'm not sure my friends would believe that. Our house is much nicer than Olivera's cramped apartment with its small windows. To look at our cheerfully furnished rooms set against huge windows and balconies, anyone would think we are wealthy. And we are better off than some. But we decided as a family that all our money should go into this happy home, and that means we scrimp other places. Olivera always has stylish clothes. I wear hand-me-downs. Self-consciously, I sit at the table and slide my ragged slippers underneath.

On my real birthday, I got new pretty pajamas and lots of hugs. Now, in May, we finally have a little extra money for party food.

"Well, if it's not your birthday, don't expect any presents!" Ivona says with a mischievous wink.

"Yeah, we're just in it for the food," Olivera says.

But Nura can't keep up the act. "I skipped lunch for three days to add my share to the pot, so if you're not going to give her the present I want my money back!" Olivera gives an unladylike snort and rolls her eyes at me behind Nura's back. Nura's a sweet girl, but some things just set her off.

"Trust Nura to turn an act of generosity into personal offense!" Olivera whispers into my ear as Ivona whips out a little package wrapped in sheets of the local newspaper we call *Krajina*.

"Is it a sandwich?" I ask with a smile. "A country cheese? Raw chicken?" The old ladies who sell food in the market wrap their wares in newspaper.

"In case you don't feed us well enough today," Olivera jokes.

I tear the paper open and find a beautifully bound journal. The fabric of the cover feels like silk, and it is printed with pink peony blossoms—my favorite flower.

"We know you're more than just a math geek," Olivera says.

"Yeah, you're a writing geek, and a science geek, and a history geek, and a . . ." Nura teases in a way that has a bit too much truth. Her brilliant mother pushes her so hard to succeed, but Nura can never seem to meet her expectations.

Olivera cuts in with a sharp look. "I know you love to write, and you have beautiful thoughts, so I figured, why not give you a beautiful book to write down your beautiful thoughts!"

I pull her into a tight hug. This gift might be from all three of them, but I know that Olivera picked it out. It makes me feel warm inside to have a friend who understands me so well.

Before I can thank the others, I catch the most heavenly smell coming from the kitchen.

Bread is the smell of home—of everyone's home. Whether it is the aromatic burn of morning toast or the steamy scent of flat lepinja at dinnertime, bread is comfort. It is stability. It is unity. Now Mama brings out a huge tray of the bread I'll break with my closest friends: fluffy, fragrant brioche rolls. They smell like sweet, yeasty heaven.

Tata follows behind her, carrying a plate of red pastrma and sliced cheese so we can make our own sandwiches. He sets it down with a flourish and says in his courtly way, "And now, girls, Dino is going to visit a friend, and we adults will retreat upstairs and leave the house to you. Don't burn it down." My friends giggle. My dad looks like an old-fashioned movie star with his silky, silver hair and brilliant smile.

My mother, stylish and slim with a modish haircut, adds, "Don't worry. These young ladies are adults themselves." She kisses the top of my head, while my father hauls me out of my seat into a huge hug.

"Oh, my little girl, what happened to you?" Tata asks, not letting me go. "When did you get to be big? You must promise me that you will stop growing for a while, so the pants that hit your ankles today are not at your knees next month."

I laugh and say, "It's not my fault. We learned about heredity in school. You are tall, Mama is tall, all of my grandparents are tall." I stand six feet, towering over the girls and half of the boys in my school. "What can I do?"

"You can smoke cigarettes and drink black coffee like Emir does," my handsome younger brother, Dino, pipes up as he comes downstairs, basketball in hand. Emir is a rich boy who is so uniquely unattractive and unpleasant that no one would tolerate him if it weren't for his money. "That stuff stunts your growth." Dino is no slouch in

34

the height department either. He's catching up to me, and he has dreams of playing professional basketball.

"Our people were warriors and wolf hunters long ago," Tata says. "Of course we are giants among men." If Tata is a giant, he is a friendly one, with an open smile and an open hand.

"Nonsense," my more practical mother says. "Our ancestors were merchants and millers and farmers. We had money and good food, so generations of children grew up tall and strong. Just like you two."

Then I see Mama's and Tata's eyes meet as Mama realizes what she just said. Two children. But there should be three. Their smiles start to fade.

Amar was tall like us, taller, too tall. But never strong.

I see Olivera looking at me, distraught, and suddenly she claps her hands and starts singing a song by my pop star crush, George Michael, and the room feels cheerful again. Olivera always knows what to do.

My parents and brother leave, and my friends and I eat and drink Coca-Cola and talk about the boys we have crushes on. The Coke is a rare treat, too expensive to have often. The bubbles and the syrupy sweetness are better than champagne to us. Later, I bring out my guitar, and we sing terrible renditions of Madonna and even more George Michael.

Finally I present the highlight of our feast: Zuhra's seven-layer cake.

My friends gasp in appreciation. "Oh, it is almost too beautiful to eat!" Nura says.

"Almost," Olivera says, handing me the knife. "Give me the biggest slice, please! But first, your birthday song."

I think it is going to be one of those sappy birthday songs, but to my delight she breaks into a funny anti-birthday song by my favorite singer and other crush, Zdravko Čolić.

We're all laughing hysterically by the end of it, begging for encores.

But Olivera says, "Cake first, more music later. I can't wait any longer to taste that cake! Now make a wish and blow out the candle!"

I look into the flickering orange flame, and I make the same wish I've made for every coin toss, in every prayer since Amar's death. *Please let my family have a long life, good health, happiness . . .*

"What did you wish for?" Ivona asks.

"No!" Olivera breaks in even as I open my mouth to speak. "If she tells, it won't come true."

"You wished for a boyfriend, didn't you?" Nura asks.

"For a kiss," Ivona guesses.

"For a thousand kisses . . . from George Michael!" Olivera says with a giggle. "Now hurry and cut the cake, and may all your wishes come true!"

I take up the knife, but when I'm poised to cut the first slice, memories flood me. I think of birthdays past, when the three of us were together, my two brothers and I. One birthday in June, one in November, one in December. For each birthday, Mom would make a veritable tower of a cake, layer upon layer of sweetness and creamy filling and nuts. She would whip the cream by hand with a wire whisk, and pretend not to see when I stole it and licked the fluffy cream.

We would eat cake in front of the fire, making up stories about the shapes we saw in the dancing flames. Mama unleashed our imaginations, just as she does with her students. When the cake was gone, she would peel oranges, handing us segments that tasted like sunshine. The sweet-acid juice on our mouths would be warmed by the fire, making our lips tingle. Each of our three birthdays was filled with cake and family and happiness.

After Amar died, Mama never made another birthday cake.

This professional cake is more beautiful, and of course made with love by my cousin. But I wish I were cutting into Mom's layer cake right now.

I shake myself free of my melancholy. This is a party! My first almost-grown-up party, and my first sleepover.

"What's wrong?" Olivera asks.

"I was just deciding whether to take a quarter of the cake, or half of the cake!" I say, then decisively cut a thick slice. A little while later my melancholy is forgotten amid gooey layers and crunchy pistachios. If there's one thing I've learned in my sixteen years on this earth, it's that sugar makes almost everything better. At least for a while.

I'm halfway through my first slice—and already thinking ahead to my second—when Olivera screams.

"A spirit!" she says, pointing to the window.

My first thought is that I'd rather face a spirit than a Serb soldier any day. Then I follow her trembling finger and see . . . Maci with her paws on the window, peering in. The angle of the evening sun and her tricolored calico face do make her seem a little otherworldly.

"It's just my cat," I tell them.

"I didn't know you had a cat," says Olivera as she tries to regain her composure.

"I don't. I mean, I didn't. But . . . I think I do now."

Olivera turns her back on Maci with a little shudder, and we eat cake until we are about to burst.

"If it was a wedding cake, I could put it under my pillow and dream about who I'm going to marry," Olivera says.

"I'm going to marry Eso," Nura says. Olivera and I exchange a look behind her back, and Olivera rolls her eyes. Nura went out with Eso for a week, and she never stops talking about him, dreaming about him. Even the week is an exaggeration. They walked by the river together one Sunday with a group of friends and went to a movie the following Saturday. Two dates, that's all. But he is her life now. Her destiny, she says. It is a big world, I want to tell her, a world filled with boys who are actually interested in you. But that would only make her sulk.

"He's just playing hard to get," diplomatic Ivona says. "To make you want him more."

Nura nods, satisfied with this assessment.

"What about you, Amra?" Nura asks. "Who do you have a crush on?"

I consider the boys I know. I think some of them are handsome, but of course I want more than that. Some of them are smart. A few have shown interest in me. It's flattering, but I never took it seriously. I've never had a boyfriend, never gone out with a boy except as part of a group. That never bothered me before. It was always something that hovered pleasantly in my future. Someday, I thought vaguely and without concern, I'd meet a boy I really wanted for a boyfriend.

Now, though, the very idea of a future seems too uncertain.

"Sometimes I think I'll never have a boyfriend," I say, thinking of Serb soldiers, of guns, of bombs.

But my friends don't catch the nuances of what I say.

"Nonsense!" Olivera says. "The boys are lining up to date you. You just have to wait for the right one to get in line."

"Or get in line for him," Ivona adds.

Part of me wants to talk with them about what happened last night. But would they really understand? It would be scary to them but not quite real. Like a ghost story told at midnight. We've never talked about ethnic tensions. Politics, conflict, the war between Serbs and Croatians, we only mention in the abstract. I'd like to open their eyes. They should know how close this is coming to us.

But I look at their happy faces, bits of chocolate on their lips and cheeks like little kids, and I think, I can't tell them about it. Not today. This party is too special, a last light. I won't be the one to bring darkness to ruin it.

As dusk falls, Nura and Ivona suggest we go up to my room and change into pajamas. With the cake almost gone except for a big last slice everyone is too polite to eat, it is time for privacy and secrets, jokes and pillow fights, and all the other things that are supposed to happen at sleepovers. Olivera, who has been unusually quiet for a while, gets to her feet.

"I have to go," she mumbles.

I don't understand what she means at first. "Aren't you feeling well?" I ask.

"She ate too much cake," Ivona teases.

"No, I . . ." Olivera gulps. "I have to go home. I can't stay. My father says I can't stay after dark. In case . . . something happens."

"What does that even mean?" Ivona asks. "What could happen? You are safer here than in your own apartment."

"He's too protective," Nura says. "You're sixteen, doesn't he know that? And you are with girls. It's not like you're out with boys, drinking and dancing."

"Call him up, beg him to stay," Ivona says. "Let me talk to him. Or have him talk to Amra's parents. He'll change his mind."

But Olivera, flushed and shame-faced, won't even try. She gathers her bag, gives me a quick little hug with her face averted, and slinks away.

Nura and Ivona go on about how foolishly overprotective parents can be. But I know why my best friend abandoned me on what was supposed to be one of the best days of my life.

Her father doesn't want his Serb daughter staying at the home of a Muslim girl.

I know Olivera doesn't care about that. I know that deep in my inmost heart. What hurts is that she seems to submit to her father's prejudice without a fight.

Without her, the tone of my party has changed. We go upstairs and try to talk about the things girls talk about, but it all feels hollow now. When Maci comes to the window again, Nura shudders.

"Can't you make that ghost cat go away? She's creepy!"

We go back downstairs, and Maci follows us there too. For a while it is a game, leading Maci from room to room. But then my remaining friends start to concoct scary stories around her. *She's a ghost cat*, Ivona says. *She's the spirit of someone who died in this house*, Nura says without thinking.

No one lived in this house before us. We built it just seven years ago.

Seven years ago, my brother died.

Once they remember this, there's no wiping it from their minds. They startle at every sound, flinch at every shadow. As night falls they deliberately provoke each other to greater and greater fears. Another night, I might take part, find all this manufactured fear entertaining. But now I've known real fear, and this just seems silly.

I try to turn the conversation, but Maci leaps to a windowsill with a bang, pressing the ghostly white side of her face against the glass, and the girls shriek and run downstairs.

"I can't stay in a haunted house!" Nura says, wringing her hands. "Ivona, come with me! I can't walk home alone."

Ivona looks uncertainly at me.

Oh, how I want them to stay! But everything feels spoiled now, with Olivera gone.

"It's okay, you both go home. I had a really great time, but I'm a little tired now."

They try not to look relieved.

"Thanks for inviting us," Nura says. "The sandwiches were delicious, and that cake was amazing."

"Yeah, don't let that last piece go to waste," Ivona says, clearly hoping I'll offer to send it with her.

Not a chance.

As I close the door behind them, I hear a small meow. Bonfire eyes are looking up at me hopefully in a soft, furry face. I look over my shoulder, but my parents have made themselves scarce, giving me privacy for my failed party.

"Come in," I tell Maci. "Just be quiet."

On velvet paws she follows me upstairs, after a quick detour to the kitchen.

Alone on my bed, I cuddle Maci in my lap and balance a dish of birthday cake on her gently purring side. I chew each bite slowly, clinging to the last shred of sweetness in the day.

"This is a happy day, Maci," I whisper to her, over and over. She blinks slowly at me, believing it for my sake even as my tears fall onto her fur.

CHAPTER 4

The next day, for the first time in my life, I think about skipping school. It's all too much. The train ride with the Četniks. The refugees. My failed party. Why should I even bother going to school? We are on the cusp of war. What is important now? Not parties, that's for sure. School? I'm not certain. I think of all those meaningless tests I excelled at. How will they help if the Serbs decide to attack us?

My imagination takes off like a spooked horse, filling my head with uncontrollable thoughts of what could have happened on the train, what might happen in days or weeks to come. Or tomorrow.

Or today.

I'm feeling panic creeping up on me when suddenly a sneaky insinuating touch grazes my inner leg like an invading hand, making me scream! I stumble backward, flailing my arms . . . and almost step on Maci. She was just rubbing against my leg. I have to do a weird hopping dance not to tread on her paws, and she looks at me like I've gone completely crazy.

But there's patience and understanding in her eyes too. *Even if you've turned into a mad human who hops on one leg all day, I will stick with you,* her kind gaze seems to say. I stagger back to my room and hastily get dressed, cinching in the colorful scarf I wear in place of a belt, and sit on the floor beside her. She climbs into my lap, rumbling in contentment as I stroke her back. I have to tell myself that the war is not here yet. And it might never be. Calmed by Maci's presence, I start to think of better alternatives. Leaders will negotiate. The United

Nations will step in. The United States will flex its international muscle and put a stop to this.

So there is hope. But even with soft Maci in my lap I have to admit that there's not much hope.

"Do I even go to school today?" I ask her. It seems impossible that normal life can go on after knowing what might be coming to Bihać. But my homework is done, my bag is packed, I'm up. What's the alternative? Sitting home worrying?

So I head downstairs to see what the day will bring.

Nothing in our house hints at any change. There isn't even a bustle of extra people. Omer and Erza must still be asleep. Muhamed is gone. He must have left overnight. I feel bad that I didn't get to say goodbye.

Mama sips her coffee as she moves around the kitchen, straightening up, organizing her papers for school with her free hand. She rarely does only one thing at a time. Tata's voice comes downstairs in a faint melody. He's singing as he shaves. Dino tumbles down for breakfast, his shirt untucked, his blond hair spiky from sleep.

Everything is perfectly normal.

"What is that maci doing in here?" Mama asks sharply. But when I look at her, there's something resigned in her face. I've seen that look before spring-cleaning, and before exam time. It is a look of the unpleasant inevitable. She might not like what is coming, but she has to get through it.

"She was so well behaved," I hurry to tell her. "She sat where I told her to, in that exact spot all night. She didn't even try to jump on the bed."

Dino pats her, and she winds around his ankles in an infinity symbol.

"She has to go out," Mama says.

"But there are dogs outside, and cars," I say. I think but do not say, "And tanks, and violence, and death."

43

Mama is firm . . . but hands me a dish of milk. Dino scoops Maci up and together we sit beneath the shade of a quince tree and watch her daintily drink her milk down to the last drop. She seems to accept her fate. When we go in, she settles down under the fruit tree, looking out at the world. She reminds me of an old grandmother, sitting on her porch, watching life move past her, waiting for someone to visit.

Dino and I leave for school after Tata but before Mama. The school where she teaches is nearby. The children in this neighborhood are mostly Muslim. We should go to that school, but Mama doesn't think it would be fair. The other students would think we received special treatment because we are a teacher's kids. Instead Dino makes a daily trek across town. Dino goes to my old elementary school while I'm at a math and science prep high school. This morning, when we set off with our bags and books, Maci follows us.

"You have to stay here," I tell her.

She continues after us anyway, but near the end of the block one of the big, fierce neighborhood dogs sets up a furious barking, and she decides the quince tree is safer. She watches until we turn the corner. "Don't worry, we'll be back this afternoon."

"Amra, why do you talk to that furball like she's a human?" Dino asks.

"She listens better than you," I say. "Did you bring your pencils? No? Even after I reminded you twice." I sigh, but my irrepressible brother is unrepentant.

"Why should I bother to remember when you always have ten pencils, extra sharp?" he asks, holding out his hand.

He's right. When your older sister is a math-obsessed nerd, you don't have to remember pencils. "You'll be in high school before you know it," I tell him. "You better get your act together by then. There's no shame in being prepared."

"Overprepared," he mutters under his breath. Poor Dino has it hard in school sometimes. He's smart, but doesn't want to be seen as nerdy like me. On the first day of class the teachers hear his last name and think he'll be a top student who gets all fives. Instead he sails by with mostly fives and an occasional four, not to look too nerdy. As for me, I can't stop until I'm perfect at something. I get angry at myself if I'm not at the top of the class.

Sometimes I wish I were more like Dino: happy-go-lucky, careless, popular.

Usually I meet Olivera halfway to school, but today I want more time to talk with her, so I head to her apartment building. Now I see Olivera, but she doesn't see me—she's talking to Tatiana. Finally she looks at me, then looks quickly away and exchanges a few more words with Tatiana. That's strange. Usually Olivera runs up to me and links arms the second she spies me.

Dino is watching the interaction too. "Wow, Tatiana looks like she's in college!" he muses aloud.

Tatiana has been obsessed with her looks from a young age. Even when she's only going to school she's made up like a supermodel, with teased hair and elaborate makeup. She's one of the most popular girls in school. Now Olivera is talking to her and ignoring me?

No, I tell myself. She is ashamed of her father making her leave last night. She is embarrassed that she ruined my party. It's okay, Olivera, I want to say. Your father is not your fault. I love you anyway.

"You head on to school, Dino," I tell him. "I'll wait here for Olivera." He runs off, and I settle down on a bench, picking up a newspaper someone discarded. It is yesterday's paper, a little greasy— someone used it to wrap their snack in—but it gives me something to do as I wait for my best friend.

The lead story is about Sarajevo. Our capital city is surrounded. The city is under attack by Serb forces. Not an outside enemy, another country. By what was until only recently our own military, the Yugoslav

National Army. When Papa told me, I didn't understand. But . . . they were our own army. How can they be attacking us?

Not long ago, the article says, the people of Sarajevo held a huge march for peace. The marchers included the three main ethnic groups in our country—Bosniaks, Serbs, and Croats. About one hundred thousand people marched, singing songs, holding candles, loving each other as brothers and sisters.

But many Serbs did not want peace. They fired into the marchers. From there, the violence only got worse. There was fighting in the streets. This wasn't a battlefield, far from homes and families. Serbs were going from house to house, neighborhood to neighborhood, shooting and arresting Muslims. Children were killed on their way to school. Policemen, sworn to protect the city, instead chose sides based on their ethnicity. Now, the Muslim members of the Bihać police force are almost all we have to defend our own city.

It also happened in Bosanska Krupa, Omer and Erza's hometown. But that little town couldn't fight back. The people of Sarajevo—the Muslims, some Croats, and even a few Serbs who object to the massacre—are holding out against the Serb forces that surround the city, raining bombs down on civilians. Serbia and Bosnian Serbs control the Yugoslav National Army. They have the weapons. We don't. Olivera is Serb.

I slap the paper down on the bench when Olivera finally stops ignoring me and waves. Does she know what her people are doing? She's always been more inclined to talk about clothes and boys and music than current events.

Now she's her usual chatty self. I let her do this, not bringing up any of the things that trouble me. What if it were my people killing innocent civilians? Wouldn't I rather bury my head in the sand and pretend I had no idea? Yes, this is what we do. We distract each other. I play the game to protect her, and myself. With half of my mind I talk about homework, friends, the blue dress Olivera saw in Boutique Bolero that she simply has to have . . .

"And did you see," Olivera goes on, "they have red jeans! They are the most beautiful things I've ever seen. Mama says she'll get me a pair. Amra, are you listening?"

"Oh, what?" I reply, only catching every other word as my thoughts wrestle. "Red jeans? They would look beautiful on you!"

The subjects are so typical that I can answer without thinking. Inwardly, I'm mulling over facts like a statistician, weighing odds about the future.

Now, this morning, as I walk with Olivera I look up at the tops of the tallest buildings we pass. The article said there are snipers all over Sarajevo. A Serb with a rifle hides high in an abandoned hotel room or on a rooftop in a Bosniak neighborhood. There, like Zeus with a lightning bolt on high Olympus, he picks off anyone he sees. He targets the most traveled spots—bridges, the roads to shopping districts, schools, hospitals. People become prisoners in their own cities.

While Olivera talks about clothes, I think of a mother going to market to buy food for her family's supper, shot because she is Muslim. A little boy, running across the street to play with a puppy, shot the instant he enters the sniper's sights. A teen like Dino shot because in a year or two he'd be old enough to be a soldier.

And sometimes they can't even retrieve the bodies, the article said. A relative or medic who made the attempt would be shot too. So a victim might lie there all day, a gruesome warning, until some brave soul could sneak out under cover of darkness.

The article closed with the journalist asking a citizen of Sarajevo whether they could negotiate peace or even surrender.

"We can never surrender," the man said. "If a dog hates a cat, and the cat surrenders in a fight, what happens to the cat?"

I cringe, picturing beautiful Maci torn apart by the Bernese mountain dog who lives at the end of our street. We are not dogs and cats, I tell myself, wanting to have faith in human nature. But I know in my heart the only choices for the cat are to resist or run away. Until dogs and cats learn to live with each other, to value each other, there are no other options.

All the while, Olivera chatters on, unconcerned.

Our school is in an ethnically mixed neighborhood. Serb, Croat, Muslim—I never really thought much about the ethnic groups. Until now it meant only small differences. If I visit a Muslim friend, the grandmother might cover her hair with a bright scarf printed with a rose pattern. At the home of a Christian friend, the grandmother would cover her hair with a black scarf. With only a few small variations all of my friends speak the same language, eat the same food, wear the same clothes, take the same classes.

In Bosnia, most of the Muslim families are secular. We are Muslim by heritage, but after decades of Communist rule very few people actually practice the religion strictly. The women in my family wear bikinis at the beach, or go braless in tank tops. Some of us eat ham and prosciutto. There are a few more traditional families, but most of the Muslims in Bosnia are virtually indistinguishable from anyone else. Olivera is throwing back her hair, looking at me questioningly. "Amra, did you hear me? Where is your head today? Remember, I'm counting on you to help me with math. If you're feeling so dull, what hope is there for me? Did you see what Tatiana is wearing? False eyelashes! I helped her put them on after she was outside, so her parents didn't see. Do you think I should wear more makeup?"

Are you thinking of killing me, Olivera? I want to ask her, given our troubled times. Do you want to take my home, make me live in the streets?

But she is prattling on about Tatiana, about our handsome friend Mirza, about makeup.

No, Olivera doesn't hate me. She's my best friend. She knows nothing about this conflict, no more than I did only two days ago. Bihać isn't Sarajevo. We are peaceful, full of brotherly love. We accept differences. No one here would hurt another person just because their ancestors came from one place or another.

I have known this city all of my life. These are my people—Muslim, Croat, and Serb. It simply cannot happen here. Olivera is still on the subject of makeup. "Should I paint on big cat's eyes?" she demands. Olivera is beautiful, but she is sensitive about her appearance, and hardly a day goes by that she doesn't fish for reassurance.

"Don't bother with makeup," I tell her, making my voice sound as normal as possible. "You're beautiful without it." Act normal and things will be normal, I say to myself.

That is all she wants to hear. As long as it is something happy. That is enough for most people. Olivera and I link arms and sing a pop song as we walk. She doesn't notice if my voice cracks or if my smile is forced.

A few blocks from the school we add Mirza to our group. He's a Muslim boy with long blond hair, a popular jokester who is everyone's friend. More schoolmates appear, some joining our group, others walking slowly before or behind us. Nura and Ivona walk with us, as does a girl named Samira. As always, I check Samira for bruises. There are no new ones, only a few faded yellow marks on her arms. Good, her father must still be in Germany. I can always tell when he has returned.

Is that why this world is in trouble—because there are more fathers like hers and Olivera's than like mine?

We pass a house with beautiful rosebushes. I don't know the people who live there, but I've seen an old man tending the plants several times. It is the most beautiful garden. Some of the rosebushes are neatly pruned, with long stems of elegant deep-red blooms. Others climb on a trellis, a tangle of small pink or creamy-white buds. A few are shaggy and wild-looking, with leggy stems and exotic golden roses. I think this is the owner's choice, not negligence. This garden is such a perfect mixture of order and chaos that I always pause on the way to school to admire it.

I'm a little behind the others, looking at a rose that has bloomed for the first time—a cream-colored flower with a ruby heart and a blush of red on the petal tips. I'm just bending down to smell it when a boy hurrying out of the house almost bumps into me. When he sees me he stops, then steps back in an oddly chivalrous way to let me pass first along the lane.

"Hello," he says. For a moment I stare into his gray-green eyes. His skin is golden, like he's basking in the sun, even though it is an overcast morning. He looks like a day at the beach. He is wearing denim overalls with a white T-shirt underneath. It's the latest style, to dress like a farmer but in clothes so tailored and clean it is obvious they never got near dirt. One overall strap hangs carelessly over his shoulder.

I feel strangely tongue-tied. All I manage to do is nod as I hurry after my friends.

Somehow I know he's still watching, waiting to see if I'll turn around.

Very deliberately, I don't.

But then, of course, I do. He's still looking at me.

"Who was that?" Olivera asks with a sly grin when I start walking faster.

"I have no idea."

"Did your true love give you a rose?" Mirza jokes, miming a courtly bow.

They laugh and tease, and everything seems so normal. It makes me feel safe, until a rotten plum hits the side of my arm.

I whirl, and see a boy from our school named Bakir crouching in an alley, having obviously just ducked the missile. Behind him is a gang of older boys, seventeen and eighteen, armed with other fruit. One pelts a peach pit at the cringing boy. "Žgoljava kukavice!" they call him. *Scrawny coward.* They warn him, "Izlemaćemo te žgoljo!" *We'll pound you, weakling!*

My friends stopped at the spectacle, but now they're walking quickly away. They know better than to get involved. This is Irfan's gang. They left school early, or were kicked out, and now they sell black market cigarettes, pick pockets, and entertain themselves by beating up people weaker than they are. Bakir is Irfan's younger brother, which doesn't always save him from Irfan's bullying. Bakir is a skinny boy, quiet, and he does well on tests, though he rarely turns in any homework. I see that Irfan has Bakir's book bag, waving it tauntingly. Papers are falling out of it.

"Give it back!" Bakir shouts.

The gang just laughs. One throws an apple, which hits Bakir and rolls at my feet. My fists clench, my lips press together. My friends see—they know the signs—and call me, but now I can barely hear them. Without thinking, I charge up to Irfan and snatch the book bag from his hand.

"Don't you dare throw fruit at me!" I shout at him. I'm mad that he's teasing his brother, but I don't dare say that. Bakir would be ashamed to have someone, especially a girl, stick up for him. It would only make his brother's bullying worse.

The gang members laugh at me like I'm beneath their notice, and one spits an apple seed in my direction, but at least I have the book bag back. This could have gone much worse. I toss it to Bakir.

"Where's your weakling brother?" Irfan asks, then starts to limp around the alley. Irfan falls down dramatically, and the others all laugh.

I freeze, a dagger of ice stabbing my heart.

"Didn't you hear?" another says. "The freak is dead. You must be so glad not to have that thing following you around all day."

"And she's an heiress now," Irfan says. "Look, she inherited all of the cripple's clothes."

I look down at my outfit. The shirt belonged to a cousin, but the pants are Amar's. Were Amar's.

Tears sting my eyes. Not because I'm afraid of them, though. My sorrow and my fury are entirely separate things, but they won't understand. They'll just be happy they tormented me until I cried. But the tears won't stop, so instead of challenging them, instead of shouting back insults that will make them lie awake at night doubting their own self-worth, I turn away. I don't want to give them the satisfaction.

That's when Bakir, so long a victim of his brother's teasing and attacks, turns on me too. He points to the stretched part of my pants, which makes me look like my knee is always bent, and says, "Look, she's just like her brother." Then he, too, imitates the tortured way Amar had to walk near the end, the pained, lurching gait he used to drag himself to school every day.

I slap Bakir. I hit him so hard my entire arm tingles from fingertips to shoulder. Bakir spins and staggers to his knees, and I have him by the collar before he can think to rise. When I look at him, though, there's no shock on his face, no anger. He looks sad, resigned.

He looks like he knows he's getting what he deserves. Like he welcomes it.

"Don't you ever talk about Amar!" I scream into his face. "If you mention him again, I'll hit you so hard your teeth will go flying all over Bihać!"

I give him one hard shake and let him go. He's still on the ground as I walk away, while Irfan and his gang are in hysterics that Bakir just got hit by a girl.

"Are you okay?" Olivera asks.

"Of course," I say as lightly as I can. "I'm always okay. Now, about that math problem . . ."

CHAPTER 5

In school, I make myself stay focused. All the bad things in the world are kept at bay by science, by literature, by math. I can turn off part of my brain, I think, focus on only one thing. In school it is easier. I am so used to discipline, to concentration. In this harsh, regimented school, success and excellence are the only things that matter.

Sava, my Russian teacher, reminds me of the street bullies but one main difference is that she has no sense of humor. Not even a bad one. She doesn't hurt her students to entertain herself, but just to make sure that her students, particularly Muslim ones, know their place. The only way to get through her class is to do everything perfectly and not challenge her in any way. She insists we all be like obedient Russian soldiers. Once I suggested she might be wrong about something. The next time she walked past my desk she leaned her huge buttock on it, pinching my arm into the edge, and stayed there for the rest of her lecture. I was in too much pain even to cry out. By the time she finally moved, my fingers were blue.

In her class today Teacher Sava calls on students to translate Bosnian sentences into Russian. She scans the class like a wolf watches a herd of deer, selecting the weakest one. Usually she doesn't call on me, but today my face must look vulnerable. Glaring at me, her eyes black and beady, she orders me to translate: "Waitress, bring me a cup of coffee."

Well, to begin with, I don't like translating this because I would never use such a rude, commanding tone to a waitress. Mama and Tata always taught me to treat people equally, no matter how rich or poor they might be. Waitresses, shop clerks, poor old men, and lonely old women are treated exactly the same as the highest officials.

But it would be a waste of breath to tell Teacher Sava this, so I translate exactly, "Ofitsiantka, prinesi mne kofe."

"Wrong!" she booms at me. "You call a waitress 'girl' when you are summoning her. Again!"

Gulping back every word I would like to say, I translate again, "Devushka, prinesi mne kofe."

Teacher Sava slams her meaty fist on my desk. "Wrong! 'Dedushka' means 'old man' not 'girl.'"

"But I didn't say . . . ," I begin.

"You Muslims make me sick. Do you want to be a backward people forever? I give you a chance to better yourself, and you squander it with your willful ignorance! You should say 'Devochka, prinesi mne kofe.'"

The situation is so full of errors that it is almost laughable. Teacher Sava is not a native Russian speaker, so she makes mistakes like this often. The word I used is correct—it means girl, as in a young or unmarried woman. I might forgive my teacher mishearing me (though I think it was deliberate), but then she herself used the wrong word. "Devochka" means a very little girl—an elementary school-aged girl in pigtails. It would be a terrible insult to call a waitress—a grown woman—devochka.

But I say nothing, and of course I don't laugh. Teachers aren't officially supposed to hit students, but when it happens occasionally no one dares to object. And the only students I ever saw hit were Muslim. I bite my tongue and let Teacher Sava feel smug and superior to a sixteen-year-old girl.

She turns to her next victim, a Serb girl named Tamara. "Translate this: 'I want to write to my friend.'"

Poor Tamara is a helpless student, but her father is a prominent Serb in the local government. She stammers out a word, corrects herself, and falls silent, blushing scarlet. I can see Teacher Sava nodding encouragingly, even mouthing the right words. Tamara babbles something else, and our teacher beams. "Yes, that is the word for 'friend.' Now, do you remember last week's lesson? How do you say 'to write'?"

Tamara scrunches up her face, and at last, by some Herculean effort, she gets out a complete sentence. It is . . . almost correct.

Unfortunately, the word for *to write* is "pisat," with the accent on the "a" sound. Tamara instead puts the accent on the "i" sound.

"I want to pee on my friend," she says in Russian.

"Beautiful work, Tamara!" Teacher Sava beams. "At least some members of our class devote themselves to their studies. You will go far, Tamara . . . unlike some I could mention." Her tiny beady eyes search me out, and every other Muslim in the class.

Not all Muslims are despised by Serb teachers.

"Come here, you beautiful boy, and show me your Netherlands," my geography teacher Daliborka purrs to Mirza. With an uncomfortable blush, he hands her a drawing of northern Europe that lists major cities and rivers. She makes him sit in the seat beside her desk while she praises his work, crossing and uncrossing her legs so they brush against Mirza's knees. When she is finished, she bends over in an exaggerated way to hand him back his map. As she does so, a button on her already half-unbuttoned shirt pops off and flies across the room, exposing even more blue-veined bosom for poor Mirza to see. Stammering thanks, he scurries to his seat.

Daliborka looks like she's just closed down a discotheque. She moves languidly and talks slowly, like a drunk trying to be sensual. Her eye makeup looks left over from last night. Her punkish hair is teased and sprayed high. Between her tall, tottering heels and her tall hairdo she towers over most of the class (except me). She reminds me of a skinny skyscraper in an earthquake, swaying, always on the verge of crashing. She favors bright-red shirts and skintight miniskirts that show not only her knobby knees, but her thighs almost all the way up to her buttocks. She picked a style twenty years ago and never changed it.

Daliborka loves two things—her fellow Serbs and males.

In Mirza, she has a dilemma. He's Muslim. But he's by far the most charming young man in our school. For him, she makes an exception, fawning over him every chance she gets. (He hates it, of course. The first day it was flattering. Every day after, he feels like he is being attacked by a harpy. But, he says with his ready laugh, at least geography is an easy good grade.)

The rest of us Muslims she treats with outright contempt. She hates me especially. Mama is a history and geography teacher, so of course I do well in this class. I push myself even harder, learning the material a week ahead of time, perfecting my memory and penmanship and speed so I can do everything in the class better than any other student. I love seeing the sour look on her face when she realizes she has no choice but to give me a perfect grade.

Daliborka loves giving surprise oral examinations. Once we figured her out, Olivera and I had fun manipulating her. She wanted the Serb kids to succeed, so when Olivera was feeling confident, when she'd memorized the material, she would comment loudly to me in the teacher's hearing how well she knew the information. So Daliborka would "randomly" decide to test her that day.

Today, we try a different tactic. As we walk past Daliborka's desk, I lament that I completely forgot to study my geography last night. "I'm so far behind," I say in a carrying whisper. "I hope she doesn't call on me today."

Sure enough, as we settle into our seats she announces, "Amra, you'll be having an oral exam today. Stand up and tell me the principal rivers of Belgium and France."

For fun, I fake a nervous expression and see the smug satisfaction on her face. Then, effortlessly, I rattle off not only the major rivers but their tributaries, adding asides about the chief agricultural products grown in each region. She stares at me, bug-eyed, then collects herself enough to ask a few follow-up questions—which I answer glibly.

I can see her grinding her teeth in frustration. She'd love more than anything to fail me. But every student is a witness to my success, and she has no choice but to mark down a five—a perfect score.

"You think you're so smart," she hisses in an undertone the next time she passes my desk. "You just wait and see what the world has in store for you!"

———————

Later in the day, though, math class makes up for the indignity of my Russian and geography lessons. My teacher there is the beautiful Lepa, a tall, stunning Serb woman about forty years old. Half of the boys have crushes on her. They are absurdly fascinated by her unshaven legs. Long and muscular, covered with dark hair, those fuzzy legs make her look like the world's most appealing satyr.

As class starts she settles her oversized 1970s glasses more firmly on her nose, and in her clear, concise way teaches us a new principle. It is a math theory I've never encountered before, but thanks to her lucid style I understand it almost immediately. In Lepa's class I rarely have to open my book to study. She makes things so simple and plain when she talks about them that mathematics seems as natural as breathing. To me, anyway. Some of my classmates struggle, but Lepa is always willing to help them.

Before long she sets us to working on problems at the board. When a student is at the chalkboard, Lepa takes their empty seat and checks their work. Today, she saves a particularly hard problem for me. When I finish, I turn to her, waiting for the usual confirmation that I did it correctly. But Lepa has her head bent down and says nothing.

Did I make a mistake? Embarrassed, I go back over my work but can't find anything wrong. I go stand by my seat and wait silently for her to notice me. When she lifts her head, her huge glasses are fogged.

"Thank you, good job," she says, and gives me back my desk. As she returns to the front of the classroom she squeezes my hand, very quickly, so no one else sees.

When I sit down, I notice splotches of water on my math papers.

For the final few minutes of the class she lets us work in pairs. The desks are set up for two people side by side, and Olivera is my seatmate. We work on the problems—or rather, I show her how to do the problems—but she won't pay attention, and before long she is whispering to me about Bakir.

"I don't know how you dared to confront him like that," she says as we bend over the tricky problems.

"He isn't so big or scary," I reply. Lepa is coming near, but she doesn't usually mind what we talk about as long as we are doing our work too.

"But his brother is!" Olivera says. "And they're Muslim too. I could see how you might be brave if they were Serbs. I mean, my father says all Serbs are afraid of Muslims, but—"

I interrupt her. "What do you mean, afraid?" She said it like it was the most natural thing in the world.

"Oh, you know," she says vaguely.

"Are you afraid of me?" I ask her.

"Well, no, but that's different. You're not really Muslim. I mean, not like the others."

"Which others?"

But Olivera doesn't know. She seems confused that I'm suddenly so upset. I can hear my voice rising above the acceptable whisper as I say, "What are you afraid of, Olivera? Muslims with no weapons?"

"I didn't mean—" she begins, but I don't let her finish.

"Serbs control all of the weapons. We Bosnians voted for independence, but the Serbs took over the Yugoslav army and made it a Serb army!" I say. "What do you have to be scared of? How am I going to hurt you? Am I going to bite you like a dog?"

"Amra, really, I . . ."

But the pain of what my best friend has uttered is too much. And worse than that, she really doesn't see anything wrong with what she just said.

"I have always been your friend, ever since we first met," I remind her. "Do you remember the first day of school, when you forgot your lunch, and I shared mine with you? What could I have possibly done to make you afraid? Yet your tanks roll through Bihać terrorizing people. Your army surrounds Sarajevo."

Everyone is looking at me now. Math is forgotten. Lepa is standing over me.

"Whose army are you talking about?" Lepa asks me gently. "It is not Olivera's army, or my army, or your army—it is our army. The army of the Yugoslav people."

"Then why do they have all the weapons, and the Muslims have none?" I ask her. "Olivera's father is in the army, and Tatiana's. But I don't know a single Muslim who is still in the army. When we voted for Bosnian independence from Yugoslavia, the army was supposed to split too. But no—now there is a Serb army for Serbs, and no army for Bosnian Muslims. So who should be afraid? The people with weapons or without weapons? She says Serbs are afraid of Muslims, but I think maybe it should be I who am afraid. Who will protect me?"

"The Yugoslav National Army is the army of the people," Lepa explains, broadening her voice to address the whole class. "We have nothing to fear from it. It is there to protect us from our enemies." She sounds like she really believes this as she looks around at other students. "Are any more of you worried about this?"

No one else quite dares to speak, but some people nod, very small, shallow nods as if they are afraid of being seen.

"Very well then, I know a powerful, very great man high up in the army." We immediately know who she is talking about. No one ever says anything, but it is common knowledge that her lover is a general in the YNA. He's married, but his wife lives in another city.

"He knows everything that is happening in the military," Lepa continues. "Tomorrow, after school, I will take you all to visit him. You may ask him anything you wish, and he will explain exactly how safe you are. All of you. But I have spoken with him myself, and he gave me his word. I trust him. I promise that each and every one of you is completely safe. Our army will protect us all."

"Protect us from who?" I need to know.

But just then the bell rings, and I leave without getting any answer.

My final class is music, where we are studying the great composers. My teacher plays us a record of Mozart's *Requiem*, but I can't pay any attention to the majestic and sorrowful music of the master. After school I wait for Olivera to walk home with her, thinking we can finally talk about real things. But she runs up to tell me that she's meeting her mother for some shopping in town, and I should go without her. I see her mother across the street, tapping her foot impatiently.

I want so much to talk to my other friends about what happened in class, but I can't quite think how to bring it up. I decide to just wait for tomorrow. I trust Lepa. She is my favorite teacher, and I think I may be her favorite student. If her friend the general promises us what he promised her, I will feel safe.

When I get home, I expect to find Maci waiting patiently at the door. Already she is a fixture in my life. But when I get there, the stoop is empty. Dino, who arrives home at the same time as I do, makes a mewing sound, but there is no reply.

"Maci!" I call softly, and poke around the peony and rosebushes in the front of our house. There is no sign of her.

My heart feels suddenly hollow. One of the things that got me through the day was the thought of squeezing her in my arms, stroking her fur while she purred with half-closed eyes. And now she is gone. Everything feels on the verge of falling apart.

We go inside . . . and there is Tata, home early from work, sitting in his favorite dark grass-green armchair, with Maci perched on his knee. He is teaching her to do a trick: standing on her hind legs to reach a piece of string he dangles just out of reach. Maci snakes one clever paw up to catch it, then settles down on his thigh to chew on her prize. Tata is beaming.

They both look over when they notice us, and Maci jumps down, running straight for me. After rubbing luxuriously against my hand she gives Dino a quick greeting, then goes back to me.

"Er, is your mama home?" Tata asks nervously.

"No, she won't be home for another hour at least."

"Good, good. I have time to put Maci out."

Despite everything that is troubling me, I can't help laughing. "You are afraid of Mama too?"

"Not afraid, Amra. But you know how she'll look at me if she catches the cat in the house." He fakes a shiver, and I take Maci outside.

We sit on the stairs, and I tell her about my day. The bad parts I brush quickly over. But I tell her about the boy in the rosebushes, and about Tamara's atrocious Russian. I feel like she is listening as she grooms her paws, carefully cleaning between each toe.

When I get to Lepa's promise to take us to meet her friend the general, Maci crawls into my lap. She's there, curled up in a tight ball, when Mama comes home.

"Have you finished your homework?" Mama asks.

Unusually for me, I haven't even started it yet. I jump up, startling Maci out of her nap.

"Make sure you work in your room tonight," Mama says as I follow her inside. Sometimes I work in different rooms of the house—in the living room to catch the best evening light, or in the kitchen in winter, to bask in the oven's lingering heat.

"Why?" I ask.

"Because your father and I have to talk about something," she says brusquely, putting down her bag full of tests and papers to grade.

Before I go upstairs to do my homework, I run to Tata and remind him to brush the cat hair off his pants. "Mama wants to talk to you about something," I whisper as I kiss the evening stubble on his cheek. "If it is about Maci, you'll be on my side, right? You want her to stay, to be a house cat?"

"Of course, Amra. But . . ." Then Mama comes in, and I make myself scarce.

Upstairs, I breeze through my math, read a chapter of history, and in physics calculate the trajectory of a projectile. I'm just opening up the first pages of a translation of a book—reading for fun, not homework—when there is a knock at my door.

This in itself is enough to alarm me. Here in Bosnia there is no such thing as privacy or personal space. Usually we just walk into each other's rooms. At most we might call out from the hall. Even our front door is rarely locked, whether we are home or not. If an aunt comes to visit, and we don't answer the door, she just walks in and starts making coffee until we come home. Now suddenly my parents are knocking? They remind me of door-to-door salespeople. What can my parents be selling?

I'm sitting at my desk and turn around awkwardly to look at them. Tata perches on my bed, stands nervously, then sits again. Mama stands, just like she stands in front of the classroom.

"Amra," Mama begins. "We've been talking."

"I know," I say. "And I've been staying out of the way."

Tata pretends a laugh is a cough and takes over. "We think it might be a nice idea if you went on a vacation. Just for a while."

"Where?" I ask. "School is in session, so I couldn't be away more than a few days at most."

"We were thinking longer than that. Your Tetka Aida and Tetak Đorđe have invited you to stay in Serbia with them for a while. Žana really wants you to pay them a nice long visit."

Aida is Mama's first cousin, close as a sister, and a Muslim like us. Đorđe is a Serb who has a degree in civil and military engineering. His main job is designing airports. He lives in Serbia but comes to Bihać often because of our famous airport. Their daughter Žana—my cousin—is one of my favorite friends. I always love it when she visits Bihać. So does she. She tells me she never feels truly at home in Belgrade, a city dominated by Serbs.

"Just me? Not Dino, or you two?"

"We have our work," Mama says. "And Dino is safe here. They asked for you specifically. Đorđe has arranged passage on a military plane leaving the airport tonight."

"Tonight?"

"There is only one small thing," Tata says.

64

"Just a formality," Mama adds. "You would have to change your name."

"What do you mean?" I ask. "Why?"

Mama bites her lip, her teacher-calm slipping. "It would be easier, living there, if you pretended to be a Serb girl. You would pretend to be one of Đorđe's distant relatives, and . . ."

"No!" I say loudly. "I am Amra Šabić, and I will never be anyone else!"

Haltingly, in a way that makes it clear there are many things they could say, but would rather not say, Mama and Tata explain why it might be a good idea to leave Bosnia. They are careful, gentle, because they don't realize how keenly I'm aware of the danger that is creeping nearer every day.

"There might be disruptions here," Mama argues. "Your studies will be interrupted."

"And won't it be fun to have a girl your own age in the house?" Tata asks. "You can talk about . . ." Here he draws a blank.

"Math?" I suggest.

"If you don't like it in Belgrade," Tata cajoles, "after a while maybe you can go to my brother in Slovenia. You remember him, the one with the mustache?"

"And the weird son who never speaks?" I ask. "No thank you."

"You have to be practical about this," Mama says. "Even if it might not be what we all would like in a perfect world."

"If I am to go, why not Dino?" I ask.

Mama hesitates, then at last says, "To do this would require a certain amount of . . . acting. You are old enough, steady enough, to play the part. Dino is not."

"Tata, Mama, are you telling me that I am going to Serbia? Or are you asking me if I want to go?"

"Let's say we're asking you," Mama says. "How would you answer?"

"I would say no," I declare. "My home is here, my family is here. I am Bosnian, a Muslim. I will not change my identity."

"And if we tell you that you have to go?" Mama asks gently. Tata opens his mouth to protest, but she holds up her hand, silencing him. "If we don't give you a choice?"

I take a deep breath. "I can't do it," I tell them. "I would forget my pretend name, I would say something only a Muslim would say. Whatever you want to keep me from, I would give myself away. You know I've never been good at lying."

"This isn't exactly lying, Amra," Tata tells me. "It is . . . make believe."

"It is survival," Mama says bluntly.

For a moment I turn inward, imagining life as another person. As a Serb girl, with a new name and a new family. I think of the way my Russian teacher calls me an ignorant Muslim. I think of the confused look in Olivera's eyes when she says I'm a Muslim, but not that kind of Muslim. If I were a Serb girl, I would never have to face that again.

But I would leave Mama and Tata and Dino. I would leave my beloved city. I would leave Maci. Would I ever come home? Would everything I love still be here when I returned?

An uncertain future looms ahead of me. I'm afraid of it. But I would rather face it as Amra Šabić than as anyone else.

"No," I tell them firmly. "I will stay here."

Mama begins to protest, but this time it is Tata who stops her. "She is our daughter. She stays." They both kiss me. Tata has tears in his eyes.

Mama is dry-eyed, but she looks proud of me. "Finish your homework," is all she says, but she takes Tata's hand as they walk out.

But I'm already finished with my homework. There is nothing to distract my mind. What I yearn for is math problems, physics problems, the harder the better. Anything to focus my brain on so I don't have to think . . .

Maci meows at the window, and without hesitation I let her in. She has wormed her way into our house. I know that Mama will object, strongly at first, but eventually her protests will become mere habit. Maci has found her family.

She rubs against my legs, but frankly she doesn't take my mind off my worries as well as solving complicated algebra problems does. "I must be the only kid in the world who is wishing for more homework," I tell her.

Suddenly my thoughts return to the last class of the day, music. I hadn't been paying close attention that final hour. I know we listened to Mozart, but had our teacher given us an assignment to read about Mozart's life? I run downstairs, Maci at my heels, and call Olivera to ask her.

"Hello?" she says, and it is a relief to hear her voice. I've talked to her almost every day for years. In a flash I think of the summer days we've spent swimming in the river, the hours we've spent gazing into shop windows at impossible clothes, the nights poring over homework. We are so close that nothing, not the fact that she is Serb and I am Muslim, could ever part us.

"Olivera, it's me! I wanted to ask you, did we have any music home-work? I thought maybe . . ."

There is a click, and then the monotone drone of the dial tone. The line is dead. That's odd. It happens in heavy storms sometimes, but tonight the sky is clear.

I call her back. "Olivera, what happened? The line suddenly—"

She hisses to me in a low whisper, so low I can almost pretend I don't hear the perplexing thing she says to me now. "Never call me again!"

"What? I—"

The line goes dead again. Numb, I lay down the phone in its cradle.

Dino ambles up. "That was fast. Usually you two talk for hours, and I actually need to call a friend. He has a recording of the last Chicago Bulls game. He's going to tell me everything that happens over the phone."

"I think the phone is broken," I say.

"Nope," he answers a moment later. "It's working fine for me."

I go back upstairs, and Maci helps me through another almost sleepless night.

CHAPTER 6

In the morning, the first thing I do is memorize Mozart's biography just in case there is a test on it after all. Maci sits in my lap, purring like the basso continuo that runs through the *Requiem* we listened to in class yesterday. I slept for three hours at most, mere minutes broken by nightmares. Now, after another night of bad sleep, the world seems askew. As the words of the text blur, I'm not completely sure what is real anymore.

Dino and I walk to school down strangely quiet streets. The only sound is Dino chattering about the relative merits of Michael Jordan and Magic Johnson. Emboldened by the quiet, Maci follows us farther this time. I expect her to turn back near the end of the block where the fierce Bernese mountain dog lives, but today even he is silent. She stops by the gate and stares through the bars intently, her slim body taut as an arrow string, ready to fly. But the yard is empty. Every curtain in the house is pulled shut.

"See, Maci, it's safe," I tell her, and she trots along with us.

"Should we send her home?" Dino asks. "Won't she get lost?"

I'm a little worried about this myself, but Maci seems to know what she wants. "She is a special cat," I tell him before he branches off toward his own school. "She can find her way home."

Mostly, though, I'm thinking about Olivera. Like a butterfly in a garden, my mind flits from one fanciful possibility to another. I called the wrong number. It wasn't her but some spiteful cousin visiting, jealous of her attention. It could be a misguided joke. Or maybe Olivera is planning some wonderful surprise, and she knew she would give it away if she talked to me. Is it another party? Maybe she pestered her dad until he agreed to let her spend the night.

Fueled by these fantasies I head straight to Olivera's apartment again. But she's not there. I wait as long as I can with Maci at my feet, but she doesn't come out. As I hurry on to school I give one last look up to Olivera's apartment. The windows are shut, the curtains drawn. Just like every window in the building except one. On the ground floor there is a shop that sells coffee and salami sandwiches. The store owner's curtain cracks open, and I see her beady eyes watching us suspiciously.

Where could Olivera be? The butterfly of my thoughts lands on another possibility: Olivera is sick with a fever and didn't know what she was saying. If she isn't in class, I'll stop by afterward to check on her.

There has to be a reasonable explanation. It is impossible that Olivera would suddenly just stop being my best friend.

I'm already on the school grounds when I realize Maci is still with me.

"Oh, you silly cat, you can't come into school with me!" I tickle her chin and gently turn her away, hoping she'll run back home. But she persistently follows me.

Now the first bell rings. I wasted so much time waiting for Olivera. Two more minutes and the final bell will sound. I've never been late to school in my life! "Maci, you have to go!" I insist. I can't think how to turn her away. I refuse to scare her, to stomp my foot. But if Teacher Sava sees her on school property I don't know what calamity might happen. It is completely possible she'd literally kick Maci out of the school!

I pick Maci up, cuddling her softness to my cheek for a moment, then deposit her firmly outside the school.

She thinks it is a game. I'd swear she's smiling as she trots back up to me, putting one paw on my leg.

I feel in a panic. I can't be late! Even with everything else happening in my country this is ingrained in me: be a good, dependable student. After Amar's death, I feel like I don't dare be the cause of any more strife for my poor parents. So I have to be perfect.

As I bend over Maci, pleading with her, I suddenly see feet in front of me. Big feet, wearing Converse All Star sneakers. I look up and see the boy from the rose garden. He's carrying a wrapped sandwich. I recognize the paper around it from the Alhambra, the popular café where students go to get lunch or a caffeine fix and alternate between arguing about politics and flirting.

I can feel my face flush.

"She won't leave you?" he asks. I shake my head. Very softly, he says, "I know how she feels." Then more loudly, "You go to class, let me take her outside."

"You go to another high school?" I ask. "Won't you be late for your own class?" In my head I'm counting the seconds. I have no more than a minute left.

"I'm in college, at the University of Sarajevo," he explains. "I'm just home visiting for a few days."

No wonder I haven't seen him before.

"She might not let you pick her up," I warn. But he flashes a disarming smile. His teeth are so white in his summer-bronze face. He bends down to Maci and scoops her up. To my surprise Maci lets him drape her across his shoulders like a fur stole. She hangs there limp and sleepy-eyed, perfectly content.

"I'll take her to the park across the street. She can wait for you there."

"But . . ."

"Go!"

I turn and run for class, while the boy carries Maci to a tiny triangle of greenery, a park with two trees and a bench. I slide into the classroom just after the final bell. Luckily my first class is engineering science with Teacher Živko. He looks like a dark dandelion: tall and thin, with a puff of hair and a huge beard. He is brilliant and gentle and absentminded. Half the time he is so deep in thought he wanders right past the classroom. He's not even there when I enter, so I have time to peek out the window overlooking the park.

There is the young man, sitting on the bench with Maci at his side, stroking her head. I can tell he is talking to her. Explaining things to her, maybe? Dino would laugh.

Only then do I look around for Olivera. She's not there.

Neither is at least half the class.

I'm amazed at my own stupidity, how long it took for it all to click. On the walk to school, I saw my Muslim friends, but not my Serb friends. And now as I look around and match absent faces to the empty desks I realize that every Serb student in the class is missing.

Teacher Živko is Serb, and he's missing too.

Suddenly our teacher strides in on his gangling legs, his hair looking like he stuck his finger in an electrical socket. For a moment I'm confused by the break in the pattern. Then I remember: Teacher Živko has a Muslim wife.

I sit down in my seat, numb, confused, but falling back on what is deeply ingrained in me. I am a good student. I behave in class; I learn whatever I am given. Whatever is happening, the lesson will go on.

I take out my notebook and balance two super-sharp pencils on top of it, waiting for class to start. The other students are milling around, but when Teacher Živko takes his place at the front of the room they settle into their seats too.

I want him to start talking about engineering and math and physics. I want this day to be normal. Yesterday he taught us how fast objects fall due to gravity—9.8 meters per second squared. I feel like I'm falling, accelerating faster and faster toward an inevitable crash. Teacher Živko, tell me again about terminal velocity. Tell me when this downward plummet will stop and I'll feel like I'm floating, even if I'm really still falling.

He stands in front of the class, and none of us know what to do. We fiddle with pencils, we wait, we watch.

Teacher Živko pushes his thumb and forefinger under the bridge of his glasses, rubbing the sides of his nose. I can see the sun shining through the electrified nimbus of his hair. Finally, he clears his throat and tells us in his scientific fashion what everyone else has hesitated to tell us outright.

"Children . . . children . . ." For a moment he looks like he is going to break down, but he settles his spectacles firmly back on his nose and goes on. "For me, the world is full of atoms and molecules, of forces and light and energy. It is not so for other people. To me, people are all the same—basic biology. But other people look at someone and see their parents, their ancestors back a thousand years. They see skin color, and religion, and politics. They do not see simply a lump of DNA struggling to survive."

As he speaks, his voice grows weaker, until on the last few words it cracks. He clears his throat but cannot go on. I wonder if he rehearsed that first part. It sounds like him, the words precisely chosen. Usually he will rattle on that way in long monologues, going off on wondrous tangents. Now, suddenly, he is at a loss for words.

"Children, I . . ." He turns away from us, and I hear him mutter to himself, "How can I tell them? I can hardly even tell myself."

Finally he forces himself to speak the simple, terrible truth. "The Serbs are gone. They have left the city. You who are left—the Muslims and the Catholics—will soon be under attack."

We absorb it in stunned silence. Now he speaks quickly, his words tumbling over each other as he tries to get them out as quickly as possible, before he breaks down. His eyes are glistening behind his spectacles.

"The Serbs, who would call themselves my people, sent secret messages to every Serb family to evacuate," he says. "Your friends, your study partners, your crushes—if they are Serbs, they have fled. Outside Bihać, the army, which is no longer your army but the Serb army, stands ready to destroy you."

He is weeping silently but doesn't seem to notice.

"I am ashamed for my people," he says, and now anger flashes through his despair. "For the Serbs, and for the human race. We have been humans for two hundred thousand years. We have had written language for five thousand years. We have been to space!" He runs his hands through his hair, making it wilder than ever. "Yet somehow we cannot learn not to hate each other."

He falls silent. At last I know what happened to Olivera. *Forget the filthy Muslims*, her parents must have told her. *Leave the rats in their nest to be destroyed.*

Did she fight them, I wonder. Did she weep and scream and tell them, *No, Amra is just like me. She's not a filthy rat. I will talk to her! I won't leave Bihać!*

Was she dragged away kicking and screaming?

Did she bow her head like a good girl and decide her parents must be right?

Did she even think of warning me?

"But you stayed, Teacher Živko," I say.

"I am not my ancestors," our teacher says firmly. "I am not bound by hate. My wife is Muslim. If those who call themselves my people hate her—the most gentle, generous, intelligent woman I know—then let them hate me too. I will not leave my city. I will not turn against my neighbors."

"What do we do?" I ask. I know whatever he says, the true answer won't be simple.

"You must go home, children," he says, his voice dull now as he takes off his glasses and methodically polishes them with a white handkerchief. "There is nothing more I can teach you."

I wander out of the school like a zombie. People pass me in a blur. Voices sound like they are underwater. I am moving in slow motion. "Get home as fast as you can!" a teacher shouts as she herds us out the doors. "Get to a basement!" I can scarcely make sense of her words. The world is in confusion, and I turn in a circle, clueless what to do next.

I feel hands grab my shoulders from behind. It is the boy from the rose garden. Funny, I think in a haze, I don't even know his name.

"What's going on?" he asks me. "All of a sudden everyone was running out of the school in a panic. Is there a fire?"

"The Serbs are gone!"

For a moment his eyes widen. Then he says with a wry smile, "Well, at least I know you're Muslim now. Or are you Croat?"

I don't answer; it's not the time for joking. "You don't understand. They didn't come to school. All the Serbs left the city. They know. They were told. War is coming to Bihać!"

He quickly catches my alarm now. "Where are you going?"

There's a strange roaring in my head that seems to drown out everything else.

"Dino!" is all I can utter.

"Who?"

"My brother!" He starts to run back into my school, but I pull him back. "Not here. He's at another school. I have to find him, get him home!"

"I'll come with you."

"No, you . . ."

He doesn't give me a chance to object. "Which way?"

But now my voice won't work, my legs won't work. I am paralyzed, hating myself because of the weakness of terror. I should be stronger than this! I should be getting my little brother to safety. But I stand there, legs rooted to the ground.

"Which way?" he asks again, giving me a little shake.

Then it is as if my legs wake up from a long sleep. Startled to alertness, now they are wild, running so fast the young man stumbles as I drag him along. All around us, students are flying from the campus like agitated bees, buzzing rumors.

We are down the street, almost at the nearest major intersection, when I suddenly remember. "Maci!" I cry, and skid to a halt.

Anyone else would have argued, I think. Get home, they'd say. Cats can take care of themselves. But the boy from the rose garden understands. "We have time. We'll grab Maci, then your brother." Immediately we turn to go back, leaving the intersection behind us, heading for the little park where he left Maci.

A sharp crack resonates behind us, breaking the day in two.

I know that sound.

When I was five, we visited my father's family in Šumatac, a land of forests and mountains, bears and wolves. One day I came upon Uncle Husein staring intently out the window on the second floor. He held a rifle. "See, Amra, there is a wolf stalking the livestock. Would you like to save the little lambs from the bad wolf?" He helped me put the rifle against my shoulder, showed me how to look down the sight. "Now squeeze the trigger." I did . . . and went flying back halfway across the room. My shoulder felt smashed, and my bottom hurt from the landing. Of course I didn't hit the wolf. I might have even hit a sheep!

I was terrified, heartsick, in pain. From that moment on, guns revolted me. If they could hurt me so much from the safe side, how terrible they must be from the dangerous side.

And so I know that sound.

It came from above.

"Sniper!" I scream.

At that moment we see a uniformed man stumbling toward us. He's limping, clutching his leg, waving his other arm to clear us away, a grimace of pain on his face. The man used to be a police officer but now he is part of the new, self-organized reserve force that protects our city, the Territorial Defense. "Run!" he gasps to everyone. "Get away from the intersection."

"It could have been us," the boy from the rose garden cries as we sprint away.

We hurry to the little park, but there is no Maci. We search the shrubs, the two trees, call her name, and meow at the top of our lungs, but she is nowhere to be found.

I want to search longer, but I have to get Dino, get him to safety. I remember how loyally Maci followed me home on the day of the tanks, how resolutely she stuck to our home, her new home. She will feel so lost without me!

I feel lost without her.

But at least the shock of the gunshot snapped me completely out of my paralysis. My mind is working like a whirlwind. This is my city. I know it better than anyone. I am the one who leads us safely through back roads and alleys, where the buildings are low, where no sniper would think to hide. We make it to Dino's school without encountering any more sniper fire.

Dino is outside, talking to some of his friends when we run up.

"What's going on?" Dino asks. "The teacher just sat at her desk crying, and when I reminded her that I'm supposed to give my presentation today she just said, 'It doesn't matter. Nothing matters.' Do you think that means I get a good grade?"

"You have to get home," the young man says. "We all do, right now. Come on!"

"You should go to your own home," I tell the young man. "We're close to home. We can make it."

But he won't leave. He insists on taking Dino and me home.

Only at our doorstep do I finally get the chance to ask his name.

"Davor," he says with a quirky grin.

"And I am . . ."

"Amra," he finishes for me. "I asked around at Alhambra this morning."

A moment later he is running down our street, homeward. "Be careful!" I shout after him. He stops, halfway down the block, and looks back. For a moment I am stricken with terror that in that precise moment a sniper will shoot him, a bomb will fall on him. But he only waves, then jogs away.

Just inside our door I meet Tata. Home from work? Mama is there too. Tata embraces first Dino, then me, then squeezes us both together until it is hard to breathe. Mama says, "Thank goodness you came home. Your father was just going to get you. Pack a bag, we're leaving in ten minutes."

"Where are we going?" Dino asks. "To the bee farm? To Šumatac? To the seaside?" Those are the places we normally go on holiday.

"No, we can't leave the city just now," Mama says. "We're going to Cousin Vesna's house."

"Why?" Dino asks.

She doesn't answer, but sends him to pack, not wanting to add to his worry. When he's gone, though, she tells me honestly that the army is besieging the city. She doesn't know if we're surrounded or not, but right now it would be too dangerous to try to leave.

But we need someplace safer than our home. As we fled school, the teacher advised everyone to go to a basement. Our house doesn't have one. I remember when Mama and Tata were sitting down with the architect he asked if they wanted one, even a small unfinished basement to store things in. *No*, Mama said with a shudder. *I hate close, dark places. Please give us light!* And so the house is filled with windows, and we store our things in an attic with a skylight, or the small second floor of our detached garage. It once seemed so wonderful to have a house with no dark corners, a house of glass.

Now I picture all that glass shattering with the first bomb. Even if the bomb doesn't kill us, the glass will shred the flesh from our bones.

But Cousin Vesna and her husband own several ćevapi restaurants, and their nearby house has a huge finished basement where they store all the food and restaurant supplies. I immediately see the wisdom of staying there: safety and provisions all in one place.

But it is not home. And Maci won't find us there.

War does not leave anyone with good choices.

"Mama, we can't go without Maci!"

"Don't worry about a cat at a time like this," she says impatiently.

"But she saved me from the sniper." I don't mention Davor, since the outbreak of war isn't the best time to tell Mama I'm interested in a boy.

"What? How did she . . . oh, Amra!" She hugs me as I tell her, then runs to the window. "Where is that animal? Maci, come on!" She still sounds cross, like she wants nothing to do with a cat, but when Maci comes bounding across the grass even Mama looks relieved. I let her in and go to pack my bag.

What do I bring? At first I pack as if I'm just staying for the weekend with one of the aunts: shorts and sandals and a bathing suit. Then I dump it all out. No, this is survival. Long pants, long sleeves. There might be rubble, glass. A book, to take my mind away from reality.

I shove the book in my bag. My schoolwork, because when this is over I don't want to fall behind.

I look down at the shoes I wore today, inherited from some male cousin. (I can't wear Amar's old shoes because his all had orthopedic elevations.) This pair is old, beat-down, with the sole flapping away at the toe like a talking mouth. The bottom is so thin I can feel every pebble in the pavement under my feet. They barely protect my feet on good roads. What rough, sharp things will I have to run over in a war, or afterward? What will I have to run away from?

I go to my closet and take out a sturdy shoebox. I open the top and take out the most beautiful sneakers. White, pristine, unscuffed, they have never touched a dirty road or blade of grass, only the polished indoor court. They are my volleyball shoes, bought after great deliberation and saving, two sizes too big so they'll last. I wear them with doubled socks, and still they are too big, but I lace them tightly and feel like with those shoes on I could jump over the net if I wanted to.

I'd promised these shoes they would only touch the wood court. After practice, I take them off and lovingly buff them with a soft cloth. They are like midwinter snow, pure and unsullied.

I put them in the bag too. I won't wear them yet, but I think maybe I will need the most dependable shoes before this is over.

Maci squeezes into the now-empty shoebox but can't quite fit no matter how she maneuvers. She switches instead to my bag, settling on top of my clothes as if saying, "Of course I'm coming with you!"

"How long will it last?" I ask my parents when we gather downstairs to leave.

"Not long," Mama reassures me. "The United States always intervenes in situations like this. They will put a stop to it soon."

"But how long?" I ask again.

"Two, maybe three days," Tata says with confidence, then pats my head, smoothing my hair back from my brow.

We are welcomed by Vesna, and at first it is like any visit, with coffee and food and chatter. But the voices are tense, and before long the children are ushered downstairs. At sixteen I would usually resent being classified with the children, but now I am grateful that someone else is making the decisions. Maci, seeing all the unfamiliar faces, jumps out of my bag and elects to stay outside. When a big German shepherd next door starts barking, I see Maci run back toward our house. I want to chase after her, but Mama pulls me close. "Your safety is more important."

In the basement there are several cots, a pile of blankets, and many of the big cushions they use around the sofra, the low traditional table some families have, where guests sit or lounge on the floor.

Later most of the adults come down, too, except for a couple of the women who are cooking. They descend with worried faces but beautifully prepared, scrumptious-smelling food.

"Why can't we eat upstairs?" Dino asks.

"Because this is a picnic," Mama tells him casually, and immediately Dino starts to enjoy himself, trading tidbits with his cousins.

We talk and play games until nightfall—which we know only by the clock, for there are no windows, only glaring, naked bulbs dangling over our heads. The room is so crowded and stuffy that even these few bulbs make an unbearable heat. There are many people here now: relatives and those from the neighborhood who don't have basements of their own. We make beds on the floor from the pillows and blankets. The oldest women get the few cots.

"A picnic, and then camping," Dino says sleepily as he settles under a blanket. For him, all this feels like an adventure. Anything out of the ordinary is exciting.

As I go to sleep that night I wish I had Maci to cuddle in my arms. She'll be at home, waiting for us to return.

That night we are packed like herring swimming in a school. The next day, more people come: other relatives, more neighbors without basements. So the second night we are like herring in a net, flopping so close we hit each other every time we move. The children stay below all day and night. The adults go upstairs one or two at a time to get food, to bring news.

I beg to be allowed out to look for Maci. Tata says he went back to our house and looked, but there was no sign of her. "She was probably frightened by the commotion. She'll turn up when this is all over."

"A few days, right?"

His mouth trembles as he smiles. "At most, my love."

Everyone is afraid and snappish. All the children beg for sunlight, for freedom, for anything except this airless basement. It smells like too many bodies. Now we are like herring in a can.

And I come to understand the torture of waiting.

For a day we hold our breath, waiting for what will come next.

For two days.

For three.

When the first bombs fall on the fourth day I am almost glad. Anything is better than the terrible anticipation.

Just before dawn I am woken by a rumbling. Thunder, the old, safe Amra thinks sleepily. A summer storm, no more. But the sound comes closer, and soon it is not rumbling but booming. Bombs!

No one else is awake yet, and though I want to scream I think, *Let them get another minute of sleep. Another minute of peace.*

Then one bomb falls so close it seems like it is on top of our heads, and the whole house shakes. I feel the feather touch of dust falling from the ceiling. My very bones seem to shake.

Everyone jolts awake, calling for their loved ones, screaming, crying, crawling for the lights. But the electricity is out, and we are trapped in the dark. My eyes are wide, staring at nothing.

I'm certain the world is ending.

It doesn't end. Not for us anyway. Not that morning.

The bombing doesn't stop for hours. We are rattled and shaken, but that bomb that woke us all is the closest hit. I can still hear them, though, every one. Some bombs are distant, muffled like the footsteps of someone in the night. The closest are like stampeding elephants, like freight trains. Sometimes there is a lull, and we begin to hope it might be over.

"They've made their point," Tata says. "The world is watching, and now the world will stop it."

But the bombing continues until noon.

Someone has lit candles, and we count the minutes by the loudly ticking clock. By three in the afternoon, it seems like the bombing must be over.

Tata and an uncle go upstairs. When they come back they report that our greatest fear is unrealized—there are no Serb soldiers in the street.

"Surely that means the United Nations has made them see reason," Tata assures us. "We will negotiate, we will rebuild."

We will bury the dead, I think.

One of the neighbors staying with us bursts into tears when Tata tells her the blast that woke us destroyed her house.

"But your family is safe," Mama chides her. "Things can be replaced. People can't."

For a long time the children remain still with fear. The hours of bombing have subdued us. But we've been locked up for three days, and after a while even our fear can't keep us still and quiet. We start to beg to be allowed outside. Upstairs, at least! Anything, just to see the sun after our long confinement. I can tell Tata wants Dino and me to stay below, but then he is swept up in the work of checking on neighbors, clearing rubble, marshaling supplies, putting out fires. We are on our own. We don't get official permission, but when Tata and Mama aren't paying attention Dino and I slip outside.

We set off, hand in hand. I clench him tightly, sure something awful will happen. But soon he breaks free and is skipping through the debris like it is a holiday. He was afraid during the explosions, but he seems like he's already over it. Is he that brave? Or only that young? He's fascinated by the cross section of the house that was hit. With half the walls sheared off, the private becomes public. A toilet perches at the edge of a ragged precipice in the bisected bathroom, staring at the street.

Dino dodges playfully around glass, peers into a crater in the street. I realize that I didn't wear my volleyball shoes. It doesn't matter. After seeing the devastation, I think this is too much for one girl to outrun, no matter what shoes she is wearing.

Because it's all luck, isn't it? Good luck for one, bad luck for another. Why was Vesna's house spared, while their neighbor's was peeled open like a sardine can? I see smoke rising in parts of the city, and I imagine people creeping out of their houses thinking, how lucky I was!

Now, watching Dino cavort through the ruined street, I have a sudden reckless feeling. We could all die at any moment. I've been an obedient girl, a good student all my life. But this danger would be no different if I were bad. Suddenly I want to do something bad, for once in my life.

We are passing the house of Kudić, an old architect with a pretentious French beret and opinions on everything. The yard is filled with fruit trees and bordered by a limestone wall. The neighborhood kids love to climb the wall, reach over, and steal a piece of his fruit. Most of the time it is hard and unripe apples and plums, so bitter and nasty they call it driskulje, or *diarrhea fruit*. The kids don't care. The fun is in being yelled at and chased by Kudić.

Of course, a goody-goody like me has never done it. But now, what do I have to lose?

I climb the wall, snatch a rock-hard green apple, and take a bitter bite of the criminal life.

Then I can pretend it is the driskulje that makes my stomach queasy as we round the corner to our home street.

I exhale a deep sigh. Our street is untouched. To look at our house, you would think there had been no bombs this morning. There are kids on the street, even. I see four girls, all close to my age. One of them, Maida, I grew up with; her father is a music teacher in Mama's school.

"Come walk with us!" Maida calls out.

"I have to look for my cat!" I call back, but Dino, who I think has a crush on one of the girls, runs to join them.

"Be careful!" I shout, though how on earth can he be careful of something dropping from the sky?

Then, finally, I can do what I've longed to do for three days: I look for Maci.

I call her name, search all around the garden, peer into the canopy of every tree. She's not there. As a last resort I go inside to look, though I don't know how she'd have gotten in. Maybe I left a window open?

It is strange being back in my house, even though only three days have passed. It seems so much longer, a lifetime ago. There is still a coffee cup on the table, the remnants dried to black sludge. My cousin Žana's grandmother used to read our fortunes in the coffee grounds. She gave Žana many loves, but me just one. The coffee grounds showed long life for all of us. I peer into Mama's coffee cup but have no idea what fate her coffee grounds foretell.

I can hear my own breathing echoing in the empty room. The house feels hollow.

"Maci!" I call, but of course there is no answer. Maybe she is in my room, her favorite place. I run upstairs, but there is no sign of her. Crushed, I walk out onto my balcony and look down the block, where I can just make out several tiny figures at the end of the street, Dino with the four girls.

Then an explosion, so much louder than what I heard from the basement. This bomb is like a dragon. I see its fiery breath through the window as it explodes at the end of the street.

When the smoke clears, there is only fire and wreckage in the place Dino and the girls were walking.

CHAPTER 7

I'm down the stairs, out of the house, and halfway down the block before I even know what I'm doing. Then, in the middle of the street, I skid to a halt. If I go to him, to that smoking tree and cleft pavement and deadly metal shards where my brother and friends were walking, it will be real. Some part of me commands me to stop, to delay what I know must be true: my brother is dead. Amar, now Dino. My first thought isn't for my own grief, but for my parents'. Losing Amar almost destroyed them.

I see people around me. Some, who have come out of hiding for a few breaths of air, are running back to the dubious safety of the indoors. Others, hearing the bomb so close, are running out of their shelters to help.

I force myself to walk toward the end of the street. I hear the shouts, the lamentations. I'm close enough to see carnage in the rubble, and I steel myself, willing myself forward, wishing I were anywhere else, to confirm what I already know.

Then from behind me I hear the voice that has teased me almost as long as I can remember. The voice that wakes me too early, that asks for a pencil, for the last roll, for help with homework. I turn, and there is Dino, his face crunched with concern, clutching Maci in his arms. His knees are cut and bleeding.

"I heard her meow from the second story of the garage," he says in a weak, frightened voice. "I told them I'd be right back." He stares blankly at the place the bombs fell, rubbing his chin into Maci's soft fur as she dangles in his arms.

"You're alive!" I pull him into a tight embrace. I feel like I'll never let him go again. Maci must be half suffocated, squeezed between us like pastrma in a sandwich. She squirms out of his hold and drops lightly to the ground, but she stays at our feet.

"I was climbing down the ladder, and then it felt like an earthquake. The whole garage shook, and spiders fell out of the rafters. I fell . . ." He sounds like he's in a daze.

"Maci saved you," I gasp as I look down at her. She's cleaning her face with one paw, but she cocks her head to look back at me quizzically. "You would have been killed."

"Did they . . . ," he begins, looking down the street where the girls last were. Where he would have been, if not for Maci. "Were they . . ."

Our friends are gone. "Look away, Dino!" I turn him around, make a wall with my body between him and the things no child should witness. Because there are parts. There are pieces. Where four girls once stood breathing fresh air after days of confinement, girls with hopes, dreams, a future, there is now only carnage.

Dino is pulling away from me. "We have to go and help them."

Just then I hear Tata calling us, out of breath as he runs from Vesna's house searching for us. The relief in his face when he spots us is overwhelming . . . followed by his grief when he realizes that someone else's children have been killed.

"Come, my darlings," he says as he pulls us away from the terrible scene at the end of the street. "There's nothing you can do." People are already there, carrying away broken bodies.

As we walk back I think of Maida, who was my best friend before I started school. Why did we grow apart? Mostly because we made other friends. I always liked her, but after we got older we never really got together anymore, though we always greeted each other happily in the neighborhood. Maida had such a welcoming smile and huge beautiful eyes. I remember our parents used to take us to the school where they both taught, and we'd sneak into her music-teacher father's office and play with all his instruments, making a cacophony that delighted us and offended the other teachers. After we were punished (which consisted of her father shaking a finger at us and telling us not to do it again) Mama would soothe us with sandwiches of butter and plum jam.

How can Maida have been snuffed out just like that? At Vesna's door, Mama looks frightened but resolute. "Get back inside, hurry!" Mama says.

But we don't go in, not yet. We sink to our knees on the porch and cover Maci with strokes, with kisses, with praise. She accepts it patiently.

"You're a hero, Maci," I whisper to her. "A guardian angel."

Cousins and neighbors come outside, and we tell them how Dino would have been killed if it hadn't been for Maci.

"She didn't save his life," a skeptical teen boy says. "It's not like she dragged him out of the way of the bomb."

But a grandmother hushes him and shares her wisdom as she looks at Dino: "That cat is a lucky spirit. I can see it in her eyes. Someone has come to look after your family."

"Who?" Dino wants to know. The grandmother can't answer that, but in a flash of inspiration I have my guess.

Once, my family had a peaceful, brilliant, compassionate spirit—my brother Amar. He was the heart of our household, a beacon of happiness that shone even through his pain and difficulty. When he died, a spark was extinguished.

I look into Maci's orange eyes. Can I see that same spark there?

I don't know how these things work; I don't know what is possible. Science teaches us the rules of the universe, but it also shows us that there are vast unknowable things that we humans can only dimly comprehend. I know that if it were possible, Amar would find a way to keep us safe.

Is there a piece of Amar's spirit in Maci? Did he send her to look after us?

Or was it just coincidence that because of Maci, Dino is alive? That because of Maci, I was not shot.

I don't know. But when I look in Maci's eyes I feel a comfort I haven't experienced in seven years.

Far away, in another part of the city, a bomb falls. I flinch, but Maci's warm body is still and calm beneath my hand.

Despite my scientific mindset, I realize I don't need evidence. Cat or spirit, good luck or coincidence, I am grateful this gentle soul has come to us at exactly the right time.

There's a sharp edge of guilt to my gratitude, though. My brother is safe. But I hear the heartbreaking wails of four other families who have lost their daughters. They are just as deserving of luck and protection.

These are not the first casualties of the war, but they are the first ones that I know, the first deaths that are personal, real. Our family was sheltered from tragedy this time. But for how long?

Our war has begun.

I came out to see the sky. Now, as Mama and Tata come wearily back, I look up at the sky one more time. When I was trapped in the basement I longed for that piercing blue speckled with clouds. Now the sky seems a dangerous place, a savage kingdom where deadly missiles like angry dragons can fly in to shatter our peaceful lives down below. It is with some relief that I close the door behind me.

Maci isn't allowed in, not even when I tell Mama and Tata how she saved Dino. "It is not our house, and there's no space for her. Besides, where would she do her business? She is used to being outside. She doesn't look like she wants to be with all those strange people."

I know Mama is right. Maci puts up with other people—out of politeness, I think—but she seems to only want to be with our family.

Mama bends down and tickles Maci under the chin, and I know for a fact that she loves Maci now too. "But you can feed her. I know she'll stay close."

"Because she is our cat now?" I prompt.

Mama sighs. "Because she is our cat now," she echoes in confirmation.

I notice how tired and strained Mama looks. Even in disaster she keeps herself so neat that it is hard to see signs of stress unless I pay close attention. But though her hair is smooth and neat, there's brick dust in it. The dust is on her face, too, and I can see the lines of sweat, or tears, or both down her cheeks. When she tucks a stray bit of hair behind her ear, I see a streak of blood on the back of her head.

"You're hurt!" I say instinctively, catching her fingers.

Then I realize. It's not her blood.

"Oh, Mama!"

I wish I could protect them from all of this. I know their only thought is to protect Dino and me . . . but I want to be strong enough to keep them safe.

When we go inside, Maci curls up on the porch with a resigned air, and I promise to come out to feed her and check on her as often as I can.

Inside, our prison sentence resumes.

For two more weeks we stay inside, mostly in the basement. A few people make quick forays outside to get food and other supplies, but the bombs are still falling.

Twenty people sleep in the basement every night. They are relatives, neighbors, friends . . . but I have to confess that being around them is starting to drive me crazy. For two weeks I can't escape them—their breathing, their snoring, the smells of their bodies. It sounds uncharitable, I know, and I'm sure they're just as sick of me and everyone else as I am. But being trapped with so many people is torment. I have no silence, no solitude, no room for my thoughts.

Sleep is my only escape, my only peace, but even that is constantly interrupted. Sometimes it is the bombs, the roaring monsters that are shattering our world bit by bit, biting off chunks until one day there may be no Bosnia left. When they land and explode I am shocked rudely awake.

Almost as bad is the sound of a girl who sleeps near me. From stress and anxiety, she grinds her teeth. I never would have dreamed that this could make such a loud sound. But all night, every night, it fills my ears like the sound of termites eating wood. I lie awake, staring into the darkness, counting the seconds of night, hoping she will stop so I can snatch at least a few hours of sleep.

She does stop eventually, and if I can convince my own high-strung mind to relent I can sleep. But if I don't manage to lose consciousness in that brief window the grinding inevitably starts again, so irritating it feels as if it were my nerves that are being ground between her molars.

My eyes feel hot all the time. My head throbs. I tell myself to be grateful to be alive, that sleeplessness is better than death. I think of my friend killed in the bombing at the end of the street. What would she give to be alive now, even if she was sore and bored and annoyed?

And so there is a mix of both self-pity and deep guilt alongside the terror.

I try to tell Tata what I'm feeling, though it is hard to put into words. I try to explain the guilt I feel at being bothered by such petty things as grinding teeth at a time like this.

"You are only human, Amra," he tells me. "We humans aren't perfect. Don't be ashamed of the things you feel, even if they aren't perfectly good feelings. We are made up of many parts, many impulses, not all of them one hundred percent noble. As long as your actions and intentions are kind and good. You wouldn't ever criticize her to her face about grinding her teeth, would you?"

"Of course not!" I reply, shocked at the very thought.

"Well then, you are a good person. The fact that you feel guilty shows you're a good person."

"Maybe bad people never believe that they are bad," I venture. "While good people are always questioning their goodness. Maybe that's what keeps them good—the constant questioning."

"My wise daughter," Tata says, pulling me into one of his famous loving hugs.

CHAPTER 8

For the other kids and teens, it seemed like the best part of the war was that they got to skip school. Not for me. Without my lessons, without the challenge of math and physics and literature, I feel bereft.

When Tata comes back at dawn I resolve to ask him about school. Every night Tata goes to sleep at our home, making a bed on the floor just inside the entrance. He says he's protecting it in case Serbs come. What could you possibly do against Serb soldiers, I want to ask him. But I know he feels like he has to do something, anything. As the man of the family it is his job to protect us and our home. Even if we all know it is futile. If Serb soldiers came to our house, he'd be killed, simple as that.

Maci spends every night with him, and the next day, stiff and sore from sleeping on the hard floor, Tata regales us with tales of Maci's heroism. "She's as good as a guard dog!" he praises her. "Up at every sound, glaring at the door like she's ready to take on the whole Serb army!" When he leaves, she stays by our house, continuing to guard it in our absence, waiting for us to come home.

"The system has to start again," I say to Tata one morning. "A country can't exist without certain things—hospitals and fire stations and schools. How can we have a future without those basic things?"

Tata and Mama exchange looks, and I know what they're thinking. Our country might not have a future.

"I'll go and find out if anyone knows when school will resume," Tata says. "At the very least, I should get your records so that when all of this is over, you can start up again."

"It would be a shame to let that perfect grade point average go to waste," Mama says, looking at me.

"Er, maybe when you get my records you can smudge the ink a bit?" Dino suggests. "Turn a four into a five, if you see one?"

We laugh, huddled together in our designated nook of the crowded basement. But we don't laugh for long. Bad enough that Tata goes to our house just a short distance away every night. But anything could happen on a longer trip into the city to our schools.

"Tata, is it safe to go out?" Dino asks.

"I will be perfectly fine!" he assures us. Which, I notice, doesn't exactly answer the question.

"I should go with you," Mama offers.

"No!" Tata says at once, very firmly, slamming his hand on a table. Mama raises her eyebrows, and without meaning to, I giggle. Tata and Mama have a very equal and loving relationship, but for a moment he sounds like one of those domineering men who keep their wives cowed and obedient. The very thought of my parents having this kind of relationship, where one orders the other around, is ludicrous.

I stifle the laugh at once, though, because Tata looks so upset.

"No," he says more softly. "I don't want you to take the risk." I can see his imaginings in his moist eyes.

Very tenderly, Mama takes his hands in hers. "This is our life now. We have to work and eat. We have to take care of our friends and family. We have to learn and we have to . . . to thrive. No matter what else is happening. Yes, we might have bad luck and be hit by a bomb or a bullet. But it doesn't matter."

"Doesn't matter!" Tata says, aghast.

"The risk doesn't matter. Life must go on. We can't be afraid."

"I can. I'm afraid for you."

"And I for you, and for our children. But someday we'll have to go out into our city as if there is nothing wrong. If we don't, the Serbs have already won."

She kisses him on the cheek, lingering against him for the space of a sigh. "We can't be afraid for each other all the time."

"I can be brave for myself," Tata says finally, bringing Mama's hands to his lips. "Not for you. However," he adds with an attempt at cheer, "I am a very skilled actor. So if it is what you need, I'll pretend not to be afraid for you. How's that?"

"I'll take what I can get," Mama says with a wry laugh. "I won't go out this time—though we can't stay inside forever."

With a sigh, Tata sets out into our besieged, beleaguered city.

It is extremely hard to pace nervously in a room jam-packed with people, but I manage it, weaving around cots and kids and grannies with a restless pace, waiting for Tata to come back. Once while he is gone I hear a distant rumble and I want to run to Mama, to get her reassurance that out of all the places a bomb could fall, it won't seek out Tata. I find her talking with an elderly woman, seated on a cushion on the floor helping her thread a needle. I don't think she heard the faraway blast over her conversation. I can't add to her fears. Comforting me would only trouble her.

And so we wait, until at last Tata comes back.

Mama runs to him, and we're not far behind. Mama is good at keeping her emotions in check. She feels things as deeply as Tata, I think, but she knows one of the two has to be stoic, so she keeps her feelings inside much of the time. Now, though, her relief and love are plain on her face.

"What was it like out there?" I ask.

"It hurts to look at Bihać," Tata says. "As you walk along, so much of it is just the same as ever, the pretty houses with colorful flower borders, the neat shops. I could almost ignore the fact that there are hardly any people on the streets, and most of the stores are closed. I said hello to a few people, but no one stopped to chat. They scurry on their errands with their heads down, their shoulders hunched, as if by making themselves smaller they will be too insignificant for a bomb to notice."

He rubs his temples as Mama leads him to a seat.

"Then I round a corner, and suddenly I'm hit with the stark, terrible reality of what is happening: a pile of rubble where my favorite café used to be. Smoke rising from the elementary school. A mourning procession. Another. And another. Oh, Dilka, how can this be happening?"

Then, with a grim face, he tells us about his mission to our schools.

"Your school records are gone."

"What do you mean gone?" Mama asks.

"I mean Amra's favorite teacher, Lepa, the one in charge of the records for your grade, pulled out all of the documents relating to her. Not only her, but all the Muslim students. It's like they never existed. If you try to go to school after this, there's no record of your grades and accomplishments. You've been wiped out!"

"Why would she do that?" I ask. Lepa is a Serb, but she cares about all her students. I try to think of an excuse. Maybe things aren't as they appear. She could have taken the records away to keep them safe. Maybe a Serb administrator ordered her to destroy them, so she hid them, and after the war she'll reappear, reveal our records, and go back to teaching. Or she fears that Serb soldiers entering the city will come after Muslim girls if there is an easy way to find them, and what better than school records with our names and addresses on them?

She had to be protecting us. She's not like the others.

I remember Olivera saying the same thing. *Amra, you're not really a Muslim. Not like the others.*

"Your entire educational record is gone," Tata says. "You've been erased."

Tata and Mama decide it is still far too dangerous for us to leave our shelter. I endure a few more days, and then when Tata comes back from his nightly vigil with Maci he brings terrible news. Strangely, Maci has followed him inside this time.

"Dilka, sit down," he says very gently. Maci sits next to Mama's feet, almost on them, in her compact bread-loaf shape.

"Who is it?" she asks at once, almost sharply, and I realize that like me, she has been bracing herself for this kind of news for weeks. I fill my time making long lists of people I love, all my relatives and friends, just so I can specifically hope that nothing happens to them. I feel like if I leave anyone off my list I'll jinx them. I am so powerless that anything, even a superstition or nonsensical charm, feels like it might do some good.

"It is your brother, Ejub. He . . . he died last night."

I see Mama crumple, deflate. She hides her face in her hands, and her body starts to heave. I can feel the grief pouring off her like heat from a fire. She wants to wail, to tear her hair, to scream her sorrow to the world. But here, surrounded by people, she manages to contain the raging of her grief.

Ejub is the only boy in a family of girls, and my mother and her sisters adore him, dote on him. Mama and Tetka Fatma, in particular, make it their mission in life to spoil him. He is the most handsome man in a good-looking family, with the charisma of an American movie star. It's not surprising that a man like that—so beautiful, so used to being spoiled by a gaggle of women—will have a lot of female attention. Women's eyes follow him in the streets. We've never gotten along with his wife, Sado, or his children, Adnan and Azra.

"What happened to him, Tata?" I ask. Mama can't speak yet.

"Mensur told me," Tata says softly. The people around us can't hear, but they know what is happening. It has happened to all of them so far. Someone comes with news about a relative, a friend.

"He had been standing outside his home, right by the lilac trees, when a bomb hit. Neighbors took him to the hospital, where Mensur treated him."

"Mensur is a gynecologist," Mama says. "Why was he treating Ejub?"

"There aren't enough doctors. Everyone is doing what they can." He enfolds Mama gently. "It wouldn't have mattered. Mensur said his legs were almost completely severed. Mensur clamped the arteries, but there's no blood for transfusions. He was too far gone. I'm so sorry, my love."

Then Mama's self-control shatters and she begins to keen, a low and terrible sound I never want to hear her make again. I put my arms around her. So does Dino. But though we're comforting her, we're also reminding her of how much more she has to lose in this war.

"We have to go home," she says between her fingers. Then in one smooth movement she wipes the tears away from her eyes and cheeks, drawing herself upright, suddenly aware of all the eyes on her. She's such a controlled person, so public in her joy but so private in any darker emotions. She can't mourn properly here surrounded by people.

Tata nods, and without another word Dino and I begin to pack. Just a few minutes later we leave the safety and stagnation of our bunker and go back to living our lives.

Only now death is an inescapable part of living.

It is strange being outside again, fully outside, after so long in the basement. The ceilings were so low I felt as if I were being crushed by the building even without the help of any bombs.

But now, stretching tall and walking out in the middle of the street under an open sky, I feel naked, exposed. I squint into the bright light and watch the skies for peril. Maci isn't worried about danger. She's in a festive mood. She leads the way to our home, stopping to pounce on blowing leaves or roll on her back to flash her appealing tummy fur. If we slow down, she meows to encourage us.

I came here to find a family, a home, she seems to say. *It is about time you all remembered what you're supposed to do!*

The bomb that killed Maida and the other girls is the closest damage. Our home, and the ones nearest to us, are intact.

"See, no bombs hit here," Dino says as he scampers inside. "We could have just stayed home." I follow more sedately, thinking, yes, but what if . . . ?

The house seems strange, as if I've been gone a much longer time. The air smells stale (though not nearly as bad as the basement), and Mama immediately goes from room to room, opening windows. I follow her, letting my hands trail over all the furniture, the billowing curtains, becoming reacquainted with all our possessions again. I only realize now that in my mind, I'd said goodbye to them. I'd told myself—tried to convince myself—that things aren't important. And in a logical, rational way, they aren't. Not as important as the people I love. But as I stroke the familiar cuts and grooves on our kitchen table, I realize that things do matter. I think we put a little bit of our souls into our household goods. Taking a drink of water from my favorite cup feels like meeting an old friend. My bed seems to welcome me happily.

And there on the wall are the little tapestries I stitched as a young child. Under Tetka Fatma's patient guidance I embroidered cheerful scenes. One shows a little girl in shorts chasing a butterfly with a net, in front of a red-roofed house. It is an idyllic scene, so full of innocent joy. I couldn't have been more than six or seven when I sewed it. I can see the places where I messed up a little on the roof.

Another shows a happy boy running through a field of flowers. I always thought of him as my brother Amar, only the boy in the tapestry is happy and healthy. It is the way Amar could have been. And then there's one of a little girl in a gorgeous frilly party dress. I always loved that one because she had what I never did—fancy clothes. I was glad that someone had them, even if it wasn't me.

The house makes one of its little settling sounds. I know it is just from the change in temperature and humidity that came from opening the windows, one of those little noises every house makes. But at that moment, to me, it feels like our house is sighing, getting comfortable again after many weeks of loneliness and tension.

For a while, it almost feels like the sojourn underground was no more than a long vacation. A bad vacation, where no one bothered to read the travel brochure too carefully beforehand.

But some things have changed. When I automatically flip on the light switch to unpack my bag, nothing happens. That's right, no power. With a sigh I move closer to the window to use the natural light.

It doesn't seem so bad until I look ahead. No reading late at night by the light of my bedside lamp! When will I do my homework?

Then I stop myself. Why am I worried about school when it is a question of whether I'll be blown to bits in my sleep? School may never start up again, and if it does, I might not be around to attend.

I go back downstairs and find Mama sitting alone at the kitchen table. "The men have gone to do manly things in the garage," Mama says. "Something with the fluids in the car, since it has been sitting so long."

"I was thinking about Uncle Ejub," I say as I sit beside her. "The last time I saw him was that day he picked me up from school. Remember?"

Ejub had been passing by just as my classes got out. When he spotted me, he offered to drive me home. He was strangely emotional, like he was worried about something, but very kind. He told me that I was an incredible young woman and that my life will be amazing if I stay true to myself. *Be happy, Amra, no matter what it takes. Stay committed to school, and keep your loved ones close always.* Then he went inside and talked to Mama while I started my homework.

Mama dabs at her eyes. "I'll tell you what we talked about that day. I didn't tell you then, because I felt like you were too young. But now . . ."

Our eyes lock, and I understand that even though that was only a few weeks ago, I've become practically an adult since then. I'll have to take on more grown-up responsibilities—and one of the greatest responsibilities is knowledge.

"Your uncle Ejub has a sad history," Mama tells me. "You know how the women all fawn over him. He dated many women, but I think he was only ever truly in love with one. Naja was loving and patient and kind, an open-minded woman of education and wit who fit in well with me and my sisters. She would have been welcomed to the family. They were together for ten years. I don't say that he didn't make mistakes all that time, but she loved him. She stuck with him.

"Then he met another woman at a party. It was Sado. Naja found out and married someone else to spite him. Ejub got drunk on the night of Naja's wedding. He married Sado soon after."

"Poor Ejub!" I say, though I can't help thinking that if he was really in love he should have been more loyal.

"Naja mourned the separation," Mama goes on, "but she married a fine, well-to-do man and slipped out of Ejub's life. I know he kept a cheerful face for you, but he and Sado didn't always get along."

"He hurt Naja, who loved him so much," I say.

"Yes . . . but . . ." Mama breaks off and sighs. "I don't know. It was a bad situation. Someone was going to end up unhappy, suffering."

"It makes me realize how lucky we are," I say. "You and Tata never fight."

"Of course we do! We just love and respect each other, so our fights come out as mild disagreements and friendly discussions. If we disliked each other like some couples do, the same tiny issues would lead to screaming and smashed dishes." She shudders at the thought.

"That day he picked you up, though, Ejub talked to me about Naja. Her husband had recently died, and a respectable period of mourning had passed. She was free now. Could he run away with her?"

"It's right out of a novel!" I say, entranced by the idea of handsome middle-aged Uncle Ejub having a late-life romance fit for a fairy tale.

"It wasn't so easy," Mama tells me. "I could feel the joy emanating from him. It was the first time in years that I saw him so full of enthusiasm. 'You say she's free,' I told him. 'But you're not free. What about Sado? What about your children?' His face fell, but he pointed out that his children are grown. His son moved away, his daughter is of legal age. And then, like some kind of Victorian prude, I found myself saying, 'But think of the scandal!'"

It was such an old-fashioned thing for my liberal, progressive mother to say. She and her sisters have never been religious or conservative in any way. They run around in bikinis in the summer, sunbathe topless and forget to tie their straps when they sit up, noticing with no more than a giggle. They all live good lives because they are good people, not because they are following some imposed moral code.

"I didn't know how to advise him, and he desperately needed advice," Mama continued. "So we went to Fatma." Fatma is the oldest of the living sisters, old enough to be Mama's own mother. "I went back and forth. It is such an amazing, glamorous love story, isn't it?" She is smiling through her tears, and I know she is picturing Ejub happy with his long-lost love. "People don't usually get a second chance like that."

But Fatma was convinced it was a bad idea. "It would make our family look ridiculous," she said, "for him to run away from his responsibilities." Though as liberal as Mama was on most issues, on the subject of marriage bonds she was firm. You stick with your family.

"She was so strongly against Ejub running away that eventually she convinced me. Just before the war we told him. 'Sometimes you have to live with your decisions,' Fatma told him. 'You don't get to choose your own happiness at other people's expense.'"

"And he took your advice?"

"He did. It killed me to see him then. He seemed to deflate, like his soul flew out of his body. But he never called Naja again. He stayed." Mama begins to sob again. "He stayed, and he died. Because of me! Because I didn't let him go. He could have been safe and far away with Naja. But no, he stayed, and had his legs blown off, and died, because of my advice."

"It's not your fault, Mama."

"I should have let him run away with her," Mama says through bitter tears. "I should have let him be happy . . ."

CHAPTER 9

All that morning, Maci is a busybody, prowling from room to room, smelling every corner, leaping in and out of the open windows to inspect the perimeter before coming back inside to resume her surveillance. Every few minutes she'll come and find me, catching my attention by flopping at my feet, meowing insistently until I pet her, then continuing her rounds. She is smelling everything, rubbing her cheeks against furniture, marking it as her own, and making sure everything is safe.

"Don't worry, Maci," I tell her. "We're home now. Everything will be fine." She blinks at me, detecting the lie as easily as I now see through my parents' reassurances. "Well, maybe not. But whatever happens will be easier to bear here at home, together."

She grabs my wrist with her velvet paws, keeping her claws carefully sheathed, and pulls my hand to her head, rubbing it with her whiskery jowls. Her purr is a deep, contented rumble. This little creature has seen horror, I'm sure. She's known loneliness. Now all she needs is family. If she has us, she can get through anything.

I tell myself I will be the same.

Suddenly Maci jumps to her feet, fully alert. The hair along her back stands up in a ridge, and her ears are pricked sharply forward. I don't hear anything alarming. "What is it?" I ask her.

Like she's stalking a dangerous animal, she pads carefully toward the open window, her tail lashing back and forth. She places her paws on the windowsill and peers intently out. I follow her, leaning on the windowsill too, framing her with my arms.

"Well, that's not right," I murmur to her. Then I call over my shoulder, "Tata, Mama, Dino, come look at this!"

Across the street, Bakir, the hoodlum's younger brother who I had to punish after he teased me about Amar, is standing in our neighbor's driveway. He looks around nervously, shifting from foot to foot, swinging his arms. He doesn't live anywhere near here, and isn't related to our neighbor . . . so what is he doing here?

As I watch, wondering why Maci is so alarmed at this, I remember a curious incident that happened right after the weekend. I hadn't given it a moment's thought after it was over—there was so much else going on—but now it comes back to me. As Tata and Mama come behind me to peer over my shoulder, I tell them about our neighbor Jovanka.

"She came over on Monday with a jar of plum jam." They have a huge plum tree in their front yard, and every year it is laden with fruit. "You were both out, and I didn't know where you were. You didn't leave a note." I say this with just a hint of accusation. My parents go crazy if I don't leave a note when I go out, sure I've been kidnapped. However, they always forget to leave one for me when they go out.

"There's nothing unusual about that," Mama says as she peers at Bakir, who is now whistling and I think trying not to look nervous. He's failing miserably. "What is that young man doing?"

I shrug and go on. "The thing is, she said she was going away for a couple of days, to Bosanski Petrovac, where they have their weekend home. She said she'd like me to go with her."

I remember how she stood awkwardly in the doorway, refusing to come in even though I reluctantly invited her. I both don't like and always feel sorry for Jovanka. She looks like all the moisture evaporated from her body decades ago. Her skin is sunken and wrinkled. Not the nice wrinkles of the old women in my family—laugh lines and crow's-feet, the wrinkles of a life well-lived. Jovanka's lines are the wrinkles of collapse, of surrender, as if her skin just gave up.

Her husband is sleek and smug, and always looks cared for and well rested, unlike his permanently exhausted wife. She has spent her life caring for him. He never seems to have a care in the world.

She stood there that day in a brown flowered dress covered in an immaculately clean apron, and all but begged me to come with them. "It's so nice this time of year," she wheedled. "I talked about it with your parents a while ago. Didn't they tell you?"

"I was confused," I tell my parents now. "We aren't exactly friends." In fact, she had never spoken a word to me in all my life. Our families are cordial as neighbors, friendly and polite. My parents say hello, and when we give Jovanka some of Tetak Ale's honey, she reciprocates with plum jam. But we've never been invited into their home, never met for lunch or coffee. When her grandsons visited, when I was younger, I was never invited to play with them.

"So I told her that you two weren't home, and I'd have to ask you. I didn't want to go, and I never dreamed you'd let me."

"We wouldn't," Tata says. "She never asked us."

"She wanted to kidnap me?" I ask, incredulous. "Her husband was already loading things in their car, and in a little trailer pulled behind. She made me promise if you came home before they left that I'd ask you. Luckily, you didn't."

"They are Serb," Mama says. "They knew what was coming. I think word spread through all the Serb residents, from family to family. Get out of the city so we can kill the Muslims. Bosanski Petrovac is a mostly Serb city."

"Then why would she want a Muslim girl with her?" I ask, perplexed.

Tata frowns a moment, thinking. "Things were already getting tense then. The local police—mostly Muslim—had already set up some checkpoints in Bihać, and along the local roads. Maybe she worried that Serbs would be stopped, but if she had a Muslim with her, they'd be allowed safe passage."

It certainly is a cynical way of looking at things. But that is what my world is like now. We all expect the worst.

"Then what?" I ask. "Would she have really taken me to Bosanski Petrovac?"

Tata bites his lip, but Mama says, "She probably would have abandoned you right in the middle of a Serb stronghold, once she and her husband were safe." The war has robbed Mama of any remaining naiveté.

It's so hard to believe! Even if they weren't friendly, is it possible that someone—an old lady who has known me for years—could so cold-heartedly use me like that? Use me and abandon me?

To my surprise, Dino is nodding. "I believe it," he says. "There's always been something off about that family. Wrong. The grandsons are monsters. Do you know I found them trying to set a cat on fire? They caught it and were trying to light its tail. My friends and I had to fight them to make them let it go."

I flinch, picturing my little Maci at their mercy.

Just then there is a flurry of new activity at Jovanka's abandoned house. Several men come out. They are in their late teens. I recognize one of them as Irfan, Bakir's older brother, head of his little gang of street criminals.

"He's got a gun!" I cry.

Mama pulls me back from the window, while Tata starts uncertainly for the door, then hesitates. He has the impulses of a hero, but what could he do? We watch a while longer.

A moment later more young men come out. One is carrying a television, its cords dangling in the grass. Two more are carrying a pretty settee, upholstered in a rose pattern, with gilded armrests. They load these things in a van parked at the curb, while Irfan shouts instructions, waving the gun around.

"Why are you bothering with furniture?" we hear him shout. "We want cash, jewelry, guns."

"My mom will like the roses on that little sofa thing," a thuggish-looking man answers sheepishly.

"Well, you can take what you like after we clear out the good stuff. You know, that's not a bad idea. It might be a long time before the city will get any new deliveries. We have to think differently." He turns to Bakir. "Why are you standing out here kicking your heels?"

"You told me to be lookout," Bakir answers sulkily.

"What's to look out for? Who will stop us? Now, if there's nothing valuable left, look for useful things. Food that will last a long time—dried beans, grains, and oils. Then get blankets and winter coats."

"But it's summer!" Bakir says.

"Now. But winter always follows." He cuffs his younger brother on the side of the head and sends him into the house. Then he stands outside for a while, admiring his handgun, periodically shouting orders and advice to his minions as they loot Jovanka's house. Two come out lugging a desk. Its drawers are open, spilling papers that blow across the lawn.

"I can't believe they're doing that in broad daylight!" I say, patting Maci to soothe her.

"I'm calling the police," Tata announces, and I'm just glad he doesn't try to confront the burglars himself.

Luckily the phone is still working, for now, though we can't place any calls outside the city. Tata dials the police, and after many rings someone finally picks up. Mama and I stand close enough to hear the muted response on the other line.

"I'd like to report a burglary," he says, polite as ever.

"Is it at your house?" the man on the other end asks.

"No, the neighbors' across the street." He gives them the address. "Are you writing it down? I don't hear you writing it down. They are taking everything out like moving people! In broad daylight!"

"Yes, well . . ."

"One of them has a gun!"

"Is he shooting? Threatening anyone?"

"No, but . . ."

"Tell me, my friend, is this house they're robbing a Serb house?"

Tata is silent for a moment. "Yes."

"Let me tell you something, friend. You sound like a nice person. A family man, no? Let me tell you that even if those robbers were in your home this moment with a gun to your head, I could not come and help you. I couldn't send any of my men. Do you know why? We are busy defending the city against Serbs! I haven't slept for three days. I only came back to the station to look for more ammunition, and I only answered the phone in case it was my wife. Twelve of my men have died, shot by stinking Serbs at the city border."

The policeman isn't yelling. He's explaining things as patiently as Mama might explain something to the class dunce. He sounds utterly exhausted.

"There's no rule of law anymore, sir. There is only survival. Look after yourself and your family. The police can't help you. And my advice? When those robbers are done, go into that Serb house and see if there is anything useful you can take. Food and guns. Each man is his own law now. Good luck, my friend."

The line clicks, the dial tone sounds, and Tata gently replaces the receiver.

"Come on, let's go into the kitchen," he says, turning away from the crime.

"It doesn't matter, Tata," I tell him. "They're probably never coming back. You know that many of the refugees have already moved into houses abandoned by Serb families. Omer and Erza said they'll be doing the same thing any day now. And if our neighbors do come back, so what?" I think of Maida and her friends, killed in the bombing. I think of Lepa, my favorite teacher, wiping out all evidence that I existed. I think of the twelve dead policemen. "They deserve to be robbed," I say bitterly. "They deserve to have nothing, after what they have done!"

"Oh, my Amra," Tata says, taking my face in his hands and kissing my forehead. "You must never let yourself think like that. Jovanka and her husband, they are just people. The Serbs, they are just people. Most of them are like us, just trying to be happy and get along. A few of them have been corrupted by hate, or greed, or . . . I don't know what. But inside we are all the same. Just because some of the Serbs have forgotten that, you shouldn't. Ever. One day this will be over. We'll all go back to being just people again. Make sure you haven't forgotten your humanity by then."

Part of me knows he's right. Another part of me can't help but hate the Serbs. All of them.

They go into the kitchen, and I go to the window to pick up Maci. She's still watching the gang strip Jovanka's house of its possessions, staring unblinkingly. Bakir comes out carrying a rolled-up rug. He looks ashamed of himself as he puts it into the van.

Then he looks across the road to my house. Looks directly at me.

I duck behind the curtain, but I'm sure he's seen me. When I peek out again he's walking across the street. He stops at the curb before my house.

Maci makes a low threatening sound, flicks her tail, and leaps out of the open window.

"Maci, come back!" I hiss at her. But she's stalking across the grass, staring menacingly at Bakir, her lips curled back from her teeth. She knows he's trouble . . . and trouble is coming too close to her family.

When she doesn't listen to me, I have no choice. I dash out the front door without even putting my shoes on. Running barefoot across the grass I scoop her up and plan to be back inside within three seconds . . . but Bakir calls my name.

I turn at the door as Maci struggles in my arms.

Why don't I hurry inside and lock the door? Bakir might have a gun too. What if he's angry about me slapping him?

But he doesn't look angry. He looks bewildered, younger than his years, like Muhamed. Young people just barely out of childhood are being forced to become men and women before they're ready.

"I found something in your neighbor's house," he says.

Suddenly I'm angry at him again, not afraid at all. "Whatever it is, it doesn't belong to you. You should be ashamed of yourself, Bakir. Your brother might be a thief, but you're better than that."

"No, I'm not," he says, bowing his head.

"You could be. You're smart. I've seen your test scores. You shouldn't do what your brother tells you." Because it is obvious that Irfan completely manipulates him.

"Bad things are coming, Amra," he says.

I make a noise of exasperation. In better days it would have been a laugh. "Coming? Where have you been the last few weeks? Bad things are here."

"I mean worse things, if the Serbs come into the city. My brother says we need guns. He says the cops are next to useless, we have hardly any weapons. There aren't any soldiers on our side, only a few who defected in time. It is up to the citizens to fight, General Irfan says."

"General Irfan?" I ask, incredulous.

Bakir grins, embarrassed. "He calls his gang a militia, to protect the city, and named himself general. But so far he hasn't done anything to help Bihać, only himself."

"Our safety depends on your criminal brother?" I roll my eyes, he laughs, and it's almost like we're just two teens again. "So what are you, Major Bakir?"

"Nah, I'm just a private. He won't even give me a gun." He sobers quickly after that. "Listen, Amra, I found this." He pulls several sheets of folded paper from his pocket. He angles it so I catch a quick glimpse of the headings—schools, factories—and names and addresses listed below them, but he turns it away before I can read much.

"What are these?" I ask, puzzled. "Evacuation plans, or . . . shelters?"

"Let me read you some of the names," he says. They all sound Muslim. None of them are characteristically Serb.

"I asked Irfan," Bakir says solemnly. "The schools and factories were going to be used as concentration camps, like in the Second World War."

My blood feels like ice.

"The Serbs didn't expect so much resistance. They thought they could take the city in a day or two. When they did . . ." He swallows hard. "They had lists of all the Muslims in the city. They were going to round us all up. Your family's names are on the list."

He flips to the third page and points. I can't bear to look, but he reads out Mama's name, Tata's, and Dino's.

But not mine.

"What were the Serbs going to do with them?" I ask. But I can imagine, and Bakir only shakes his head.

"My name isn't on there?" I ask him. If my family is condemned, I have to stand by them, even through the worst.

"Yes it is. Just not on that page." He flips to another page. Under the name of a local school is a long list of names. "Only female names," Bakir says as he runs a finger down the list, then stops. "Your name is here."

He tries to show me, but I flinch away, squeezing my eyes shut. He reads out other names, some strangers, some girls I know. Samira's name is there. So are two girls I went to elementary school with. There's a woman in her twenties who I met at Alhambra. And a mother of two who used to teach at Mama's school.

With a shaking voice I ask, "Why is my name on that list? Where are these girls going?" Bakir won't meet my eyes as he tells me.

"I won't let them in, Amra," he vows, his voice louder but shaking. "I'll make Irfan give me a gun. I'll keep those bastards out!"

But he's just a boy. What can he do? What can any of us do?

Maci falls from my arms. I don't even notice. My body is nerveless.

Without another word I go back inside. It feels like a crushing weight is pressing on my body, but somehow I make it upstairs and fall into my bed. I feel like I'll never rise again.

CHAPTER 10

I get out of bed. Of course I do. I have to go to the bathroom. I have to help Mama around the house. I have to keep Tata from the despair he would feel if he thought I'd given up my will to live.

But for as long as possible, whenever I can get away with it, I just lie on my bed, staring at the ceiling, alternating between thinking and not thinking. Eventually I stop getting out of bed altogether. I don't want to do anything, talk to anyone.

The thinking comes against my will and is almost uncontrollable. Like a horrid sick fantasy, a waking nightmare I conjure up, I imagine the future when the Serbs come into Bihać. Over and over I see my family being dragged from our home. Tata and Dino are shot. Mama is dragged away by a group of bearded Četniks. And as for me . . .

What every Muslim woman now fears above all else. Above even death.

The rape camps.

I envision it so clearly that it feels like it has already happened. Every day, in my mind, they are binding my wrists with barbed wire, spreading my legs, violating me. I see the dark, windowless room that is my prison with three other girls. My skin prickles with the cold as I'm left in tattered clothes. In my head I live through day after day of torture and humiliation, degraded by so many Serb soldiers, until at last my belly starts to grow with a child I hate. I feel the sacrilege of this—to bear a child you cannot love.

I feel my imaginings multiplied a thousandfold. Ten thousandfold. For every girl and woman who will be captured by the Serb soldiers.

Better to be one of the men, forced to dig a ditch and then shot and buried in it.

Better to be killed by a bomb, snuffed out with only an instant of suffering.

And then, when I'm overwhelmed by fear and disgust and disillusionment, something in my brain snaps and I don't think of anything at all. Somehow this is even worse. All my life, I've been a thinker, a dreamer. I love to learn, to process information. I revel in stories—reading them and telling them. But when my brain shuts down, desperate to protect itself, I feel like the living dead. I stare at the same spot for hours. I count my own breaths, then lose count and begin again. I lie there in a state of almost comatose indifference, rising only when someone calls me.

For a while I have to hide the fact that I'm lying down all day. But after a few more weeks pass, and food becomes scarce, we all spend our days moving as little as possible anyway.

The city is closed, besieged. The Serbs thought they could bomb us into submission in a few days and then march in with their lists, divide us and break us, execute us. But we are stronger than they expected. What did they expect? That when pushed against the wall we wouldn't fight back? Even though they had been plotting for months, many Serb civilians in the city weren't prepared for the secret order to evacuate. Many, who had planned for fighting, thought they were just going away for the weekend until their soldiers took the city. So they left plenty of guns and ammunition behind. Now civilians raiding houses, like Irfan and Bakir did, are supplementing their supplies.

The Serbs are bombing us day and night. Even as I lie in bed I hear the mortar rounds from the hill encampments outside the city. But if the Serbs try to enter the city they risk terrible casualties. We will make them pay for every inch they come into Bihać.

The Serbs fight for land, for ideology. We fight for our lives. They are careful and want to survive this war. We know if they take our city we are dead, so we fight with everything we have—with guns we take from them. With our hands. With our teeth if we have to. They fight to win. We fight to the death.

So they trap us here, bombing us, demoralizing us.

Starving us.

Now both sides have hunkered down for a long standoff. My little cat is the only thing that ever brings light to my eyes. Every day Maci stays near me, curled up patiently at my side, waiting for me to take an interest in life again. When I don't, she doesn't begrudge my indifference. She just stays, loyally, lovingly.

"I wish I could give you more food," I tell her as I listlessly stroke her rounded sides. "But you seem to be plump enough. Are you hunting mice at night, Maci?" For even though she curls up with me when I sleep, I know she creeps away later to prowl on her own outdoor errands. In the morning she's waiting for me outside. I never know what she gets up to, but I suppose all cats have their own business.

With the constant threat of bombs, we have shoved every piece of furniture against the downstairs windows. What they don't cover, we block with plywood and other scraps. We only have enough to cover the first-story windows. So Tata and Mama decide we should close off the second story and only live on the first. Our once bright and airy house is now dark and musty. The summer is humid, and the air hangs damp and still around us, an atmospheric swamp.

After a while, black mold begins to grow on our walls.

The first days of autumn come, but they bring no relief. The air is less humid but just as heavy and dank, and the first whisper of chill only reminds me of coming winter. What will we do with no electricity in the bitter Bosnian winter? What will we do with no food?

What does it matter, some little part of me says. You will be dead by winter.

I curl around Maci and return to that living-dead state, staring at nothing, doing my best to think of nothing. Most days I lie on a flowery rug. With one finger I trace the pattern of petals, over and over. Dino, who for all his life has followed the example of his strong older sister, loses his energy too and lies on the other side of the rug, as listless as I am.

Mama and Tata are more active than we are. They still go out, creating a makeshift economy of friends and relatives, trading this for that. They bring home food, though in pitifully small quantities. Mama tries to make the best of it, cooking unpalatable dishes with as much gusto as the finest French chef.

Once we get some unidentifiable grain. It isn't a proper grain like wheat or barley. It is tiny, like birdseed. Like the seeds that would grow on a roadside weed. Mama raves about a dish she had on the Dalmatian coast when she was a girl, a delicious savory rustic porridge. "This will be just the same, I'm sure of it. These grains are a delicacy in other places."

So she cooks them, all the while regaling us with tales of meals she had in other regions of the former Yugoslavia. That, more than the unpalatable smell of the grains, makes my mouth water. I thought our stomachs had learned not to protest against the constant hunger, but now Dino's tummy makes a loud growl that makes us laugh as we haven't in weeks.

After half an hour, Mama tastes the grains. She almost hides her distaste, but can't disguise the crunching sound. "Not quite ready."

An hour later they are still too hard for anything except a horse to eat.

Three hours later they are a gluey, disgusting mess.

"It's not quite like I remember," Mama admits as she spoons out a bowl for me. "But of course, we don't have the right spices."

I manage to choke half the mess down, then I feel like I'm going to vomit. It is full of sharp little husks that stick in my teeth and tonsils. I think we were supposed to do something to the grain first to remove them and make it edible.

I give the rest to Dino when our parents aren't looking.

Still, it is better than most meals. Some days are watery soup with a few leaves of cabbage, or sorrel gathered from the roadside.

Other days we eat nothing.

It is the need for solitude that finally stirs me a little bit. I love my family dearly, but all my life I was always able to escape from them. One afternoon the need for a few moments alone is enough to combat my lethargy. Tata and Mama are in the kitchen, talking over coffee made from twice-brewed dregs. Dino is napping. Maci paid me a quick visit in the morning after her nightly prowls and then disappeared, which was strange. She usually sticks by my side all day.

The world swims when I stand up. For a moment my vision fogs at the periphery, leaving only a pinprick of clarity straight ahead of me. Gradually, as if a street artist were coloring in my world, the fog fades and my sight clears. I take a deep breath, fighting the dizziness of malnutrition, and head upstairs.

I love my room. Not long ago my parents realized it was time to transition from a child's room to a teen's room. Somehow (I suspect with Tetka Fatma's help) they got me a new bedroom set, off-white with red and brown dots, very modern and low to the ground. They made me a room to be social in, with lots of seating—an armchair, a two-seater, and a three-seater, all of which can open up to sleep on.

Now that I'm sixteen I'd expected to have people over all the time, to be able to entertain in my own realm. My birthday slumber party was supposed to inaugurate that new era of my life . . .

I open my windows wide and flop down in the armchair. My guitar is in arm's reach. If it weren't, I don't think I'd have the willpower to cross the room to get it. But it's easy, automatic, to pick it up and angle it across my lap, strumming a gentle chord. It has been a while since I practiced, but my fingers remember.

Looking out my window, I see my neighborhood, and beyond that my city. The view stirs me, and for the first time in days I feel a slight interest in something. How I love my city. My poor suffering city.

I need to see it more closely. Gathering my will, I walk out to my balcony and sit in a chair out there. I see a speck in the sky, and at first think it might be a stork, a good luck bird. I almost smile. Then it flies closer, on a straight line toward me, and I hear the low-pitched engine drone. It is a plane.

So much for luck.

I don't know what I'm thinking. Hunger has put me in a dreamland. As the plane drops lower and buzzes toward me, my fingers start to pick out a Bach prelude. I'm playing for the pilot. Surely if he hears the gentle complexity of those notes he'll come to his senses. How can violence and hatred exist in a world that created Bach? How can the same species that makes exquisite music also make machines of destruction?

I switch to a piece by Fernando Sor, a Spanish composer who wrote pieces for classical guitar. The low, thrilling melody fills the air.

"Listen to me," I whisper to the pilot. In my delirium I'm sure he can hear me. I put every ounce of passion into the melody, sending each vibration through the air directly to his heart. "Turn your plane around," I beg him. "Fly across the border to some neutral land and give up fighting. Live a life of peace, and let us do the same."

But the plane doesn't stop, and a moment later I see red, I see a trail of smoke.

It's shooting at my city.

My fingers fumble, tearing discord from my guitar as the plane shoots buildings downtown.

No, not the plane. The plane is an object. It has no volition. It is the man inside the cockpit doing this. He has a choice.

The plane wings closer, leaving havoc in its wake, and I stare it down, unafraid. The firing ceases momentarily. "Go on, you bastard!" I scream out into the clouds. "Shoot me! Get it over with! You stinking coward up in the sky!"

The plane flies so close I'm sure I can see the pilot's face. Maybe I'm imagining it. I see a young man, like Muhamed, his face twisted in hate. I see headphones on his head. He can't hear my music. He can't be saved.

I stare in frozen horror as bullets dig into the street, raking huge gashes like the claws of some giant leopard. The plane is low, roaring in my ears. Is he shooting at me? Surely he can see me, out here on the patio.

What a fool I was, thinking I could tame a savage beast with music like in the stories. "I hate you!" I scream at him as he flies by. My body is shaking as if I have a fever.

Then I hurl my guitar back into my room. It crashes into my black bookcase with a bang and a twang. What can a guitar do against guns? Culture and education are powerless now.

What is the point of trying? The world is broken. Everything is hopeless.

I hurl myself into my disheveled bed and pull the covers over my head. I cry with abandon, with utter despair, feeling so useless and hopeless.

Then my feet touch something warm.

I hear a meow. Then I hear tinier sounds, like the squeak of a rusty hinge.

I pull back the covers, and there is Maci.

She's not alone.

Curled up at her side, stretching and rolling shakily, are three tiny, slimy newborn kittens. Maci looks at me with one of her long, slow blinks of love, then sets about licking her children clean. As I watch with wonder, they become spiky-fluffy and almost dry. Two are like her, with lovely calico fur. The other is like a smear of marmalade, completely orange. Their eyes are closed, but their tiny ears perk at each sound. The marmalade kitten staggers on unsteady pink feet toward the edge of the bed, and Maci takes him tenderly by the scruff and tucks him against her belly.

"Maci, you made them?" I ask in wonder. I still have tears in my eyes, but now it is for a completely different reason. "They're beautiful, Maci. They're . . . perfect!"

Look at that new life, squirming and warm and full of hope. Something bright kindles inside me, a flame I thought this war had extinguished forever.

"I don't care what's happening around me," I tell Maci as I stroke the orange kitten's head. "This war is one place, one moment. It is not everything." The kitten gives a tiny mew, and Maci tumbles him over to lick his belly.

A paper on my desk flutters in the breeze that drifts in through the window, and that makes me think about the list Bakir showed me. I brace myself for the onslaught of fearful imaginings, but instead something strange happens. I remember Jovanka's weathered, wrinkled face, the strange urgency as she asked me to go away with her.

What if she saw her husband's list? Maybe she was shocked to see someone she knew on the list. That made this real to her. It was no longer abstract hate and cruelty, one group against another. It was someone hurting a young woman she'd seen out her window for years, even if she never spoke to her.

What if tired old Jovanka tried to commit one heroic act in her life? Faced with horror she couldn't fight, what if saving me was her attempt to make things not right but better?

What if every Serb tried to do one small thing to fight the hate that has taken over our world now?

What if everyone on the planet did?

Maci's kittens are a reminder that life continues. With them before me, I have to recognize that there may be the capacity for good in everyone after all.

"I was wrong, Maci," I say. "The world is a beautiful place. It's not beautiful everywhere, but that just makes it more important to look for the beauty." I sniff back the last of my tears and feel strength fill my body again. "We'll get through this, Maci. We will."

I decide to let Maci stay in my bed for a day at least. Mama would have a fit about the somewhat messy birth in my bed. I know Maci and her kits will have to move outside, just not yet.

I caution her to be quiet, and go downstairs to see if I can find anything edible for her. After all her hard work, she deserves it. What a clever cat, keeping her pregnancy a secret.

As soon as I go into the kitchen Mama greets me with a huge smile. "Muvehida from my school just came by. She told me the schools are reopening next week!"

"Next week!" I exclaim, and Mama's face lights up at my animation. Suddenly I have purpose again. "I have so much to do! So much to catch up on!" I turn to fetch my schoolbooks, and as I do so I spy the unsightly, unhealthy black mold creeping across the apple-green wall. "But first, I have plenty to do here."

I rummage for a bucket and rags and start scrubbing the wall. I work like a maniac until nightfall, until not only the mold but most of the green paint is gone.

There can't be mold, or sorrow, or despair in a world that has three newborn kittens in it.

CHAPTER 11

My mind feels better—alert and motivated—but my body isn't physically able to follow its example. After all that maniacal scrubbing I'm exhausted. Weeks of thin broth and strange grains have taken their toll.

"We only have a few days to get you two strong again before school starts," Tata says. "I have an idea." But he won't tell us what it is. The next morning he starts out on foot. In the afternoon he comes home with a big, unwieldy cardboard box. His fingertips just barely manage to curl around the edges. He's having even more trouble holding on to it because the box seems to be . . . moving.

And clucking.

He carries the box around to the back of the house, and we all gather around it. Even Maci. When Tata opens the top she stands on her hind legs to peer in . . . then flinches when a beak pecks toward her nose.

Inside are a dozen scrawny chickens, looking up at us with interested, beady eyes. I reach for one, and it pecks at me, too, but not hard. It feels like a quick clumsy kiss. I leave my hand there, and the other chickens take turns pecking and chewing on my fingers.

"They don't look like real chickens," Dino says. "They're scrawny. And why are their feet so big?"

"They're young chickens," Tata says. "Teenage chickens. They've grown up but not out."

They're malnourished, too, just like us. A factory farm on the edge of town had just gotten a huge shipment of young chicks right before the war. With no new supplies coming in, they quickly ran out of feed for them. So they started giving the chickens away to citizens before they starved.

Tata scoops them out one by one, and they start to explore our yard, pecking at bugs and our shoelaces. "Won't they run away?" I ask. But they show no inclination to leave. Maci stalks around them. They're too big for her to eat, so she decides to accept them as part of the family. Sitting with crossed paws, she watches them like an older sister. But when they don't do anything more interesting than cluck and peck, she loses interest and strolls back to the garage, where we've set up a nursery for her and her kittens on the second story.

I like the noises the chickens make. They talk to themselves or to each other as they scratch at the grass, making low, soothing warbles. It is a very peaceful, sociable sound. I decide I'll like having these chickens around.

"So we're going to have eggs?" Dino asks hopefully. "I'd love a nice, fluffy omelet."

"They're too young to lay eggs yet," Tata says. "If they're even hens. They might be roosters for all I know. It's hard to tell at this age, and I just took whichever chickens were easiest to catch."

"I wish I could have seen you chasing down chickens!" I say with a giggle. Imagine my tall, dignified Tata stooped over, bent in half as he runs after a squawking fowl.

"So we have to wait before they give us any eggs?" Mama asks. "How long?"

Tata takes off his hat and smooths his hair back, clearly stalling. "Um, these chickens aren't for eggs. Egg-layers need a lot of food in order to make an egg every day or two. We can't give them that much food."

"So they're pets?" Dino asks, eternally optimistic, too young to immediately understand that the worst is always a distinct possibility now. As for me, I realize I shouldn't get too used to the calming sound of chickens.

"No . . . no," Tata says. "These are food chickens."

We all stare at the foraging feathery creatures, trying to reconcile their strange vitality with the roasted chickens we're used to. These animals are all feet and head. There can't be much meat under those funny feathers.

"You mean we have to . . . ," Dino begins. "No! They're too cute. I don't want to personally know the chicken I'm eating."

"We don't have any choice," Mama says in a dispassionate voice. "We haven't had a decent meal in weeks. If you're going to have the strength to walk to school, you're going to need some good healthy protein. There's no other way."

I wonder if Mama even knows what to do with a whole feathered chicken with its head and feet and guts. How do you turn these clucking animals into the plump, pinkish, anonymous thing we stuff with sliced lemons and rosemary and roast in the oven?

"But . . . ," Dino objects with a stricken look. "We can't!"

I put my arms around him. "Sometimes you have to do things you don't want to do. To survive. Remember, these chickens were going to be killed anyway. They were at the factory farm, destined for the slaughterhouse. If we weren't at war, we'd have bought these same chickens in the market."

"I know," he says with a sniff. "But when you buy a chicken in the store it doesn't look you in the eye. It doesn't nibble on your fingers."

"Who's going to do it?" I ask.

Tata sighs. He knows it has to be him.

We know we should go inside, but we stay. Tata looks over the milling chickens. What a terrible responsibility, to choose one of them to doom. I see him weighing the options. Maybe the biggest one, because it might be older and have had more of a chance at life. Maybe the smallest, because it might not survive very long. Maybe one of the chickens has a bad personality.

Or maybe we should choose the one who volunteers, I think, looking down at a chicken pecking at my shoe. When I bend down, she lets me scoop her up. Yes, I think it is a she. She seems pleased to be picked up, staying still as I tuck her under my arm. I stroke her head, and she closes her eyes, making that contented little cooing rumble that could almost be a purr.

This happens every day on farms, I tell myself. It's how humans have been living for thousands of years. It's how I've been living. I just had the luxury of not thinking about where my meat comes from.

From a living animal that trusts me.

"This one," I say, handing her over. Tata takes her with a grim, sorrowful face. He walks to the wood pile where we get firewood ready for winter. There are two axes—a big one for splitting logs, and a little hatchet for kindling. Tata approaches the chopping block as if he were heading to his own execution.

Mama goes in the house, but Dino and I can't look away. Tata is patting her feathers, whispering gentle words to her. The chicken closes her eyes again, lulled almost to sleep against Tata's side. Stealthily, he picks up the smaller ax.

He lays her down across the block and raises the hatchet over his head.

Then he pauses, and I can see him weighing the morality of this, our need against the life of a living thing.

He should have struck quickly. The chicken isn't comfortable in this position, stretched out on the block, and just as Tata makes the ultimate decision she starts to squirm. The hatchet comes down, I scream, Tata and the chicken flinch at the same time, and I close my eyes as I hear a solid *thwack*.

128

Then I'm covered with a hot wet spray. I open my eyes. Half of the chicken's head is hanging off. She slides off the block and starts running blindly, spraying blood everywhere, making a sickening gurgling sound. She deflates like a balloon as the blood shoots out of her neck. The eyes on her hanging head are still beady and bright.

Finally she crashes into Tata's legs and falls over. But she's still alive. Her legs are kicking. Bubbles rise from the hole in her throat.

Tata staggers to the corner of our yard and vomits. Then he goes into the house.

A moment later Mama comes out, her lips pressed firmly together. Without a word she picks up the dying chicken, lays it on the block, and with one confident movement chops its head cleanly off. Her face shows no remorse or regret, but I know what it costs her to be the strong one.

———

That night, our new friend has been turned into soup. While the other chickens roost on our terrace, tucking their heads beneath their wings, we sit around the dining table. Maci sits below the table, half draped over my feet.

The soup has a greasy sheen on top. Mama has used all the parts efficiently. Everything edible has gone into our meal, except for some of the viscera, which Maci gobbled up. As Mama stirs it with a ladle, I see a grotesque yellow scaly foot circle the tureen.

I set down my spoon. "I can't eat this."

"You will eat this," Mama says evenly. "The chicken is already dead. It died to give you strength, to keep you alive. Do you want it to have died for nothing?"

And so we eat.

CHAPTER 12

As disturbing as that meal was, I have to admit I'm feeling better for getting a little nutrition in me. The next day Ale and Fatma bring us a few small jars of honey from their bee farm, and also some eggs, beans, onions, and rice.

"The honey is what will save us," Fatma says as she sits down at the kitchen table with Mama. "It lasts forever—bacteria can't grow in honey. It is high calorie. And what's more, it can be traded for what little food remains."

I look at the two women I admire most. Mama is the baby of the family, an afterthought, a footnote, Fatma sometimes teases. She is young enough to be Fatma's own daughter. Fatma never could have children. Instead she lavishes love and food on every member of our family. Mama is her special favorite, the baby who grew into a respected best friend. Fatma herself seems almost ageless, with a smooth face and her stylish short red hair and elegant clothes.

She's not wearing one of her usual tailored, color-coordinated suits today. Instead she's wearing a charming flowered dress, the casual sort of garment that stay-at-home mothers and housewives will carelessly throw on during the day when they run errands or do chores. On some women they look dowdy. But of course Fatma has chosen the most beautiful material and added little nips and tucks to make the dress emphasize her figure.

Fatma always seems perfectly adapted to her time and place, no matter what is going on. Her style and grace transcend the moment;

they come from within. When she was a girl, around the Second World War, she was always fully covered in public. From head to toe she was draped in flowing material, with not so much as a strand of hair showing. Even her face was covered by a zar. Tetak Ale will tell stories of their courtship, when he sneakily positioned her just right so the sun would shine through the fabric, and he could glimpse the curve of her cheek, her flashing eyes, a lock of her thick, wavy hair.

She went from that to a woman with a passion for the finest Italian clothes, for custom leather shoes, for impeccably styled hair and expertly applied makeup.

Now, in our moment of distress, she's changed her standard costume again. But she takes something as utilitarian and dull as a housewife's dress and gives it a style all her own. She fits with the times, but she is always completely and absolutely herself.

"Who would have thought that your hobby would keep us from starving one day?" Mama comments as she packs away the golden jars Fatma's brought.

"There I was, like Marie Antoinette pretending to be a shepherdess!" Fatma says with a chuckle. It would take more than a war to make her lose her good spirits. "A nice house in the city, and Ale and I were always running out to the country to play at being beekeepers."

She jokes about taking her beekeeping lightly, but she has a way with the bees. You have to talk to them, she says, and then they will give lots of honey and never go too far when they get a new queen and swarm. I think her bees must be as amused by her conversation as the rest of us are. Neighbors keep an eye on the bee farm when she isn't there, but when she goes, she dons a white beekeeper's outfit, complete with protective mask and gloves, and harvests the honey herself.

There's still not a lot of food, but for a few days at least we'll have one good meal a day. Mama divides the leftovers of the unsuccessful soup. She strips every last bit of chicken from the bones and mixes the few remaining shreds with the beans, creating a thick flavorful stew. With the leftover broth, she cooks the rice like a risotto, stirring in half a cup of liquid at a time until the rice is creamy and tender.

And onions go in everything! They add crunch and flavor that our bland, basic food is usually lacking. The only problem is that onions lower blood pressure. Mine tends to be low anyway, so between the onions and my low-calorie diet I feel like I'm going to pass out sometimes.

It is hard cooking over a wood fire, but Mama is managing, and I make sure to watch and learn.

With my health and spirits revived, I'm excited to be going to school in another two days. Dino is less excited about classes, but he's thrilled he'll be able to leave the house. He misses his friends, and being able to run and climb and swim in his free time.

"I talked to your friend Damir the other day when I was visiting his grandmother," Tetka Fatma says as she's leaving. Damir is a nice boy a year ahead of me. Before the war, he'd mentioned he would lend me a couple of math and physics textbooks that I was going to need for next semester. "He hasn't forgotten," she says. "He'll stop by with them soon."

"It will be good to see him again," I say. "We always had such nice long talks about linear algebra. I'm excited to be starting it this year." With Algebra 1 and 2 behind us, linear algebra is next.

Fatma rolls her eyes comically. "In my day, linear algebra was not how we flirted with boys!" I'm sure that even covered from head to toe, Fatma found a way to be charming and flirty when she wanted to: a turn of the head, a movement of the hands, a sigh could win over any man.

"I don't flirt with him," I reply indignantly. "He's just a friend."

"Well, you should flirt with him," she replies. "Or if not him, there's a lovely young man who lives down the street from me. I used to know his grandmother very well. A college boy studying to be a veterinarian, with a big Šarplaninac dog."

"You know I'm not a fan of dogs," I remind her.

"Fine, not him, but you should still flirt with every young man. Especially now." Her merry face grows more serious. "Amra, don't pass up any opportunities. Now, more than ever, you must seize life. You must grab hold of every happiness. Here, I have a little something for you."

She digs in her purse and takes out a golden tube of lipstick with a pretty green bow tied around it. I think even in a nuclear winter she'd find a way to not only give gifts, but make them elegant.

I twist it open and find a color just a shade lighter than the burgundy I borrowed from Mama for my slumber party.

"Try it on," she urges, handing me a compact from her purse. I smooth it on my lips. "Perfect!" she says with delight. "Just your shade, especially since you're so pale from being trapped indoors. You need to get out more, dear. Go to the river, swim, bask in the sun. Live!"

"But the bombs!" I protest.

"They can't hit everyone, can they? And if you're destined to die, isn't it better to go out of this world in a bikini on the banks of the Una than cowering in a dark basement? Enjoy yourself, and once you get a tan again I have the perfect shade of bright-pink lipstick for you." She laughs, gives me a kiss, and goes out into our war-torn city without any apparent fear.

"And don't forget to flirt!" she calls over her shoulder as she goes.

But when she leaves, I'm not thinking of the perfectly nice Damir. Instead, for almost the first time since this all began, I remember the boy with the summer-bronze skin and the gray-green eyes. Fatma's advice about taking advantage of opportunities really resonates now. I could die at any moment. I'm getting more used to that idea as a concept, but when I think about what I might miss out on, it is another story.

What if I die without ever having a boyfriend?

I think about all the boys I know. Mirza is handsome but too frivolous. Damir is smart, but when I think of him I feel nothing beyond friendship. There is no one in school or in the neighborhood who makes me think twice.

But Davor. Even Maci liked him. What better recommendation could there be?

I wish there was someone I could talk to about this. If only Olivera were here, she'd understand. There's a sour taste in my mouth at the thought of my friend. Is she still my friend? I wish I could write to her, tell her what is happening in Bihać. She's always been so warm and compassionate. If she knew . . .

Or is she just a Serb? Not a friend but a Serb, first and only?

When she is sad does she wish she could talk to me?

I shake my head, unwilling to fall into a depression again. Olivera might be gone, and probably Ivona too, though I don't know for sure about her. But I still have my Muslim friends. There are Nura, Asmira, Lana, and Samira. They were always my second-best friends, back when friendships could happen organically and weren't based on religion and heritage.

Suddenly I'm determined to see Nura, the closest of the ones who remained. I tell myself I want to make sure she got the message that school is starting up again. But really I want to talk about Olivera, and maybe, if I'm brave enough, about boys.

The only problem is that Nura lives on the other side of the Blue Bridge. And the Serbs have been doing everything they can to bomb the bridge to oblivion. The river Una divides the city in two, and the Blue Bridge connects us. Destroy that bridge, and the city will be crippled.

What's more, the strategically valuable railway station is in my half of the city. If the city is cut in two, it will be that much easier for the Serbs to take the side with the railroad.

I head to my parents to tell them where I'm going . . . then stop. There's a good chance they'll say no.

Before the war I was such a good girl. Now my tactics change. It's not lying if I just don't tell them, right?

Unfortunately, Dino catches me as I'm slipping out. "Where are you going?"

I don't yet know how to lie to a direct question from someone I love. "To see Nura."

"Mama and Tata are letting you? I'm coming! I heard the mjesna zajednica has power since it's near the firehouse." The community center also has a television, and it is a popular place for kids to hang out. "Mama!" He turns to call her, and I grab him back, clapping a hand over his mouth.

"Shh! They don't know! I just want to go out for a while. Just to make sure she knows about school opening."

He puts on a sulky face. "It's not fair! I haven't gone farther than the front yard in forever."

"If you come they'll get suspicious. Please, Dino, if they ask can you just tell them I'm in the garage with the kittens or something?"

"I don't know . . ."

"Please? I'll cover for you tomorrow if you want to go to the mjesna zajednica."

Reluctantly, he agrees, but says, "Hurry back. I don't know how long I can keep it up." I slip on a green sweater, another thing that Tetka Fatma brought on her visit. It is part of the humanitarian aid that is slowly trickling in. Fatma had looked at it disapprovingly as she handed it to me. "There were twenty of them in a shipment," she'd said. "All just alike, a pretty color but such rough nubbly material, and no style to the cut! Still, it is getting chilly at night already, and it will keep you warm."

I tell Dino goodbye and head out.

A little while later I'm hurrying across town. Well, not exactly hurrying. A couple of meals can only do so much after so many weeks of malnutrition and lethargy. And I'm sure the onions didn't help. My blood feels like it is barely moving around my body. I can't believe I can feel so weak at sixteen! Each step feels like I'm climbing a mountain. I break out in a sweat before I cover two blocks.

But I keep on, slowly making my way across the bridge. The glimpse I got of destruction near my home is nothing compared to what I now see in my city. I'm overwhelmed by the devastation. I pass a bank that looks like it has been dissected, one outer wall sheared off, its insides hanging out: beams and wires and steel. The streets are pitted with craters and deeply gouged with bullet holes. A smell of smoke hangs in the air, and I see black clouds rising from several distant places where buildings are still on fire.

Even houses that are still standing show signs of shrapnel from bombs that fell nearby. After a while I can tell where the bomb must have hit just from the angle of the damage. One building is scarred with a million marks as if it were splattered with paint. As I pass I can't help but examine those wounds on the facade. Some of the marks are rusty red. Did shrapnel pass through a person on the way to the building? Whose life was erased at that moment?

All around me, at sporadic intervals, I hear gunfire. It is hard to tell where it is coming from. The sound reverberates through the city. After a while I notice it no more than I notice birdsong on a summer day. The echoing reports don't even make me flinch. What's the point? They're not a warning of immediate danger. There is no warning. The first sign that the gunfire has come to you is when someone drops dead next to you. Then you know to run.

When I reach the Blue Bridge I stand under the shade of the broad-leaved linden trees, looking out over the Una and to the city beyond. Some buildings are completely destroyed. A few are untouched, but most show signs of damage. When I look around I see plenty of destruction, true, but now my eyes go to what is still standing. Despite months of bombardment, most of the shops and houses are still largely intact. Many have some kind of damage, like broken windows, but I am astonished that after all the effort the Serbs have gone through to crush our city, it still stands.

But so empty! These streets used to be bustling at every hour of the day. Now I only pass a person here and there, hurrying with downcast eyes. The bridge ahead is a little more crowded, though. It is like a funnel, and even the small amount of foot traffic comes together here to cross. I see maybe a dozen people picking their way carefully across the Blue Bridge. Everyone is silent. No chatter, no cars, no factories humming. It is the strangest thing in the world to hear my city so quiet, the only sound the occasional boom of a gunshot.

The bridge still stands, enduring, but it is a sorry sight. As I make my way tentatively across I can see the river below me through gaping holes. Parts of the rail on the side are gone. Once I step on what looks like solid pavement beneath my feet, but it shifts, and the second after I jump away it crumbles, bits of masonry tumbling into the river. I look down at the rushing water beneath and think how close I came to taking a swim. From this height, into the rocks and current, it could have been fatal.

When I'm past the middle of the bridge I pause to look around again, and to rest. I see another girl doing the same on the opposite side of the bridge. She's wearing a green sweater too—my twin! She must have gotten it from the humanitarian aid shipment too. When she turns I smile at her, and point to my sweater. Her face crinkles in a giggle, and for a second life is normal. She waves as she continues her

137

journey to my home side of the bridge, and I'm left with a feeling of almost-calm.

When I glance after her I notice a tall young man walking a huge shaggy Šarplaninac dog just at the beginning of the bridge. He's wearing red jeans and a stylish black shirt with white polka dots. His beautiful eyes are hidden behind Ray-Ban sunglasses. He's pretty far away, but I recognize him immediately. It's Davor.

Could that be who Tetka Fatma was talking about? The veterinary student with the big dog? What a remarkable coincidence!

Instantly, the small crowd on the bridge seems to vanish. A woman in a fox-fur hat and wrap around her shoulders pulls at the arm of a small blond boy. She's dressed too well and too warmly for the season. Maybe keeping up stylish appearances helps her cope. Her little boy is trying to look over the edge of the bridge, hoping to see fish, and he's making a fuss while his mom hisses at him to hurry. I scarcely hear them.

Something unfamiliar stirs within me as I look at Davor. It is a strange, fluttery feeling.

Is it a crush?

Or is it just low blood sugar?

This makes me giggle, and just at that moment Davor looks up and notices me.

He stops, though the dog tries to keep going and almost pulls him off his feet. He laughs, too, and waves at me. He opens his mouth to shout something, and then we both notice: the gunshots have become louder, closer, more frequent.

Then I hear a whistling overhead, a thin, reedy sound. An instant later I see a flash as a missile hits a house on the bank of the Una, on my home side of the bridge. The sound of the explosion comes an instant later, and I stand frozen, bizarrely thinking about physics, about the relative speed of light and sound that cleaves the experience in two. First the sight of fire and flame, then, disconnected by a second or two, sound waves that roll over me like messengers eager to bear bad news.

I hear another missile overhead, launched from the mountains surrounding our town. Someone told Tata, who told me in turn: The bomb that you hear is not the one with your name on it. If you hear it whistle, it is because it is flying over your head to somewhere else. You never hear a whisper from the bomb that kills you.

The air raid siren starts its high-pitched howl then. We have no radar, nothing to tell us that the missiles are inbound, so the siren is a joke. It just serves to remind us that people are being killed. It gives no warning, just wails and mourns with the rest of us.

Davor and I find each other again. We're still frozen in place, not knowing if we're about to die, but our eyes meet across the bridge. Between us I see the mother and her little boy, the girl in the green sweater, a trio of middle-aged women who look like sisters. Davor takes a step toward me . . .

Then the air seems to be sucked out of the world as I'm hit with an earth-shattering, deafening explosion. There's a flash between Davor and me, and I'm blinded. Metal and stone are flying around me. I turn to run, and its only when my legs are moving that I realize I'm not dead.

I only make it a few steps before I fall, scraping my knees. In the dust and chaos I hear screams, and I drag myself to my feet, stunned. My ears are ringing, and the air is choked with dust. I smell smoke. I taste smoke. There's grit on my tongue.

The Blue Bridge is still standing. The bomb struck a glancing blow that didn't do anything much to the structure.

But the pedestrians on the bridge . . .

Against every survival instinct I make myself walk back toward the other end of the bridge. I look all around but don't see Davor. The little boy, the one who wanted to look at fish over the side of the bridge, is standing in the middle of a cloud of masonry dust. His mouth is open, and at first I think the sound he's making is part of the loud ringing in my ears, because everything sounds weirdly muffled at first. The sounds are returning to my ears one at a time. Then I realize he's screaming, a long, drawn-out, terrible cry that stops only when he's out of breath, then starts again after a ragged gasp.

I go to him. He's blond, tousle-haired, and blue eyed, just like Dino when he was younger. But his little face looks impossibly old. I wish he could be confused. I wish he didn't know exactly what just happened. But this little boy understands his loss, and he is suffused with helpless, inarticulate rage.

I go to him, reaching out my hand. He just stares at me with his prematurely aged face. I look beyond him. Blood on a stylish suit. The fox-fur collar, made from a whole fox, its sharp white teeth grinning as it grasps its own tail. Its black glass eyes are staring at me. Above that, nothing. There is nothing where his mother's head should be.

He finds words now, and his screams turn into a desperate wail for his mother. He's not looking at her, but he must have seen. He's calling to her like his words could turn back time, undo the bomb. Like if he begs the universe loudly enough he can make his mother alive again.

I take his little hand, and he looks at me like I'm an alien thing. I try to lead him off the bridge, but he is like a boulder, immovable. All this time, he never stops screaming his feral fury against the world. An old man staggers beside us. A couple clings to each other as they walk through the smoke. Though it is midday, the smoke and dust make it look like a foggy evening. Survivors are like ghosts in the haze.

I still don't see Davor. Not among the bodies or the survivors.

The little boy's grief shatters me. There's nothing I can do. So I leave him. It's a wrenching decision. But someone will come to help him.

I look at the other people on the bridge. The three middle-aged sisters are strewn about like old clothes—that's what I see, their old-lady sweaters and their sensible shoes. A man is hanging half off the bridge, draped over the rail. Blood is dripping in a puddle at his feet.

Then I see the girl in the green sweater like mine. She's on the ground, curled on her side, facing away from me. Her sweater is perfectly clean and tidy, like she just decided to take a nap in this odd place. I think she's unconscious. Maybe she was knocked out by the shock wave.

I kneel at her side and take her shoulder, gently turning her over as I say, "Don't worry, I'm here. I'll help you."

I roll her and find a bloody horror. The front of her body is stripped of clothes, stripped of skin, shredded from a hail of metal and stone shrapnel. From the front she doesn't look human. She looks like meat.

I scream and scramble backward on my hands and feet like a crab, wiping my bloody hands on the ground. They make a red paste with the dust.

I roll to my knees, haul myself to my feet, look around for somebody, anybody, who can do something.

Suddenly there are lights up ahead in the middle of the road where we're walking. It's a big square white lorry with tall blue letters on the side: UN. The United Nations is supposed to be here to help the suffering, to facilitate peace.

With a gasp of relief I run to meet the truck, waving my hand to stop them. "Help is here," I shout to the little boy as I pass him. "These men will help you."

I'm standing in the middle of the road, right in the truck's path. It slows. The driver sees me. He meets my eye. Please have medics, I think. Please have some kind counselor who can take care of this poor child. Please have someone to compassionately tend to that poor girl's body, to cover her ravaged face.

But the UN truck swerves around me, increasing speed.

Okay, I think, they're going to the wounded in the center of the bridge.

But the truck doesn't stop. It drives fast enough to make the damaged bridge shake. It swerves carefully around the carnage and rubble and carries on as if dead Bosnians weren't sprawled on the streets.

The world is watching, and it doesn't care.

CHAPTER 13

I make a split-second decision to continue to Nura's house. The homing instinct of every hunted animal to seek its den tells me I should go back to my family, but logic says that they're bombing my side of the river. Going back that way is slightly more likely to end in death.

But as I leave the cries, the screams, the blood on the bridge behind me, I wonder what the next five minutes will bring. I hear one more missile hit, and I barely flinch. I walk mechanically, with an empty mind. It terrifies me that I don't feel more. How can I be standing after what I've just seen? How can I breathe, knowing other people's breath was just snuffed out forever in an explosion?

I think the brain and body do what they have to do. If I thought about what just happened too much, if I let myself feel too much, I'd fall down and never get up. I'd die of a broken heart.

So I walk on, numb, thinking only of putting one foot in front of another, of not missing the turn to Nura's street.

And a part of me wonders, will I ever be allowed to feel again? How will I mourn the dead when my mind has built this protective wall?

By the time I make it to Nura's I'm utterly exhausted in body and spirit. My walls are weaker now, and all the pent-up emotion threatens to burst out. I feel like I'm pressing a lid down on furiously boiling water. The steam needs to escape or the pot will explode. But I know the second I loose the lid it will scald not only me but anyone close to me.

At first the numbness was instinctive, involuntary—survival. The pain and fear I felt were immeasurable. There was no way to deal with it, so to get through each minute I had to block it out.

Now, though, with the critical moment past, it takes a supreme effort of will to keep my emotions in check. If I let those feelings free they will take over, and I'll never be able to force them back down.

I want to unburden myself to Nura, to lessen my share of the horror by giving some to her. But when she opens the door and sees me her face lights up so happily that I immediately change my mind. She knows what's happening. She's probably seen things just as bad or worse. I don't even know if her family is all safe. What would it serve to add to her suffering by sharing mine? I think everyone in this city already has their fair share.

She hugs me and pulls me inside. "Amra, what a wonderful surprise! I wanted to come and see you, but my mother wouldn't let me. How is your family? Is your house still standing? A bomb hit our street, but it didn't explode, and for three days we had to go to my cousin's house until someone managed to defuse it. It's still sitting in the middle of the road, half buried in pavement. Do you want to see? It's completely safe, I promise you. Some of the boys are writing their names on it."

I smile at her, so happy to be on the receiving end of this animated chatter. Nura was always a little more melancholic, less talkative than Olivera. But she must be going crazy with only her mother and sister to talk to. (Her father is always a silent presence in the house. I think he's probably a nice man, but since he never says anything I don't really know. Nura's mother is the charismatic spirit in the household.)

"What's that?" Nura asks as she draws me into her home. Her family hasn't boarded up the windows, and I feel at the same time more free and more vulnerable with light pouring in. She points to my sleeve. "Are you hurt?" I look and see a splash of red. My hands, too, have rusty stains, where the dust didn't quite wipe away the blood.

Again I want to tell her, to collapse in a flood of tears and let her comfort me, sympathize with me. But after a quick moment of weakness it passes again, and I feel strong. I realize that the emotional stoniness doesn't just protect me—it protects other people too. What has this war done to me that I can bear such a weight, keep such an awful thing to myself?

I've found a strength I didn't know I had.

"Oh, that's nothing," I say. "I just fell. I guess I scraped myself a bit. I'll wash my hands, and clean that too."

Lies are coming more easily to me—the lies that protect other people.

Nura forgets about it instantly. "Did you hear what happened to Selma's house? It caught on fire, not even from a bomb, just from her mother trying to make musaka on a wood stove. Her brother, you know, the one who runs track, sprinted to the fire station, and they sent a truck but they didn't have any water. So she and her family and the firemen just stood in the street and watched her house burn down! It was terrible! Now the community center is organizing volunteers, bucket brigades, stationing buckets of sand to smother fires for the next time that happens. It's neighbors taking care of neighbors."

"I can't believe Olivera is gone," I say as we sit on the couch. "What about Ivona? Have you heard from her?"

"I went by her apartment and it's empty," Nura says bitterly. "They're all gone. Every last Serb. And good riddance, I say. What fake friends they were. I wish we'd known earlier."

"I don't think Olivera was a fake friend," I tell her.

"Of course she was. It was all an act. It had to be. The Serbs were just lulling us into a false sense of security so they could attack—so we'd never see it coming."

"Maybe, but Olivera wasn't doing that. She didn't know anything about what her people were planning."

"Oh didn't she?" asks the cynical Nura. "You know how your parents feel about things, don't you? You don't have to be nosy, you just overhear. You know what they're making for dinner, what they're fighting about, who is going to get the promotion at their job. Nothing is secret in a family. Believe me, Olivera knew. So did Ivona and all the others. But they kept their secrets like good little Serb soldiers until they could escape and their soldiers could start to kill us all!" Her voice has risen to a hysterical pitch.

"But Olivera was different," I try to say.

"What's wrong with you? Olivera or a Četnik, they're all the same. They would both kill me as soon as they would kill a Bosnian soldier."

"But . . ."

"Why are you defending her? One word, that's all she had to say. Go. Be careful. Take a vacation. Anything. But she didn't. Because she's a traitor."

I understand what she's saying—and they are all things that I've been thinking myself. I feel betrayed by my best friend. But I also try to understand what she must have gone through, to be torn between her own beliefs and her parents' beliefs. To be told to think that Bosnians are dirty subhumans, and then see proof to the contrary in her best friend. Or did she come to believe it too?

"But we don't have to worry about her anymore," Nura says briskly, settling back into the couch. "Now you have me. And you know that you can trust the people who are left. We Muslims will all look after each other. Now tell me, who have you seen from our class?"

We talk about Samira, Lana, Asmira, and the others who remain.

"Dani is here too," Nura tells me.

"Really?" That's surprising. Dani's mother is Croat, someone who used to be high up in government, a determined woman born with only half an arm. His father is Serb. I really like Dani. He's one of the kids who competes with me in math class, each of us vying for top grades. I remember there was one extra-hard test, and his parents were mad at him for getting a less than perfect score. They thought he had goofed off with friends instead of studying, and were going to ground him. His excuse was, *But Amra didn't do so well either!* His mom actually called Tata to make sure he was telling the truth. Then his parents accepted that it really was an unusually hard test, if both the top students had difficulty.

"He's the only close non-Muslim friend who's still in the city."

"We have to look out for him," I decide. "Some might think well of him because his family chose to stay and work for peace. But others might see him as just another Serb."

We talk about other friends, and then I ask what I know Nura is just dying for me to ask. "Have you seen Eso?" Her one-week date, the love of her life, who I think doesn't remember she's alive half the time.

She brightens. "Yes! He didn't leave the city! Oh, I'm so glad he's still here. What would I do without him?"

I open my mouth to say that if you truly loved him, you'd rather he'd escaped to somewhere safe. But I have to tread carefully with Nura. I've known her since first grade, and I know what will offend her. It can be hard censoring myself, but she's one of the few friends I have left now.

How I miss Olivera. We spoke from the heart and forgave any offense.

"You've seen him? How is he?" I ask instead, unleashing a flood of syrupy praise about his handsomeness (he's nice-looking at best), his brilliance (three or four out of five), and the way he is secretly pining for her affection.

"His parents don't like me, you see."

This is new to me. As far as I know, I don't think his parents are aware of or think anything about her. But she sees it as a doomed love, a Romeo and Juliet affair. Poor Eso, he doesn't know he's been cast in a teen tragedy!

When she runs out of things to say about him (because really, what can she say after having spent only a few hours in his company?), I say very tentatively, "I think I might have met someone too. At least, I met him, and then I saw him again today."

"Oh, a date! Tell me all about it! Did you kiss him?"

"No, no, it was nothing like that," I say, embarrassed now, because how can I explain the connection that comes from a brief meeting of eyes? How can I say that from only a few words I understand this young man's character?

I'd sound like Nura, going from nothing to true love in a heartbeat!

Before I can embarrass myself further, Nura's mother comes through the front door, with Nura's serious little sister trailing behind.

Nura's mom has a successful career in science and is one of the most ambitious women I've ever met. But her success has made her hard and cold with the person who needs her most—Nura. People should recognize their own intelligence and ability, but Nura's mother rubs it in people's faces. Her sensitive daughter never stops trying—and failing—to live up to her expectations. She demands that her two daughters be exactly like her. They don't have to follow exactly in her footsteps, but she insists that her girls become famous at something. They can be scientists or poets, artists or politicians, as long as they shine. Nura's little sister is as ambitious as her mother, always striving, never still. But poor sensitive Nura's flustered under pressure, and I think she would be happy just having a normal job, or being a wife and mother.

"Still sitting around, Nura?" her mother asks as she sails in. "Have you finished the history chapters I told you to read? Oh, hello, Amra. Has she made you coffee yet? Nura, would you . . . never mind, we're out of coffee beans." She sighs and sits down at the table, while we have to scoot aside to make room for her enormous hat. "What a time we live in, when you can't even get coffee anymore. I always tell Nura, drink more coffee! If you have enough caffeine you just fly through schoolwork."

"Coffee just makes me nervous," she tells her mother with downcast eyes and a sigh. Nura is smart, but she just doesn't have the capacity to be a top student. Her little sister is the best in her year, so Nura stands out as the dunce of her family, even if she'd be considered a good student in most other families.

"You're falling so far behind," her mother says, ignoring her complaint. "How will you get a good job if you don't go to school? How will you be a success?"

"Mom, how can you think of school in the middle of a war? We're on hold."

"Life is never on hold! Look at me—I still go to work, even if the factory is closed temporarily. And I just negotiated for supplies for the factory. We need metal, fuel, if we want to build . . ." She bites her tongue, realizing she's saying too much. Who is she negotiating with, and for what? What is her factory trying to build? Maybe bombs to fight the Serbs? She is a scientist, and though her factory makes civilian components, the factory could have been repurposed. I want to ask, for that little bit of reassurance that we can fight back. But I know she won't tell me, and she concludes, "Life never stops!"

She sweeps off her hat and puts it down on the table. "So, Amra, what news do you have? Is your family well?" But she's looking over my shoulder toward the door, and I know she's itching to be out again. There's nothing domestic about her. She'd rather be at a committee meeting than with her family.

So I don't tell her about my family. Instead I bring up the one thing that will truly interest her, the reason for my visit, which, amid the gossip, I haven't even gotten around to telling Nura.

"I just got word that school will be back in session on Monday."

Her mother is delighted, of course.

Nura slumps back in her chair.

"Just when I thought this war couldn't get any worse!" she groans.

I spend two hours feeling almost like a normal teen. There might not be coffee, but when Nura's mother goes out again her little sister confesses she'd been hiding half a nut cake for the last two weeks. It's stale and hard but not moldy, and when we slice it we pretend it's biscotti. We fake Italian accents and pretend to be supermodels in a café, talking about make-believe boyfriends (which is much easier than talking about real boys we like). For a little while we have an impromptu party, and our laughter and conversation drown out the sporadic sound of gunfire outside.

When we fall silent over our cake crumbs, though, the ticking of a wind-up clock makes me jump. "How long have I been here? Oh no! My parents will be so worried. I have to run! See you in school!"

As the door closes behind me the happy party vanishes as if it had never been, and I'm back in a world of gunfire and smoke, of danger and death.

The sugar from the cake has given me more energy, and I walk very fast through the streets. Has Dino managed to cover for me? I don't know which I'm more afraid of: that I'll get in trouble or that my parents will be worried about me.

When I get to the Blue Bridge I balk. The bodies are gone, and some workers are shoring up the damage the missile caused. The evidence of tragedy has been hastily swept away, the way you sweep crumbs under a rug when guests are at the door.

Crossing that bridge again is the hardest thing I've ever had to do. Ghosts seem to whisper at me, but I can't hear what they're saying— begging for help, warning me to stay away? I stare straight ahead, knowing that if I look down at the ground I'll see the tell-tale red . . .

Somehow I make it across the bridge without having a full-blown panic attack. Pressing on, I make it to the end of my own street and stop. I know this half of the city was hit in the same attack that dam- aged the bridge. What if my house is gone?

I come to the grassy field, the empty, undeveloped lots that lead to the stretch of the river that snakes near our neighborhood. Late-season butterflies flit through the few drooping flowers that remain amid the browning grass and seed heads. As I watch them, Maci springs from her ambush like a tigress, leaping high in the air to bat at a white butterfly. I think she misses on purpose—she doesn't want to catch the butterfly, it is just a challenge, a joy, to leap into the air.

For a moment I share her joy. What a simple and wonderful thing it is to be alive, to move, to breathe!

She sees me and bounds through the tall grass to rub my legs in greeting. When I reach my arms down she leaps into them and nuzzles her head against my chin. My fears for my family evaporate. I know Maci wouldn't be playing if anything was wrong with her humans.

She mews as we near the house and squirms out of my arms. I fol- low her to the peony bush, my favorite hiding spot, until I see the white toes of Dino's sneakers peeking out.

When I crawl in beside him he looks like he sees a ghost. His mouth gapes, his tear-streaked face blanches. His whole body is shaking.

"What happened?" I ask in a panic at his distraught face. "Were Mama and Tata hit?"

"You . . . you!" He's touching my cheeks, my hair, shaking his head. "I saw you. You were . . . Oh, Amra, is it really you?"

"It's me. Dino, what's wrong?"

"I went to the bridge. When you didn't come home in an hour they were asking where you were. I kept telling them different places, but they were getting suspicious. So I went out to find you, to bring you home before we got in trouble. I started to cross the bridge and . . . it was you. I was sure. I saw your green sweater, and your face was . . . was . . ."

He throws his arms around me, sobbing into my hair. I pat his head, this little boy I've seen grow up. He's a teenager now too, but to me he will always be a little golden-haired boy toddling after his big sister.

"I came home, but I couldn't tell them," he says. "I couldn't break their hearts."

"It wasn't me. I saw her too. The other girl."

And then we cry together for her, for the girl that could have been me. I tell him about the mother with the fox-fur collar, about the little boy. Unburdened, we weep with sorrow and fury . . . and relief.

"We can't tell Mama and Tata," I say.

He gives a rueful laugh. "They'd never let us out of the house again."

"It's not just that," I explain. "Do you know how they'll feel if they think about what could have happened? If every time they leave the house they think about us dying?"

"They'll be doing that anyway. We'll all do that."

"I know. But I think as much as possible we have to spare them. Protect them. They love us so much, I think worry would kill them as much as any bomb."

"It's all upside-down, isn't it?" Dino asks. "Parents are supposed to be the ones keeping the ugly truth from their children."

"They're not as strong as they'd like us to believe," I tell him.

And so we make a pact that whatever we witness, whatever happens to us, we'll keep the worst of it from our parents.

CHAPTER 14

So what if school is in the middle of missile attacks and strafing from planes. School is the place I feel most comfortable. School is my way to be normal.

Of course, school will be a little different now. Our old school, which was in a cluster of other schools all in the same neighborhood, is a constant target for bombs. Now our class has been relocated to a sturdy redbrick building, right next to another similar building where the United Nations set up their headquarters. Their Protection Force is made up of military members of dozens of different countries. They are supposed to be a humanitarian security force, to guard aid shipments that come into the country and to make sure hospitals stay open. By their presence, they are supposed to keep us—the civilians—from being targets.

But they're a passive force. They're not really supposed to intervene. They're just supposed to be there, with the awesome power of their blue helmets, and they think the Serbs will respect them? What army has ever respected anything but guns and planes and death? Half the time, the Serbs just hijack the aid convoys, and the UNPROFOR just stands around doing nothing. America and the rest of Europe can't be seen turning a blind eye when atrocities are happening in what is supposed to be a civilized region. So they send token peacekeepers who say a lot but accomplish little. They don't want to invest money or lives into helping us. After all, we're Muslims: not quite white, not quite like them. One thing the UN can do is be visible. Their headquarters in

Bihać is clearly marked, and even the Serbs know that to bomb that building would probably bring swift international retaliation (whereas, say, bombing a shelter full of women and children doesn't make the West bat an eye).

So our new school is parked right next to the UN building, and even the Serbs who would like to wipe out our next generation won't dare attack it.

Dino and I start out extra early because we don't know what we'll encounter. Tata and Mama see us off with faces that are obviously rehearsed, not looking too worried. But they can't hide it completely, especially Tata.

"I remember when you were a little girl I didn't even want to let you go outside in the rain," Tata says, kissing my brow. "What if you got hit by lightning? What if it started to hail? But now?" He looks quickly up at the sky. "Worse things might rain down on you."

Mama flashes him a look. I know they've talked about this moment. With everyone living in the living room and kitchen it is hard to keep conversations secret. Tata promised Mama he'd be brave and not make a fuss when we left.

"Education is the most important thing in life," Mama says. "It opens every door for you. Some say that fate is a roll of the dice. But I say that without an education you don't even get to roll."

"Maybe with enough education you'll get an extra roll or two!" Tata says, laughing though there are tears in his eyes he's struggling not to shed.

"We'll be fine," Dino says. "After all, we have our guard cat with us!" Maci is at our feet waiting for us to go. She is anxious for a walk with us.

"We'll be careful," I amend, worried that too much confidence might jinx us.

Dino has a little satchel with a few pencils and a notebook from last year with half the pages ripped out. I don't have any books for this year's courses, and I haven't yet heard from Damir, my older friend who was going to lend me his math books. So I bring whatever might be useful: pencils, paper, a ruler and compass, a calculator, several books from last year that we hadn't quite finished before the war began, and a few of Tata's old textbooks. I stoop under the weight, but I want to be prepared for anything. This feels like a momentous day.

"Stick together!" Tata calls after us. "Protect each other!"

Dino and I act normal until we are out of our parents' sight, then we put our plan into action.

"It would kill them if anything happened to both of us," I say, reminding him of what we talked about. "So we can't walk together. At the very least we should stay across the street, or one far ahead of the other. That way if a bomb hits it will probably only get one of us."

Such morbid calculations. I can't wait to be seated in the classroom, where the only calculations are for clean, safe, abstract math problems.

We keep an eye on each other, though. Maci runs from me to Dino and back again, making sure we're okay.

When we come to the Una we have a problem. The bridge is the most dangerous place. Even if we cross separately it is more likely we'll be killed.

"Here, hold my stuff," Dino says, and before I can stop him he's peeled off his shirt, kicked off his shoes, and is picking his way downstream. He reaches a rocky place. It is a little shallower than most of the river, but that just makes it more dangerous because the water rushes even more swiftly over the rocks.

"Dino, are you crazy?" I ask as he plunges in up to the waist and then scrambles onto a broad flat rock before the current can drag him away.

"Yup!" he shouts back, and then plunges in again, just for fun, swimming like an otter.

He never could resist swimming. I think not being able to play in the water and show off his diving and cannonball jumps to girls has been the hardest part of this summer of war for him.

I can't help smiling as I watch him shake himself off, then pick his way across the shallow rocky waterfalls until he reaches the concrete strip that's just underwater but has more secure footing. I guess this really isn't a normal school day. We can't hang on to the usual way of doing things. We have to do whatever works for this new normal.

Maci waits in the center of the bridge while I go to the other side and Dino crosses the river below. She heads home once she sees us meet up again. I hand Dino his clothes. Here we separate, Dino going to his school, I to mine. Dino is still soaking, shivering, bare chested, and barefooted. But as he pulls his shirt back on he looks happier than I've seen him in months.

The UN compound is surrounded by spiky rolls of barbed wire, telling us in no uncertain terms the difference between Us and Them.

There are a lot of students from my old school, and more besides—people from other schools combined into this building for ease, as well as some refugees. Our usual serious, disciplined order goes out the window as old friends find each other. There is Dani, looking a little nervous, so I make sure to give him a big hug to let him know that even though he's not a Muslim, we don't have any prejudice. And there is handsome Mirza with his long blond hair, looking like a poet and teasing like a court jester. He takes a seat behind me, and I hear him talking with one of his friends about volunteering for the war, going to the front to fight. His friend is all for it. Mirza isn't so sure. "I don't even know which end of the gun a bullet comes out of!" he confesses, then starts teasing me by tweaking my hair.

"Same old Mirza," I say to Nura, but loud enough for him to hear it. "Are you still going to try to unhook my bra strap to convince me to give you math answers, or have you outgrown that?"

"I'll never get over teasing pretty girls," he says with a grin most people find irresistible.

We are called to attention by the principal, Zulić. He was the head of the engineering school prior to the war, but now that he is principal of our school, he makes sure we know that he isn't going to make our experience any easier because of the war. Quite the opposite, in fact. We know him by reputation, and when we see him up there everyone around me looks terrified. I'm not sure what to think myself. He's known for his high expectations and academic rigor as well as his sternness, which makes me think I might come to like or at least respect him despite his foreboding demeanor.

He jumps right in. "In the future I expect you to be in your seats and ready to learn without all this extraneous conversation. War or no war, this is a school, the most serious thing in your lives. Tardiness will not be excused. Absences are forbidden." He frowns down over his lectern at us.

"The authorities feel that meeting on a regular basis would make us targets." He scowls like he thinks the authorities are fools, and we should attend classes every day no matter how many bombs fall. "So on the few days we do meet, you will be driven all that much harder. Teachers will explain concepts, recommend resources, and make assignments. You'll work on your own and turn them in whenever we reconvene. In a few months you'll be tested, just as if you'd been in school all the time. So don't get lazy!"

I'm sad that school won't be meeting every day, but I understand the risk of putting all Bihać's future in one building. The UN proximity should protect us, but mistakes happen. Even deliberate mistakes.

"One more thing," the principal adds before he dismisses us. "Your grades were, ahem, lost in the transition. Your teachers, the ones who stayed, have been doing their best to compile your academic history from memory. It would be helpful if tonight you could all write as much as you remember of your grades over the past several years. We'll corroborate your notes with our teachers' and create a new record. Don't get any bright ideas about giving yourselves all fives." He looks directly at Mirza, who gives a sheepish grin. "We teachers all have good memories. We just want your help to double-check." He looks at me now. "You don't have to bother, Amra. We know what your grades are."

I flush with pride and embarrassment.

We go from class to class—math, physics, history, literature. In history, we were supposed to study European history, but our teacher switches it to Asian history. "European history is borders changing and people fighting people across the next border, over and over again. You've had enough of that. Think about Feudal Japan for a change."

Our literature teacher assigns us a task that would have been simple only a few months ago. "Write an essay about the first day of the war." That starts a conversation about when the war actually began. Was it on the day war was officially declared? The day we realized in our hearts what the war meant to us? Or some other moment? Some of us tell our stories.

I don't.

I can't. I don't know if I'll ever be ready to talk about the things I've seen.

But here, I don't have to. My friends and I can just look at one another and get some comfort from the knowledge that each of us understands what the others are going through.

Mirza starts his essay while we're still in class. "I died the day the war began," he writes. His opening alone is enough to move Teacher Safeta almost to tears. I have a feeling Mirza might get his first five in literature.

When class is over, we receive instructions to meet the next day. "But it won't always be day to day like this," we're told. "Keep in touch with your friends. Spread the word when school is in session. Don't let anyone get left behind."

I don't like leaving my friends. It feels so normal, being in a little room behind a desk, with the regular cycle of classes, chatting with friends in between.

Normalcy has become my highest aspiration.

But I'm also excited to get home and start studying. I just have one stop to make on the way.

"Who is this again?" Dino shouts from across the street. This walking separately idea might get a little ridiculous.

"Damir, the boy a year ahead of me. He told Tetka Fatma that I could borrow his old math textbooks, but he never came around to deliver them. We're just stopping to see if he's home."

We reach his house, and his father answers my knock. I'm just so happy about school, happy to be out, happy at the idea of learning new math concepts, that I don't pay attention to his drawn face. "Hi, is Damir in? He said I could borrow some schoolbooks. Classes started today!"

Damir's father doesn't ask me in, a very strange thing in this hospitable country. Instead he tells me to wait and comes back with a big stack of books in several subjects, far more than I was expecting. One is for calculus, which I won't need for another year.

"But these are for his current year, and beyond," I say, trying to give some of them back to his father. "He'll need these himself."

"No, he won't," his father says.

"You should check with him first," I say, dubious. "He'll be mad if he goes to start his work and his books are gone!"

I smile, but no smile answers me in return.

"He won't need his books," Damir's father says in a low, flat voice.

"He was killed by a missile yesterday." He piles the books I tried to return back in my arms, in a stack so high it almost covers my face. "You can have them. He'd want someone smart to use them."

"I . . . I'm so sorry," I begin, but with a look of apology he closes the door gently in my face. Different people deal with grief different ways, and Damir's father needs solitude and silence.

I found a little light this day, and once again it is extinguished.

No, I tell myself as I head home. I won't let the world go black around me. I'll kindle a new light. With study and knowledge and persistence . . . and hope.

When I get home I go to the second floor of the garage, where Maci is nursing her fast-growing kittens. Her calico twins nestle close by her side, but Žućko, the brave little cat with the marmalade fur, tumbles out of his nest and pounces on my fingers while I open up the first book and start to read the introduction:

> The scope of this book is broad, beginning with linear equation systems and proceeding to matrix algebra, finite dimensional vector spaces, and concluding with matrix representations of linear transformations. Students will be pleased to know that proper attention is also paid to determinants and eigenvalues . . .

I can hear gunfire in the distance, and the grief for Damir hangs heavy in the background of my thoughts. Yet as the numbers and concepts in the textbook coalesce into something I can comprehend, I feel strangely calm. Maybe somehow with pure mathematics and kittens I can build a better world.

From her cozy bed, Maci gives me a long, slow blink as if I've finally understood something important.

1993
SUMMER

CHAPTER 15

With long, sure strokes I swim from the island to the beach. It's hot, blissfully hot, and I relish the sensation of my flesh baking like a potato skin in the oven. It makes me remember our family trips to Croatia, though the Adriatic Sea was much warmer than the Una, which is chilly even in the height of summer. I would stay outside from sunrise to sunset and always get sunburned. Mama would slather cooling yogurt over my red skin, and that cooled it better than aloe.

Winter seems so far away now, those bitter days huddled beside the wood-burning stove, or shivering in the unheated classroom in our parkas. My old shoes were separating at the seam and snow seeped in, melting in my wool socks and leaving my feet frozen. There were times when I didn't feel my feet all day. I didn't undress completely for months.

Now my body is free in the sun and the warm gentle breeze, and I never want it to end.

"Thanks again for the swimsuit, Armela," I tell the gorgeous girl sprawled luxuriously on the sand in a scanty bikini.

"I'm happy for you to have it," she says, adjusting her straps so she won't have a tan line. "I've decided I only want to wear two-piece suits. As long as my father doesn't find out. I love feeling the water and sun on my body!"

Another girl might have said it lasciviously. But Armela is as innocent as she is beautiful. She's never vain about her looks, but the other girls hate her for being so pretty.

Nura is sunbathing on my other side, being polite to Armela but mostly ignoring her. Samira and Lana are here too. Lana is talking about how glad she is that the war made her skinny. Samira is looking happier than usual, probably because her abusive father is too busy now to bother her.

My cousin Azra—the ill-tempered daughter of my uncle Ejub who was killed in front of his house at the beginning of the war—is here too. She's a couple of years ahead of me, in college.

And in the middle of the river—boys. Teens and young men, taking a day for nothing but fun. They sit on each other's shoulders to wrestle, the loser toppling with a curse and a splash, the winner shouting in triumph. They dive off a jutting dock into a deeper place, showing off their acrobatics or just trying to make a splash big enough to reach the sunbathing girls.

It is a perfect, peaceful day. I forget any past animosities. All of these young men and women are my friends, by virtue of the simple fact that they're here today. We are the survivors.

I close my eyes against the bright light, enjoying the chatter and laughter around me. I'm completely relaxed and unprepared when something starts dragging on my leg, pulling me halfway into the water. I panic and kick, memories and fears slamming me. In my mind it is a Četnik hand, a violating hand.

But even before I realize what's happening I hear Armela's giddy laughter beside me, and I know that on this day, nothing bad can happen. It's just Mirza, who swam across the river to spring on me like a crocodile. He's not flirting—he knows I'm not interested. He just likes fun and plenty of attention, no matter who it is from.

"Ugh!" Nura groans beside me. "Boys never grow up, do they?"

Mirza winks at her. "When I'm an old man, I'll still splash you!" Then he does just that, and dives back into the river to chase his friends.

"You girls should sit somewhere else," Azra says to my friends.

"With pretty Armela and Amra here, the boys won't pay any attention to you."

"I don't see the boys flirting with you either," Nura tells her.

Azra shrugs. "A boy is meeting me here later. A very special boy named Dado."

Ugh, I don't want to hear any more about Dado. Every time we run into each other (more and more now since Mama makes me bring her food every week or so), she corners me to talk about this Dado. He lives somewhere in her neighborhood, and they had gone to school together. She goes on and on about how handsome he is, how smart. Whenever he says something funny I have to hear about it. *Maybe I'll let you meet him someday*, she teases each time. *Poor lonely Amra. No one wants you, do they?* I stand up to swim again.

"Where are you going, Amra?" she snaps. "You have to stay here. I told this boy he was going to meet a very clever friend of mine."

"Me? Why would he want to meet me?"

She shrugs. "I've loved this boy for a long time. I'm going to tell him today. But I don't want it to be obvious, like I set the whole thing up. So I need you here in the beginning to make it look natural. Then after a little while you better get lost. I don't want you talking to him any more than you have to."

"Don't worry, Cousin, I have no interest in stealing your boyfriend."

"He's not my boyfriend . . . yet."

I shrug, indifferent to any boy Azra might like. There's only one young man who's captured my interest in the last year, and so far I haven't seen Davor again. School might only be in session a few days a month, but I study a lot. I also have several tutoring jobs to make extra money, and I joined the city's first Association of Muslim Women. Right now our main mission is to write impassioned letters to anyone we think might listen—the UN Security Council, heads of government, special envoys—telling them the truth of what is happening here, begging for intervention.

But busy as I am, I haven't forgotten him. Whenever I go to visit Tetka Fatma and Tetak Ale, or go to my tutoring jobs, I look for him or his big dog on their street, but I haven't run into him again. I don't want to go as far as to ask any of my friends about him. It seems silly to pursue someone I only really met once. And more important, I don't really have any experience with pursuit!

Just then I hear a shout and everyone is greeting my popular brother, who has just shown up. Whenever he is free—most of the time—he's down by the community center. Partly this is because that's one of the few remaining places in Bihać that, on rare occasions, still gets electricity. When it does, word spreads and kids flock to the television there. All the channels we receive are from Serb-controlled media, so we Muslims are called parasites and invaders. But at least it gives them a glimpse, however skewed, of what is happening in the rest of Bosnia.

He also goes for the excitement. For a teenager full of energy and a thirst for adventure, the community center provides a perfect opportunity. They are the ones who mobilize to help put out fires. They are the ones who drag away rubble with their bare hands when a building is bombed, looking for survivors. He and the other teenage boys too young to be conscripted into the army run messages and medical supplies around the city and feel very important.

"Did you hear what happened to Adis?" Dino asks the group at large. "He was stealing electricity with a couple of other boys. His family lives by the clinic, and the line was live today. His mom wanted to bake his father a birthday cake, but she didn't want to use the wood oven in this scorching weather. Adis told her he could get the electricity connected so she could use the electric oven. So she sends him up the pole, and he's messing with this wire, that wire, trying to find which one is live. Looks like none of them are, but then all of a sudden the power comes on in the house and his mom shouts out the window, 'Good job, Adis! My clever boy did it!' The rest of us look up and there is Adis electrified: frozen to the pole, his hair crackling, sparks flying, looking like Nikola Tesla in his lab!" None of us dare laugh out loud until Dino adds, "Don't worry, he's fine. He says it hurt like hell but afterward it felt like he just got a full body massage!"

I laugh too, but I know people have lost limbs, or their lives, trying to get a few hours of electricity in their homes.

The beach is getting even more full. Most of the Una is too deep or rough for swimming, but at this broad quiet bend in the river it is almost like a lake. The sandy beach makes it even more appealing, and young people and courting couples come here often.

It's also far enough away from the heart of the city that it's less likely the Serbs will target it.

Here, for a few hours, we feel safe.

I see other people I know, older people, families with kids. My cousin Aida arrives with her husband. She is a gentle, petite woman, a dental nurse. Her husband, Raja, is a giant.

He's so big that people pause their conversations to stare at him. He isn't just tall, he's massive, with shoulders like a bull and feet like cargo boxes. He's the most mild-mannered man, though. Aida told me that when she found a black beetle creeping through her bedroom and screamed for him to kill it, he instead scooped it up gently and carried it to their garden. "I swear I heard him tell that bug to be more careful where he wanders next time!" she told me. "And then, can you believe it, he gave that bug a crumb of bread!" She shook her head with pretend disapproval, but I know she appreciates her gentle giant's ways.

Raja greets me with a pat on the back as he passes—a pat that almost knocks me down. I don't think he realizes how big he is. When he sits down on a towel, he makes it look like a postage stamp.

Suddenly there's a commotion on the riverbank.

"What's that?"

"Can it be?"

"I don't believe it!" I say when look. It is a Nestlé candy bar. I'd recognize that design anywhere: milk chocolate with hazelnuts. And there it is, just drifting down the river on a matted raft of sticks and reeds like a gift from God.

My mouth begins to water immediately. I haven't had anything sweet or delicious in a year! Well, the occasional spoonful of honey, but that's just sweet and nothing else. But chocolate! Smooth, sugary, delicious, creamy, melt-in-your mouth chocolate, with crunchy rich hazelnuts! It will taste better than last year's birthday cake! How did it possibly get here? Did a Serb soldier lose his snack far upriver?

While the others are staring at it like it's an angel coming down to bless us, I take action and plunge into the water. They're after me like a pack of hunting dogs, but I'm a strong swimmer and determined. My long legs kick, my arms churn the water.

As I take a breath I see Dino and Mirza coming up close behind me on either side. It's a race to the finish!

Dino grabs for my foot, but I slip free, stretch out my hand, and suddenly my fingers close around . . .

An empty candy wrapper.

Nothing but floating garbage, tossed in the water by some overfed Serb upriver.

I keep the wrapper, though. One of Dino's favorite pastimes is remembering delicious food from before the war. We talk about which foods we miss most. Mine is fluffy white bread. We don't have any yeast now, so our bread is dense and chewy, made from soured dough.

With this candy wrapper we'll read the ingredients and our mouths will water with memory. We'll talk about it at night so we can taste it in our dreams.

Dejected, I start to swim back for shore, telling my body it has to do without a delicious treat for now.

When I get to where I can touch the bottom again I rest, look on the beach, and see Davor.

He's standing next to Azra.

But he's staring at me.

An hour later we're under the shade of a spreading tree, apart from the others. Azra has gone away in a huff. She'll never forgive me, but that doesn't bother me. After her father was killed, Mama and Tetka Fatma brought her and her mother food, but after a first flush of sorrow and gratitude they both reverted to their previous states.

I'm not worried about that. For almost the first time in this war, I don't care about anything except the present. I feel fluttery, nervous, but at the same time oddly confident.

"I've been waiting a year for this moment," Davor says, echoing exactly what I feel. "I wanted to find you, but, can you believe it, I forgot where you lived! I remembered the neighborhood, and I walked around a few times, even asked some people if they knew where a tall beautiful girl named Amra lived."

"Oh, no wonder you couldn't find me!" I say, looking down. "They thought you were looking for a beautiful girl."

"I'd say you were fishing for compliments, but if you don't know you're beautiful, my telling you wouldn't help."

"When the bridge was bombed last year, I looked for you afterward," I tell him. "I thought maybe . . ."

"Me too. When it happened, my dog, Mrki, got spooked and took off, dragging me with him. By the time I got back, you were gone. I helped with the bodies, made sure none of them were you."

"My brother thought I died that day," I say.

"We've spent the last year holding our breaths, haven't we? Waiting for bad news."

"I feel like some good news for a change," I say, looking him straight in the eyes. Beautiful, gray-green eyes that seem to shift color.

"I think I have some for you," he answers, taking my hand.

The war melts away, and I'm just a young girl falling in love.

Davor and I talk all day, until the sun settles low in the sky. Most of the swimmers have gone home, but my closest friends and Dino remain, along with some of Dino's friends. They keep a respectful distance. Dino makes teasing kissy-faces, and my friend Nura mouths, "Tell me everything," but I don't mind.

Davor, nicknamed Dado, tells me about my cousin Azra. "She's been my classmate since we were small, and our families are close. I think she has a crush on me, but what can I do about that? To me, Azra has never been more than a friend. I'm grateful that she brought us together, even if she's upset."

As I get to know Davor better I'm not disappointed. What if he had just been a tall, good-looking boy, nothing more? A young man with nothing to say for himself? But luckily he's funny and smart, and even when I get tired of trying to figure out exactly what color his eyes are, I don't get tired of him.

"What are you studying?" I ask him.

"I was in the veterinary school," he says. "I wanted to treat pets, but since the war started I've been taking care of our army's horses."

It's an important job, because with hardly any petrol, jeeps and trucks are useless. We've reverted to medieval life, relying on literal horsepower.

"What's your favorite animal?" I ask him.

"Hmm . . . right now a cow, or chicken, or goat, or fish . . . or even a pig! Anything I can eat! The only thing I love more than animals is food!"

For the past hour I've been smelling a strange scent wafting across the river, and at that moment I see the door of the house on the far shore swing open. It is Tetak Ale and Tetka Fatma's house, where they live most of the year when they're not at the bee farm.

"Amra, Dino, call your friends over! I've made a treat!"

I squint, shading my eyes, and see Tetak Ale holding a tray clutched in an oversized oven mitt. "Come on!" I say, pulling Davor to his feet. "I think he made pastries!"

I cross the river on an old small footbridge that reaches nearly to Ale's house, hoping not to be disappointed this time in my quest for deliciousness. It's more likely that Tetka Fatma baked the pastries, or at least prepared them and left them for Ale to actually cook. I expect them to be a little burned on the bottom.

"Tetak Ale!" I say, trying to hug him without getting him wet. He doesn't care about that, but holds the tray aloft and hugs me with his free arm. "I didn't know you could bake."

"Neither did I. You never know what you can do until you try."

"What kind are they?" Dino asks, sniffing and reaching. "Cheese or plum?" Fatma is famous for her pastries—for all her cooking—and usually makes either sweet, sticky plum confections or savory, salty cheese pastries.

"Well, I didn't want to make two batches, so I decided to combine them—cheese and plum jam all in one. You get sweet and savory together. The finest gourmands recommend combining flavors."

My heart starts to sink. Cheese and fruit can go well together . . . but not this kind of cheese.

Still, it is better than the onion and bean porridge I've been eating for days, and after the disappointment of the candy bar, I'm dying for anything yummy.

I take one . . .

And almost break my teeth.

Tetak Ale is watching me in happy anticipation. "Mmm, good!" I manage, covering my mouth when crumbs try to spray out.

"Yes? I thought they would be. I had most of the right ingredients."

Most? Flour and water I can believe. But there can't be a speck of butter in these baked rocks.

I chew and chew and chew, smiling though my jaw hurts. I don't want to make Tetak Ale feel bad. Dino wisely wraps a couple in a napkin. "I'm going to save mine for later. Thanks, Tetak!" He swims carefully back across the river holding them aloft, and if those concrete pastries aren't buried before sunset I'll eat my volleyball sneakers!

Davor accepts one and tries polite little nibbles, like an old lady at a tea party. He can hardly break off more than crumbs, but at least he's not dislocating his jaw like I am when I try to chew my big bite.

"Why didn't Tetka Fatma make the pastries today?" I ask, still trying to get the first bite soft enough to swallow.

"Well, she's a little under the weather," he says.

"Oh no! Why didn't you tell me? I'll go in and see her." I start past him, wondering if there's any place in the house to hide this plum and cheese rock. Tetak Ale catches me by the arm. "She's not home. She's at the hospital."

Then he tells me what happened.

War, they say, makes strange bedfellows, and nothing is stranger than the fact that we in Bihać owe our continued survival in large part to the Serbs. As always in humanity, greed vies with hate, and for a lot of Serb soldiers on the border, greed wins. The Serbs in the occupied land surrounding the Bihać pocket are turning a tidy profit by trading with the enemy—us. Under cloak of darkness, bolstered by the courage of liquor, they venture into the woodsy no-man's-land with flour and sunflower oil, powdered milk and salt, and sell their wares to this besieged city at exorbitant prices.

If they live, these black marketeers will leave the war with a fortune.

And we Muslims survive a little while longer.

Many of them sell decent-quality food, just happy to be making boatloads of money off our misery. But a few others think to line their pockets and aid their cause at the same time. They lace their flour or baking powder with rat poison or other deadly chemicals. Sometimes we catch the taint in time. Tetka Fatma didn't.

She was so happy that she could bake a real marble cake that she used the baking powder right away. The only thing that saved the rest of us from getting sick is that she made a little too much batter and baked a separate small cake in a custard cup alongside the main one. She tasted that mini cake first to check her recipe. Within the hour she was doubled over with gripping pains in her gut. Severe vomiting and diarrhea started immediately after. Tetak Ale rushed her to the hospital, where she got her stomach pumped.

"Will she be okay?" I ask. Tetak Ale nods. "She didn't have too much, and we got her to the hospital in time. They're just keeping her overnight. She was mostly upset that she wasted all those nuts, and we have to throw the whole cake away now. From her hospital bed she said, 'Can't you pick out the nuts? I'm sure they'll be fine.'"

Davor takes my hand when it's time to leave. "Can I walk you home?"

"No, that's okay." I have to hurry and tell Mama what happened to her sister, so I won't be able to enjoy his company.

"Can I come see you tomorrow?"

I want to say yes, but I'm not sure how my parents will react. Strict Mama might think he will distract me from my important studies. Vulnerable Tata will feel like he's losing his little girl to adulthood.

"I don't know . . . ," I begin.

But he smiles in understanding. He knows what families can be like. "Tell you what, you don't have to invite me, but I'll invite myself. At three o'clock I'll take a walk down your street. If you want to see me, you can come out and we can accidentally run into each other. Your parents can't object to that, can they? At worst we can go for a stroll. But if you're feeling brave you can invite me in. Or, you know parents—you don't dare invite a boy officially, but if they see you talking to a friend they'll say, 'Oh, you rude girl, why don't you invite him in for coffee!'"

I can't help laughing—he has my parents down perfectly.

I don't say yes . . . but I don't say no.

That night I dream of Davor. Nothing romantic, just the pleasure of seeing him, maybe having him over, sitting on the sofa, chatting, eating a snack.

The next morning word comes that the Serb offensive has pressed within a quarter mile of the city. If our heroic volunteer army can't stop them, we could be overrun at any moment.

"Start packing," Mama tells us. "We're all heading to Ale and Fatma's bee farm."

CHAPTER 16

In 1993, Bihać was officially designated as a "Safe Area" by the United Nations Security Council. No one must have told the Serbs, because their attacks have continued. It's almost as if the Serbs wanted people to think this place was safe, so residents would stay, and refugees would crowd into this one little area. With the population concentrated under a promise of safety, we're that much easier to kill.

Now the Serbs are launching a stronger attack than ever before, surging toward one side of the city. At any moment they could be here, on our streets, going house to house.

I think of the list that Bakir found in our neighbor's house. Even without any list, the Serbs will have no trouble finding victims when they enter the city. Kill the men. Rape the women. They see us like rats in a nest. I don't think they even consider basic humanity when dealing with us, because to them, we're not human.

So we flee in the other direction, where for the past week or two there have been no attacks. It's still terribly dangerous, especially driving during the daytime.

"I'd rather be doing this at night," Tata says as he navigates our tiny orange Stojadin. "But at least this way we can see the potholes and barricades." He swerves carefully around what he is tactfully calling a pothole, though we all know it is from a bomb.

"Just remember, if I tell you to get down, duck your head and cover it," Tata reminds us. "And if I say get out of the car and run, you go, fast as you can, and don't look back. Go in different directions, don't wait for anyone. Just run."

Dino and I are sitting in the back seat, Maci crouched on the seat beside us, her eyes wide and wild, her tail lashing. She might be more comfortable on the floor where she can't see the confusing flashes of passing scenery, but part of the floor is rusted out. I can see the pavement pass beneath us like a flowing river. It's big enough for her legs to slip through, so we keep her on the seat near us.

I've never seen Maci afraid before. Even during the worst bombings she maintains her serenity. She might be watchful and alert, but she is never frightened. If anything, she sometimes seems like she's ready and willing to attack any danger that comes near her family.

Today, though, she's terrified. Her ears are laid flat back, and she's trembling. I bet she's never been in a car before.

Driving in our tiny Stojadin is nerve-wracking in the best of times. This car is older than I am. Tata rarely pushes it past forty or fifty kilometers per hour. It rattles and squeaks, and occasionally a little piece of it will fall off along the roadside. Today, Tata is pushing it faster than it wants to go, and it is whining dangerously in protest.

I don't ride in a car very often. Usually it is on the way to something fun. This trip brings back memories of other trips, happier trips, usually with Fatma and Ale. Sometimes we would all drive in the same car to a spa town called Topusko, on the border between Bosnia and Croatia. They have mineral springs there that are supposed to heal all manner of ailments. But mostly, Mama and Fatma liked to soak and chat for hours on end. The togetherness was more healing than the magical mineral waters.

The road trips there were always fun. We piled into their beige Škoda, and Tetak Ale would keep his foot pressed all the way down on the gas pedal to force that reluctant car over the mountainous roads. When clouds of steam started to billow from under the hood he'd cheerfully pull over to the side of the road and open up the radiator cap. "Lunch time!" he'd announce, dropping hot dogs into the boiling water one by one. By the time the engine had cooled, the hot dogs were ready, and he fished them out with long tongs for us to eat on the second leg of the drive. I'm sure we were eating terrible chemicals from the car, but we didn't care. We bragged to our friends about Tetak's talented car that knew how to cook.

Other times we would go visit Tata's family in Šumatac. The family home is perched high on a hill that is shaped like a swirl of soft-serve ice cream. I think of that house as a cherry on top of a treat. The property borders a forest of chestnut trees, and in the autumn we would gather them and edible wild mushrooms, and roast them all in a bonfire. Tata's brothers would tell stories of their youth—how right after World War II, Tata, the youngest, walked barefoot through the forest in winter to deliver himself to an orphanage where he'd get food and an education. Or they would tell us spellbound children how Tata and his brother were chased through the snow by a starving wolf, only to be saved by their noble Dalmatian dog, who led the wolf away and gave up his life so the brothers could survive.

Today, though, we are fleeing danger and heading into uncertainty. We hope that the Serbs fighting on the Croatian side have all joined forces with the Serbs on the Bosnian side for their big attack, and that this area should be relatively safe. But we really don't know anything for sure.

Ale and Fatma's bee farm is only eleven kilometers outside the city, but it takes forever to reach it. We are held up at one roadblock—by Muslim soldiers, fortunately—and once have to take a long detour when the main road is completely blocked by burned-out cars, logs, cinder blocks, and sandbags filled from the Una beach: things designed to stop or at least slow advancing enemy troops. It is nearly dark by the time we near the bee farm.

We pause on a hill to give the car a break, and I look back at the distant Bihać. Orange lights flare and die over the dusky city. We're too far away to tell which parts of the city are being hit. From here, it looks like the whole city is on fire. If this were a celebration, it would be a beautiful light show of fireworks.

Even this out-of-the-way place isn't really safe. At most it is a temporary shelter. The Serbs are focusing on the main cities where most of the population is clustered. But if they take Bihać, they will come to places like this next. Nowhere is safe.

Fatma and Ale are supposed to meet us here. Ale just had to get Fatma out of the hospital. They should be here tonight or by morning at the latest. But what if they leave too late?

I think of my friends, who might have no place to go when the Serbs enter the city.

I think of Davor.

How hopeful I was only last night. How happy.

Now, if he comes to see me, there will be no one to meet him. Will he know that I fled? Maybe he'll think I just don't want to meet him. I imagine the disappointment on his face as he wanders up and down my street, trying to figure out which house might be mine, waiting for me to come out to meet him.

What if that is the last thing he thinks and feels before the Serbs take Bihać? He could die feeling disappointment in me. I wish I could have left a message for him. Now we may never see each other again.

I close my eyes as the explosions over Bihać flare and die. Once again, a spark in me that has flared seems to have died. Was it foolish, was it selfish to want just one little good thing in this war? Just one afternoon with a boy who likes me? When people are dying and suffering, how can I feel bad that I didn't get to take a walk with Davor?

Maci makes one of her strange cat noises that sounds almost

human—not a meow or a growl, but that sort of whining howl that makes it seem like she's trying to replicate speech. I pull her onto my lap, but for once she's not interested in that, returning to her place on the seat to hunker in misery.

"It will be okay, Maci," I tell her. "You'll love the bee farm. There are such beautiful flowers, and the grass is the softest I've ever felt. And maybe you can even have a reunion with your kittens!" When the kittens were weaned we gave two of them to Fatma to take to her farm. The villagers there have cows for milk, and they welcome cats who will hunt mice in their barns. We thought the kittens would have a better life there.

We kept little yellow-orange Žućko, our favorite, but he proved to be nothing like his calm and sophisticated mother. He was wild, scratching at the furniture and clawing his way up the curtains until Mama banished him outside. He lived near us for a while, but he always had his own agenda—which, as a tomcat, probably involved courting girl cats across town. For a while he came home every few days. Then he stopped coming. He'd found a new home somewhere. Maci didn't seem to mind. She is a cat who thinks of herself as a person, and she seems happier with her humans than with other cats.

Finally we make it to the farm. I pick up Maci and stagger, stiff-legged, out of the car. "You sleep inside the house," Mama tells us. "And we'll sleep in the camper." The camper is parked near the house, and it looks haunted in the evening shadows. I know they're not going to sleep, though. They'll sit out front all night, watching the firefight over our city, wondering whether our forces can hold them off.

Wondering if the fighting will make it this far.

I want to tell them that I'll stay up with them all night to keep watch.

But Maci purrs against my chest, nestling her soft cheek on my neck, and such a weariness washes over me that I do what they tell me and go into the little house to sleep.

———————

I awake to birdsong, and to Maci nose to nose with me, kneading her paws on my chest and staring into my eyes. The sun is shining, and there are no sounds of distant explosions right now. Is it over?

There are voices outside, though. Still fully dressed from last night, I step outside with Maci in my arms and find that Fatma and Ale have arrived in the night. "There's the sleepyhead!" Ale says when he spies me. "Do you think you can nap all day? This is a working farm. We have honey to harvest, the last of the strawberries to pick." He pops one of the scarlet strawberries into my mouth, and instantly the wild sweet taste casts a spell on me.

I set Maci down, and she immediately begins to stalk moths in the flower beds.

Far away, from the direction of Bihać, there is one distant boom. Maci pauses in her hunting to look at me. Then very deliberately she flops over in the clover and bats lazily at a chubby blossom. Yes, she seems to tell me, those things are still happening. But just for this moment, out here, we can relax.

Who am I to question the wisdom of such a cat as Maci?

This little bee farm has been the setting of so many happy times that it is easy to fall into old habits. The one-room house is charming, and a perfect embodiment of Tetak Ale. He taught physics and technical education—a class that is really practical engineering where students design and build things. Ale is extremely handy and artistic. In fact, his love of physics and engineering seems as much an appreciation of proportion and the beauty of the physical world as it is about abstract concepts. He is one of those men who can make things. Give him a problem—broken equipment, a need for a piece of furniture—and he will solve it by constructing something wonderful. When he and Fatma bought this property, they decided they needed a perfect little house just the right size for the two of them.

A few miles from the farm stands the Gorenje refrigerator factory. They have a dump behind the property where they toss piles and piles of old or broken merchandise, including refrigerator doors. Plenty are rusted refuse, but some are left over from discontinued models, others have some manufacturing defect. Ale stared at those piles of garbage and saw potential.

So he decided to make their vacation house out of those abandoned refrigerator doors. The result is adorable, like an industrial midcentury fairy home, a blend of practicality and whimsy.

The rest of the property is all flowers. Inside, the walls are papered in floral designs. A cunning little cabinet holds a tea set with briar roses. And outside—oh! Bounties of flowers! *For the bees*, Fatma always says, and indeed her busy little charges run riot through the blossoms, their bodies heavy and laden with pollen as they feed. But I think Fatma plants them mostly for their beauty, and their heady scent. This place is a paradise.

How can there be hell without a heaven too?

"Let's tell the bees what's going on," Tetka Fatma says as she leads me over to the hives. There are forty of them, wooden boxes made to keep the bees happy and safe, dry in the rain, but well ventilated. They reward her care by giving more honey than any other bees in Bihać.

"Their honey is sweeter too," Ale always says with a wink. "It is because all the worker bees are male, and they're all in love with her."

"Each hive already has a queen," Fatma scoffs good-naturedly.

"Well then, you are the Bee Empress!"

When she takes their honey she wears a full bee suit, covered in white from head to ankles, with her stylish Italian leather shoes the only thing sticking out. And she smokes them during the harvest, too, puffing it into their hives to make them sleepy. But now, when she's not actually touching the hive they're guarding, the bees don't see her as a threat. They're so used to her that as long as we move slowly we can get as close as we like.

"Hello, bees," she tells them in a low, mellow voice. The bees crawling over the outside of the hive seem to shiver with the vibrations of her voice. I love the smell up close to the hives, like overripe fruit in strong sunshine. Together the bees make a drone that is almost like a cat's purr. They come and go about their business, yet I get the feeling that the hive as a whole is listening to us. This city of bees wants to hear what Tetka Fatma has to say.

"There is danger coming, little bees," she tells them. "It is close. But you will be safe. Everyone wants honey, Muslim and Serb alike. So if they come here, you won't be harmed." She leans closer to the hives. One of the bees lands on her hand, and she raises it to eye level, speaking directly to that one fuzzy bee in particular as he grooms his antennae with his forelegs. "But I ask a favor of you, my bees. If the Serbs come, sting them like hell and then fly into the woods and never make a drop of honey for those monsters!"

She puffs a breath on the bee, and he flies lazily back to his hive, where he spins in a circle while the other bees gather around him.

"I'd swear they understand!" I say.

Tetka Fatma shrugs. "Sometimes we tell people things for our own benefit, not theirs. Because it makes us feel better, not because the other person needs to hear it. I wouldn't like to think of a Serb soldier enjoying their honey they worked so hard for. Now, I'm going to check for the last of the strawberries, and you can talk to the rest of the bees. Tell them anything you need to get off your chest. They're good listeners."

She goes back to the garden, and I go to the next hive. But the bees show no sign of listening to me. I'm not their empress. So instead I head to the back of the house and find Maci, my favorite confidante.

"Have you found your kittens?" I ask her. They went to two nearby farms, and they might well wander by. But I don't see any sign of them. Maci leads me into the tall grass, summer-dry and freckled with deep-red wildflowers.

"I'm going to graduate next year, Maci," I tell her as she sprawls beside me, showing her creamy belly to the sun. I lie down too, stretched out in the ticklish grass. "Well, such as it is!" I chuckle. "Last year we had eight weeks of classes, if that. But we had exams, the grades were recorded, so I suppose my graduation will be official. And then what? Mama says that education is the key to my future. And I believe her. But what will the future be? How will physics and math and literature help me get food for my family?"

By way of an answer, Maci climbs onto my belly and curls up. I stare at the clouds, watching them swirl into dragon shapes.

"And what about Davor?" I ask her a long while later.

But she's asleep, lulled by the quiet and the heat.

A few moments later, so am I.

"Amra! Where are you?" I'm jolted awake by Tata's shout. I'm close to the house but hidden in the tall grass, in my own little world of green stripes against blue sky. I hear the panic in his voice, but I lie here unmoving for another few seconds, unwilling to give up this peace to whatever is coming at us next.

Finally I sit up—easily, because Maci is no longer snoozing on my stomach.

"Here I am. What's happening?"

"We thought the Serbs had all moved to the other front, but some of our soldiers just came through and told us that the Serbs are massing on the Croatian side too. They're almost here! We have to go home!"

I climb to my feet, my eyes bleary in the noon brightness. I rub them and try to think. I didn't unpack yet, so I just have to grab my stuff and . . .

"Where's Maci?"

I look around, but don't see her anywhere.

"Hurry! Get in the car. We have to go now!" His words are punctuated by gunfire, closer than I've ever heard it before. It gives power to my feet, and I dash into the refrigerator house to grab my bag. Dino is already in the car.

"Have you seen Maci?" I shout to him. He shakes his head and starts to get out to help me, but Mama is there now, ordering him back into the car.

"We don't have time," she says.

I throw my bag into the back seat and run to the RV, which Fatma is just locking up. "Where's Maci?"

"I saw her stalk off into the grass a while ago." She points vaguely in the direction of a neighboring farm where one of Maci's kittens went.

"I can't leave without her!" I cry.

But the gunfire is even closer now. Something whizzes overhead like a supersonic flying insect, smacking into a tree with an explosion of bark.

"Get down!" Tetak Ale shouts, and I drop to my knees, calling for Maci but crawling to the car. Dino pulls me in, and we're lurching down the road even before I can close the door. Ale and Fatma are in their car right behind us.

"Maci!" I scream out the window, tears streaking my face. "Mama, Tata, stop the car! I have to find her!"

But we leave my beloved little friend behind as the Serb army advances.

CHAPTER 17

After what I have seen, I don't know if I believe in miracles anymore. But I do believe in the will of people to survive, to fight against impossible odds. The people in Bihać are not trained warriors. Beyond a few policemen, a few Muslim soldiers who fled the army, we are just citizens: shopkeepers, businesspeople, teachers, scientists, students. Yet somehow we have banded together into an army.

The Serbs think they are determined to make a Serb homeland, to kill all of us? Well, they are not half as determined as we are to survive.

Somehow, against all probability, the ragtag fighters of the Fifth Corps inside Bihać have managed to drive back the Serb offensive. They aren't defeated—nothing close to that—but they have been sent back to their borders with their tails between their legs.

I know that means they are just going to regroup and come back harder, but every day above the ground is a good one. Every day brings hope that the world will finally see and put a stop to this.

But I am bereft without my Maci. The tears dry on our journey home, but the sorrow feels like a rock in the pit of my stomach. She is family. How could we have left her behind?

"We'll go back for her," Tata assures me.

"When? Tonight? Tomorrow?"

"No . . . not so soon as that. But there are good families there, and lots of mice and birds to eat. She'll find her kittens. She'll be safe."

But she doesn't want to be safe, I think. She wants to be with her family. She must be feeling what I felt when Mama and Tata tried to send me away with my aunt at the start of the war. What does safety matter if you aren't with the people you love?

My little Maci must be so confused. Does she think we left her on purpose? She'll search all around the bee farm, sniffing in every corner, stalking through the roses and wildflowers, searching for us. What if she wanders to the front lines and steps on a mine?

Will her heart break when she realizes we're gone?

I sit on the stoop, staring at the empty street while the others go inside. Just yesterday, Davor was walking down this street, waiting for me to come out and "accidentally" run into him. Now he must think I don't care about him at all.

My family is safe, and for that I am deeply grateful. But with no Maci and probably no Davor, my world feels empty.

If she were here right now, she'd sense my unhappiness and come to cuddle in my lap. Maci always knows how to cheer me up. Just her soft, warm, calm presence is enough. She's our good luck charm, the spirit that watches over us. Look how she saved Dino! What if our luck is gone with her?

I see someone coming down the street, a man, tall, with a confident walk. For a moment my spirits lift a bit. Is it Davor?

But no, when he gets closer I see that it is a stranger. I assume he's going to keep walking to some other house. Instead, he stops in front of our house, checks a piece of paper he had folded in his pocket, and calls out to me, "Is this the home of Mehmed Šabić?"

He's wearing a military uniform with the emblem of a winged stallion sewn on the side—the symbol of the Fifth Corps.

"Yes," I say, jumping up. "Wait here." This man scares me. I know he's on our side, fighting for our lives and freedom, but there is something hard and merciless about every soldier's face that makes me shiver. So I ignore the typical Bosnian politeness and don't invite him in.

"Tata, there's a man here to see you. A fighter. What does he want?"

"I don't know," Tata answers. He gives me a big reassuring smile, but I can see apprehension in his eyes. "I suppose I'll find out."

"I'll come with you," I say.

"No, no, you stay here and help your mama with dinner." One good thing about our lightning trip to the bee farm, we took home some honey, eggs, beans, and onions.

But I don't help. I peek out the window while Tata talks to the man. Tata's back is to me, but I know him well enough to read the tension in his shoulders. The stranger looks gruff. He gestures to Tata aggressively, points in the direction of the battle lines.

A few moments later Tata comes in alone. As the soldier turns to go I see a smirk on his face.

"What was it, Tata?" I ask him, while Mama and Dino gather around.

Tata wipes the worried wrinkles from his brow, then gathers himself up to his full, impressive height. He is no longer young, no longer strong, but he has an upright dignity that makes him seem imposing.

Tata salutes us sharply, with perfect military angles in his elbow and wrist. "I've been called to war!"

"What?" all of us say at once, with a chorus of, "That's nonsense, that's ridiculous, you can't!"

I wonder what would happen if Tata said no. Of course we need everyone to fight in any way they can—even I would pick up a gun or a stick or use my teeth to defend my family if it came to that. But I wouldn't be any good on the front lines, and neither will Tata. But the Fifth Corps is our army, the only thing we have to protect us. Tata's pride wouldn't let him say no. And if he did . . . what do they do to deserters or shirkers in wartime?

"Tata, have you ever even shot a gun?" Dino asks.

"Of course he has," I tell him. "He was in the military as a young man."

"Oh, they're not about to give me a gun," Tata says with a chuckle. "More like a pickax and shovel. They need ditches and fortifications near the front lines, to protect our soldiers. The young men need to save their strength for fighting, so it's time for the old fellows like me to lend a hand and dig."

Mama and I exchange a look behind his back. Tata is a very proud man who never likes to admit to weakness. He has aches and pains. Another man might be using a cane by now, but Tata never will. He has diabetes, which isn't being properly treated now. Sometimes when he gets a cut, it takes a long time for it to stop bleeding. And ever since the war I've sometimes seen him suddenly have to sit down. When he thinks I'm not looking he'll press a hand against his chest and hold his breath as if waiting for something to pass. But if I catch him he'll just laugh it off and claim his heart was merely overcome with love for his family. Or, if he's in a mischievous mood, blame trapped wind.

But I know that the war has been harder on him than any of us. He is the provider, and whenever he can't get us what we need he feels like he's let us down. The whole city might be starving, but when his family can't eat he feels like it is his fault.

He's done so many things to help us get by. Now Tata and Mama run a store—of sorts—out of the house. We call it a store, but actually it is three shelves made by Tetak Ale. The shelves stand mostly empty, holding only the few supplies we can get hold of, and spare. We have oil and salt, occasionally potatoes. And of course honey, our most reliable product. Maci stands by in the store for part of the day as if she's guarding our merchandise.

Earlier in the war we sold soap, deciding that we would give up some personal cleanliness ourselves and sell the harsh, chemical-smelling bars whenever we could get any. But soon real soap became too much of a luxury for anyone. Food was the only priority. Each household made its own version of soap out of ashes and fat—a gritty, slimy mess that hardly lathered and left you feeling only slightly cleaner than plain water.

Now, I can tell that Tata feels a strange mixture of pride and worry. He doesn't want to spend time away from his family, and he doesn't want to take valuable time away from his various schemes to bring in a pittance of money or food.

And yet, he wants to help his beloved city hold off against the foe, even if all he can do is dig a ditch. He wants to be useful to everyone.

But he knows in his heart that he's not physically up to such backbreaking labor.

"I don't want you to go, Tata," I say.

"It is necessary," he says. "Besides, how could I look at myself in the mirror if I didn't do everything possible to help Bihać, to help Bosnia?"

"You are already doing more important things than digging ditches," Mama snaps. She's angry because she knows she has no control over this.

"Don't worry, my love," Tata tells Mama. "It's just a few days a week. I can do it. After all, if a little mole, a lowly worm, can manage to dig all day, so can I!"

We all put on so many brave fronts in this war, hiding the worst from each other. We bury our fears deep so we don't add to the fears of our loved ones.

But always before I had someone to tell my deepest worries to. A small, soft creature with whiskers and a soothing purr, who would listen with patience and understanding, and somehow help me feel better without uttering a single word.

Now I'm all alone with my fears.

CHAPTER 18

And so the tall, gray-haired intellectual, the man who recites poetry, who is too gentle to kill a chicken, who loves humanity with a deep and abiding love . . . this man, my father, departs our home the next morning to dig trenches on the front lines.

"Let me go too," Dino begs him as he leaves. "You're not strong enough to dig all day."

I see Tata wince, and realize that for every parent there will always be a moment when their children see their weakness, when the son becomes stronger than the father. Dino is still a teen, but I realize this moment has come.

Tata isn't ready for it, and I see his face go ashen all of a sudden, his smile slack and his gaze distant with the knowledge that he's not the strongest one in his family, the protector anymore. It is only there for an instant, then he pats Dino on the head. "Nonsense. I'm strong as a horse. Well, maybe a donkey. But strong enough to dig."

I want to protect him from the war, from the front lines, but at the moment all I can protect him from is the consciousness of his own frailty and mortality.

"Of course he is, Dino. Don't be silly. Look at him beside you! An oak next to a skinny aspen. You'd pass out in ten minutes, little brother." I put on such a show of confidence that Tata cheers up even more. His steps as he leaves us are jaunty.

My own smile only holds up until he is out of sight.

"They can't really put him at the front lines, can they?"

Mama just shakes her head. "Who knows what will happen with the world like this." She sends Dino to do some schoolwork in the kitchen and takes me out back, in the dusty yard where, until recently, the last of the chickens scratched. (Chicken ended up in the pot a time or two since their arrival, and our chickens vanished by slow attrition, but we never saw any more slaughter, and I think my parents traded our live chickens for prepared chicken parts, so we didn't have to eat chickens we actually knew.)

"Tell me, Amra, does war bring out the best in people, or the worst?" Mama asks me.

I think for a moment. "Both," I say at last. "Violence is the worst. But I've seen the way people here in Bihać come together, the way they help each other. Of course there are some opportunists, people profiting on others' desperation and misery. But for the most part we have become more unified, I think."

"You're right, of course. Nothing is simple. But think about who is being helpful, unselfishly helpful. It isn't everyone. It isn't even most people. There are a few societies, a few organizers, a few active people—like your Tetka Fatma—who are driving all the food collections and spearheading medical aid and keeping the schools open. Yes, there are many good and noble people here in Bihać. I'm proud of my people. But for the most part, I think war brings out the worst in people. To some extent it has to. How generous can I be when my own children are hungry?"

Mama takes my hand, circling her fingers around my gaunt, fleshless wrist.

"More than that," she goes on, "the chaos and instability of war take away the foundations, take away the control, and leave a void for the worst of the worst to rise. Do you know who is running Bihać now? Really in charge?"

I shake my head.

"Criminal gangs. Like the one that robbed the house across the street. That friend of yours, the nice boy with the vicious older brother—his gang controls half the black market in the city. And he fights with rival gangs for more. Criminals killing each other—not for money or drugs, but for sausages and tins of condensed milk."

"But those are criminals, not the real leadership," I argue, wondering why we're talking about this now. "Every society has criminals, in war or peace."

"Sweet girl, even in chaos someone is always at the top, making the decisions. The natural leadership of Bihać is mostly gone. There is a void, and the worst of our society are rising to fill that void."

I think about this a moment. Even if I were put in charge, what would I know about fighting people, defending territory? But for someone whose job is selling drugs or stealing televisions, that is all second nature. Who has viciousness and aggression and firearms? The criminals, of course. It is understandable, if unfortunate, that they are leading the fighting. Maybe it will redeem them, now that they have something important to fight for instead of turf battles with other gangs.

Mama goes on. "I don't know how it is elsewhere in Bosnia, but in this city, the cream has not risen to the top. This place is like a soup of boiling bones, where the thing that rises is scum. Opportunists are in charge, the people who didn't have power before but have something else to drive them. Greed, usually. Or nationalism. And these people, these anti-intellectuals, hate anyone who tries to moderate their worst natures. People like your father."

I nod, starting to understand where this is heading.

"Your Tata was an important man, an influential one. But he never took advantage of his position. When others skimmed money, took bribes, opened bank accounts overseas, your father played straight—and people despised him for it."

"No," I protest. "People admire Tata."

"Some do, yes—other intellectuals like him. But many people think he was a fool not to take advantage of a corrupt system to feather his own nest. Remember our old apartment, before we built this house?"

I nod. Apartments are allotted to people on a waiting list, and bribery or connections can move a person up a list. The apartments are technically rented and owned by the state, but once a person lives there the requisite thirteen years they unofficially own it. They can't be made to give it up. Most people who move out of a place like that rent it out at a huge price or trade it for a beachfront apartment.

"He could have made a fortune, but it wasn't ethical. So instead he just handed over the keys to a hardworking man who had been stuck at the bottom of the list because he couldn't afford a bribe, a man with five children. No one could believe it. People laughed at him behind his back, called him naive. Now, in this harsh new world, there's nothing but contempt for kindness."

She reminds me that the honest man is a threat to the corrupt. Tata knew all about the other people who accepted bribes. He had no interest in turning them in, but while he had influence they probably thought he might at any moment. So even though they thought he was a fool, they feared him. Now that Tata is weak and poor, now that the normal structure of life and government is broken, those corrupt people remain. And so do their old grudges against Tata.

Then Mama tells me what I didn't know—that since the war started, Tata has been meeting with the new officials, urging civility, compassion, mercy.

"Well, what's wrong with that?" I ask.

"We can't meet hate with hate," Mama says. "That's what he tells them. 'What,' they scoff, 'should we welcome the Serbs into Bihać, shake their hands while they shoot us?' 'No,' your Tata tells them. 'But nationalism, worshiping your own side, hating a person just because of their group, their clan, their state, their religion, is what led to this. The cycle has to stop somehow. Defend the city, yes, but talk,' he tells them. 'Talk whenever you can. Find a civilized way out of this. Or we will be just like our killers.'"

I understand what Mama is saying, but at the same time I can see that it is bound to be unpopular with people whose families are getting bombed.

When I tell Mama this, she answers, "War brings suffering, but it brings profit too. There are some people who are making their fortunes in this war. People will give up their life savings, their wedding rings, their artwork, all for a meal, or a gun, or a bomb shelter, or a visa. The new wartime politicians don't want to lose their position when the war ends. Their power is based on aggression, hating the Serbs. So when your father talks about peace, about compromise, about negotiation, he is a direct threat to their fortunes."

Tata talks about hard things. Right things, but hard things. How can you tell someone whose children were killed by a bomb that the Serbs are human, that they are individuals who may hate the war as much as we do, or be ignorant of exactly what is happening, or even indifferent . . . but not uniformly evil. We like to see our enemies as fairy-tale villains, thoroughly wicked. But Tata sees nuances. He sees people, not causes or countries.

He urges our side not to commit war crimes out of blind hate. We must rise above that, he says, no matter how much they hurt us. Fight, yes—but don't become animals. The world will intervene one day soon, he is sure. When that day comes we must make sure both sides don't look alike in atrocities.

It's the right way of looking at the world, I know. But unpopular. Even to me, right now.

Someone with opinions like that—it is easy to brand them a traitor or a coward.

Traitors and cowards get sent to the front lines.

Traitors and cowards are expendable.

I stay outside while Mama goes back in. I'm burning with anger at a world that can hate my father for his innate goodness. He's gone for two nights, and all that time I imagine the terrible things that might be happening to him at the front.

In the evening of the third day I meet him in the road on his way home. He's limping and trying to hide it. His face is slick with sweat, his neat clothes dirty. There's a haunted look in his eyes.

But he's not shot. He's not blown up. And for that I thank heaven.

I take his hand, and he winces. Turning his palm upward, I see blisters, and the raw, bleeding places where other blisters popped.

"Oh, Tata!" I gasp. My tears start to fall. One hits the open wound, and his fingers curl.

"Just a sign that I haven't done enough honest work in my lifetime," he jokes.

"Honest work?" I bristle. "All of your work has been honest! Every action has been good and true, and now they send you to the front lines?"

"Hush, we all have to do our part," he says soothingly. "My soft hands have pushed pencils and held books, and now they hold a shovel and haul cinder blocks and sandbags. Hands are adaptable things. They can do calligraphy, and mend a bone, and break a bone." He mimes punching me, the gentlest blow. "Now my hands will figure out how to do this."

"But your poor hands!"

"Blisters turn to calluses, Amra. It is one of life's great lessons."

"They shouldn't! Why should the world have to get hard and tough? Aren't we smart enough to make a world where people can have soft hands that only hold pencils and books?"

"Of course we are. Then that world breaks, and we have to rebuild it. Over and over again."

"It isn't fair. It isn't right. You shouldn't be in pain."

He takes my chin in his hands, in the fingertips that have been spared blisters. "Pain is always with us, dear one. I'm told that the first breath a baby takes after it leaves the womb is agony. But we persist. Don't worry about me." He lets go of my chin and smiles. "Now, tell me what you are studying. Have you mastered linear algebra yet?"

I take his arm instead of his hand, and together we go inside.

CHAPTER 19

He makes light of it, but his days at the front lines are breaking him down. I see him crumble before my eyes. His upright posture bends. The work, which over time would make a young, well-fed man stronger, only breaks him down. He doesn't build muscles: he wastes away.

Two or three days a week he digs ditches for the war effort. The other days he works to feed his family. The supplies we can get are few and monotonous: beans, grains, onions. What I wouldn't give for some summer squash or a nice tomato! Even on the rare days when we get enough calories to make us feel full, I think we all have vitamin deficiencies. There's very little fresh food.

Almost all production has shut down in the city. We have no supplies, and no one can afford to buy anything we might make. The only thing that is still being produced in any quantity is beer. Some very strict Muslims never drink, but most of us are secular, and a lot of the men (and some of the women, but almost never my own parents) enjoy their locally brewed beer. Now they probably like it more than ever, as it is one of the few things to take their minds away from reality for a little while.

Luckily, Tata knows the owner of one of the surviving breweries, a man named Adem. When Tata was powerful, Adem was always kissing up to him. But Tata thought Adem was uncouth and immoral. He was polite to him, as he is to everyone. But Adem was always struggling to impress my father.

A while ago Tata went to visit him, to see if he could get a few casks of beer to sell around Bihać to the bars and cafés that remained open. I was busy studying, but Dino was free, and bored, and cajoled Tata into taking him on the interview.

"Oh, Amra, it was horrible!" Dino tells me later. "This gross man, unshaven, greasy looking, didn't even get up out of his chair when Tata entered. He had his feet up on his desk, the dirty soles facing Tata. He was chewing a toothpick like it might bite him back. And ugh, as soon as we walked in, he . . ." Dino blows a long raspberry and makes a face of disgust.

"He made Tata beg. This rat of a man who always groveled to Tata—he insulted him, called him a fool for not putting away more money, bribes, when he was in power. Then, like he was a prince, this sniveling man says he feels sorry for Tata and will give him some beer to sell. But only if he comes in person. He wants to see Tata humiliated! And then he sent us outside, made us wait, didn't offer coffee, or a chair, or anything, until one of his men got around to bringing out a couple of casks of second-rate beer. And Tata thanked him! All humble and grateful after this worm of a man insulted him. I wanted to punch him."

"But then he would never give Tata beer to sell again," I point out.

"I know," Dino says miserably. And I realize it's hard for him, too, to not be able to defend his family. In another time, he could have broken Adem's nose. In peace, Tata could have walked out. But both of those good, proud men have to endure insults for the sake of their families.

Days pass and Tata gets weaker. I get lonelier. Every morning I wake up expecting to hear the loving meow that Maci always greeted me with. I dream that she's with me. Then in that first magical moment of being half awake, I think my dream is true.

But every day the crushing reality hits me anew—Maci is gone. We abandoned her.

She won't survive. That's not me being pessimistic. That's just reality. There are soldiers who would shoot a cat for target practice. There are land mines in the forests and fields. She's just a soft, innocent, gentle cat, alone in the world.

And then, every morning, I cry for my little lost friend. And I cry for us, for my family, struggling against impossible odds in this besieged city.

Then I wipe my tears, slap on a smile, and greet my family. They have smiles too. Big smiles and red eyes. We all stay cheerful for each other, on the outside.

Inside, we are tears and sorrow. Inside, we have given up. Our shells keep going automatically.

———————

One day, Tata is late coming home. Often we don't know when he'll return—three, four days sometimes—but this afternoon he sent a friend with a message that he'd definitely be home for dinner tonight. Five o'clock. Six o'clock. Seven . . . eight. I pace up and down our street, wanting to go looking for him, but he could have been sent anywhere along the border of Bihać. I wouldn't know where to begin. I stand on the corner of our street, looking down the next street where Tata is likely to come.

He could be wounded. He could have had a heart attack. His chest pains were coming much more quickly now. And his feet have been hurting—and even more worrying, growing numb. Now, without treatment for his diabetes and with irregular meals, who knows how that condition is?

If something happened to him, would anyone even come and tell us?

Finally, as the moon is rising, I see someone at the end of the next street. My heart leaps. No, I realize when they come nearer. It is two someones, close together. A couple?

No, one of them is limping, shuffling, walking very slowly . . . being supported by the other. I recognize the shape of Tata's shoulders from far away and run to him.

"Tata, what's wrong?" I cry, slipping my arms around him in a move that is support disguised as a hug. I hardly pay attention to the man helping him.

"I'm fine, just a little tired. I took a bit of a stumble, though, and this nice young man happened to see and insisted on helping me home. I tried to refuse, but it turned out we were going to the same place."

Finally, I look at the other man . . . and find Davor. His face is handsome by moonlight, his strong jaw touched with a silver glow.

"I meant to visit sooner," Davor says, "but you'd be surprised how demanding horses and mules are. If they're not asking for hay, they're clamoring for oats." He gives me a barely suppressed grin.

"Very important work. You didn't tell me you had a veterinarian friend, Amra. Perhaps he can look at Muret's horse." Muret is an ancient man with an ancient horse, more bones than muscle and more skin than bones—both of them—who sometimes helps Tata with his sporadic beer deliveries.

"He's a friend of Azra's," I say quickly. I'm not sure how my sentimental father will react to a boy having an interest in his daughter. If indeed Davor has any interest. After all, I wasn't there when he came before. Maybe he thinks . . .

"And a friend of Amra's," Davor adds firmly. He shakes my hand in a very businesslike way—as far as anyone else can see. But I feel his secret tickle on my palm, and I shiver.

"We all need friends, especially now," Tata says seriously. "Come along, young man. We'll see if we have any refreshments to offer you."

"If you're sure it's okay?" Davor demurs politely, catching my eye. I nod.

"What's wrong, Tata?" I ask as we walk slowly home. "Something happened today, I can tell from your face."

Tata doesn't like to talk about his days at the front. Once he joked that he and the other "volunteers" are each given an old rifle while they dig, in case the Serbs make a sudden attack. "But only one bullet," he tells us. "Who is it for, a Serb or me? I don't even know if the gun works. I'm just as likely to shoot my own foot!"

Tonight, his face looks more upset than usual in the moonlight.

"There was a man. A young man. A doctor. How they could have sent him with a shovel to the worst of the war zone . . . an old man like me, fine, but him, with his knowledge? We don't have so many doctors here that we can spare one, even one who . . . But he was right in what he did!"

"Tata, slow down. Who was it?"

"I don't even know his name, but I heard others talking about him. He treated Serb prisoners that the Fifth Corps had captured, argued that they should be treated humanely, as prisoners of war. His commander said what no one knows, no one objects to. I object, the young doctor said. And the next day, today, he was at the front, even closer to the Serbs than I. In a crazy position, no cover at all. The Serbs shot him for fun. In the head. I heard them laughing, clear as if a neighbor was shouting across the street. 'Look at that Muslim, not even a helmet to hold his brains in.'"

His legs start to shake. "I don't think he can make it to your house," Davor says. "Here, there's a tree down in this field." We lead him just off the road into the overgrown lot, half straggling grass and summer flowers, half garbage dump, on undeveloped land that leads to the Una. It's a place that Maci liked to play, and with a sharp pang of memory I can almost hear her voice. She would hide in the wildflowers and call to me with her plaintive mew, then spring at my feet, pouncing with her velvet paws, her sharp claws tucked safely away . . .

Tata sits down on the fallen tree trunk, protesting all the while that he's fine. Davor checks his pulse. "Much easier than treating a cow or a dog," Davor jokes, but he shoots me a worried look. "Your pulse is a little fast. And a little . . . It could be stronger. Are you taking any medicine for your heart?"

"No, no, there's nothing wrong. I'm just tired."

"Well, let's sit here for a while until your pulse slows a bit. I wouldn't mind a rest myself." He leans back to look at the sky. "With no electricity, nothing to blind the eyes at night, look how bright the stars are!"

"There's always beauty, if you remember to look for it," Tata says.

"I agree," Davor says, but now he's not looking at the stars. He's looking at me.

A night bird calls, and a cricket fiddles a melody, answered by another one across the field, whether mate or rival I don't know. I wonder if the insects and birds have their own troubles, their own wars and loves and heartaches, never perceived by us humans.

Then I hear another sound.

It can't be.

No, I tell myself. There's no such thing as miracles.

Maybe it is a cat, that distant mewing sound. But it is some other cat.

It can't be Maci.

But I go toward that sound, deeper into the foliage toward the river, drawn as a mother is to a baby's cry.

And like a mother, I know in my heart that this faint meow isn't just any cat. It is my own dear little friend. My steps quicken . . . I hear the crunch of grass under velvet paws . . . and Maci leaps into my arms!

"Oh, Maci! Oh, my sweet kitty!" She rubs her head against my cheeks, a deep rumble in her chest. Maybe she can't speak with words, but her entire body tells me that she loves me, she missed me, she is happy beyond belief to be home.

"What is it, Amra?" Tata calls, starting up from the fallen tree.

"It's Maci!" I shout. "She's home!"

However exhausted Tata might be, he still hurries to my side, supported by Davor. He sinks to his knees, overcome, and when Maci jumps down to greet him he reaches out a finger to stroke her nose. She licks his fingertip and gives him one of her slow blinks. "I can't believe it," he says. "She made it, all this way?"

I explain to Davor what happened, and he's impressed, but says, "Cats and dogs have incredible homing instincts. They can sense magnetic fields, you see. I read a paper about it. And she's obviously a smart kitty. I'm not surprised she found her way home."

"I still think it's amazing," Tata tells him. "All of your science might see nothing out of the ordinary, but to me, it is a miracle."

I think so too.

I have Maci again. I have my family. And now, Davor. For just a moment I feel like the luckiest young woman in the world.

Tata rises again to finish the walk home, but his legs are still unsteady. Davor is examining Maci (who is back in my arms but lets him check her paws, her eyes, her teeth), and I'm watching the process anxiously, waiting to hear that she is in top shape despite her ordeal. So neither of us are helping Tata, and he stumbles a bit as soon as he rises. He sinks back to one knee, and immediately we're beside him. Both of his hands are in the dirt. He doesn't try to get up, and I think he might have twisted his knee or ankle.

"This dirt," he says, digging his fingers into the moist loam and pulling up a handful. "This is good dirt. Here, smell it!" He thrusts it under my nose. Tentatively, I sniff. It smells rich and alive, faintly sweet . . . but mostly just like dirt.

"Don't you see?" Tata says excitedly springing up unaided. "We live in a city and just see the concrete, but look, here in this empty lot and all along the riverbank there is good, arable land, a close water source. Why didn't I think of it before? We can grow our own vegetables! Your little Maci showed us the way!"

He holds out his hands, now more callused than blistered. "See, now all that practice digging dirt won't go to waste! Just as if it were planned. Isn't it a beautiful world?"

There's a spring in his step as he walks home. He hugs Mama and doesn't tell her about the young doctor who was shot. Instead he quickly introduces Davor, then immediately calls on Omer and Erza, our refugee friends who have taken up residence in one of the abandoned Serb houses in our neighborhood. They hurry over and start planning their war garden, while Davor and I sit on the front step, basking in the moonlight and each other's company. Maci sits curled on my lap. We don't have any food for her, but she drinks a lot of water, and Mama gives her a teaspoon of oil, which she laps up.

"Your mother didn't seem to disapprove of me," Davor says. "Maybe you worried for nothing?"

"As it turns out, Mama knows your family. Which isn't surprising—Mama knows everyone. So now you seem as much a friend of Tata's as mine. Your coming here looks like an accident."

"When really I've been thinking about this moment ever since I first saw you."

"What, drinking make-believe coffee on a concrete step?" I tease. No one can get real coffee anymore, but we Bosnians are so addicted that we soon came up with passable substitutes. Grains like barley are roasted and then ground into hard nodules that, when brewed, make a bitter black liquid that everyone pretends tastes like actual coffee. As probably the only Bosnian who doesn't like coffee, I have one less reason to suffer.

"Just being with you, spending time with you."

204

"And you wanted that from the first moment you saw me?"

"Well . . . I thought you were pretty, and I like tall women!" He chuckles. "But really it was when I saw you with Maci." He reaches over to stroke her as she lounges in my lap, and it's almost like he's touching me. "Your love for her, your concern for her. Your bravery when you went back to look for her instead of running home. In a flash I saw your true character."

He takes my hand, and lets our clasped fingers rest on my knee.

Maci stretches, arching her back and elongating her body, giving a huge yawn that shows her curling pink tongue. When she finishes, one of her paws comes to rest on top of our linked hands.

In the distance, somewhere along the front lines where Tata had been digging today, I hear mortar fire, gunshots. But here, in our little world, everything is peaceful, if only for a moment.

CHAPTER 20

Even when death rains down from the skies, there is life in the earth. Tata was right—the soil in the empty land and trash dump leading down to the river Una is rich and fertile. It has grown undisturbed, self-fertilized with the plants and bugs that grow and live and die.

"Look at this—a legume!" Omer says, pulling up a nondescript, leggy weed with lumpy, almost colorless flowers. "See the little nodules on the roots? These add nitrogen to the soil, as good as any fertilizer. Vegetables will grow splendidly here."

Omer has great book-knowledge of plants, and he treats our garden like a science project. When our families and a bunch of other neighbors gather to mark out our plots, he chooses a fine, level piece of land. "Not that one," he tells my father, who is standing indecisively on a rutted and sloped area. "The water will drain right off, and you'll spend all your time just trying to make the ground level."

But Tata lets everyone else pick their patch first, and he is left with that one. No matter, Tata says—he's taken a liking to this patch, because it has the prettiest wildflowers growing on it. "They're nicer than your legumes, anyway," he teases his friend. But it is also the part with the most trash on it.

The city has agreed to let us use the land. Whoever clears away the refuse is entitled to a plot. So we make a party of it on this fine summer day, neighbors and friends all gathered together, scooping up litter until the landscape is beautiful again.

"Why did it take a war for us to clean all this up?" I ask Mama as

I wipe the sweat from my brow. She hitches up her skirt—now a size too big—and surveys our plot. With the Una as a backdrop, it is picturesque. This could be a park. Instead it will be our means of preventing scurvy. Between lack of toothpaste (we brush our teeth with superfine sand from the banks of the Una) and lack of vitamin C, many of us have bleeding gums. We can't wait for our vegetables to be ready.

Exhausted from malnutrition and our other wartime work, we're really in no shape for farming, but within a few days our families have our plots cleared. Davor even comes to help. His parents have a lovely garden, and every time he comes to see me he brings me one of their roses. Unfortunately, he doesn't have very many edible plants—sprouts of rosemary and parsley, and seeds from an exotic purple cabbage.

"It looks like a purple alien spaceship, but it is edible," he tells me. Then he gives me a little jar with what looks like dark-red, shriveled berries inside.

"Rose hips," he explains. "The fruit of the rose, with seeds inside. We always let some grow, even though that means the bush gets fewer flowers."

"Er . . . thanks? But I don't think we can spare any space for roses." This is a survival garden.

"Not to plant—to eat. Actually, you grind them up and make tea from them. They're very high in vitamin C, so until your vegetables are ready, I don't want you getting sick."

I'm so touched by his thoughtfulness that I move to hug him. Then I catch myself. Mama and Tata are right there. I've only called him my friend so far. I'm sure they have their suspicions, but I don't want to confirm them quite yet.

Instead I give him a grateful smile. He doesn't want anything more than that. Oh, he makes me so happy! He's smart but silly, and to my surprise I like the silliness best. I don't know if I'd feel the same way if there wasn't a war going on, but right now his laughter and dancing eyes keep me cheerful. It's what I need.

I think Maci noticed the missed opportunity for a hug. She stands up on her hind legs, putting her paws on Davor's knees. He picks her up and cuddles her for a moment, then hands her to me. As I take her back I'm so close to Davor I can feel his warm breath on my lips. Our hands touch lingeringly. Somehow, it is even better than a hug, this secret touch.

When we have to separate, I tell him exactly what this tea means to me, the memory it evokes. "I'd gotten rose tea in teabags before, but I never really thought what was in it—rose petals, I thought. Before the war I loved to drink it with a slice of bread, with butter and rose hip jam. Tata would bring it to Dino and me as we sat lined up on the sofa watching a rare movie on TV."

Davor secretly squeezes my hand, and it touches me how he understands what my family means to me.

He visits whenever he can, but it isn't very often. His work with the Fifth Corps keeps him busy most of the time. I worry about him less than about Tata; he tells me he treats the horses and mules just behind the front lines. Sometimes I wonder if he's telling me the whole truth. With his veterinary experience, maybe they make him double as a medic on the front lines of battle. But as far as he ever tells me, he has a nice safe job with the animals.

He's not here the day we begin planting our garden. The rest of us have rolled up our sleeves and tried to figure out how to be farmers. For the most part, our knowledge is limited to ornamental gardens. Tata worked in wheat fields when he was a little boy in the orphanage—before he got wheat chaff in his eye, which led to an infection that almost blinded him.

Omer has a decades-old book on scientific gardening, which mostly deals with soil pH (which we have no way of testing) and things like bone meal (whose bones, I wonder). Beyond that, we all have bits of advice we've picked up along the way.

Omer claims to remember a snippet from an old Communist pamphlet on efficient farming. "Corn, beans, and squash. The tall cornstalks made a support for the bean vines to grow up on, and the spreading squash plants kept weeds away. And of course the beans are legumes that help the soil."

"If I hear the word 'legume' one more time . . ." Erza lets the threat trail off. She knows little about gardening, but she's an expert seamstress, and her penchant for neat, straight lines shows in the furrows she's prepared.

Omer plants trios of corn, beans, and squash in part of his garden. Then he adds cucumbers, summer squash, peppers, and tomatoes.

"Aren't tomatoes a little temperamental?" Mama asks him. "I remember one summer Fatma spent every morning picking caterpillars off her tomato plants, and dusting them for aphids, and washing off white mold . . . and in the end a bird still took a bite out of each tomato just before it was ripe."

"True," Tata says. "Tomatoes bring nothing but heartache."

"And heartburn if you make them into a spicy sauce!" Dino teases. He's been tasked with cutting up potatoes, separating each eye that will sprout into a new plant. "Are you sure these will grow?" he asks Tata. "I'd rather have fried potatoes now than wait for more potatoes that might never come."

"Have faith, Dino. The land will provide."

"But your land won't provide as much as mine," Omer teases. "My nice, flat land."

My family plants less temperamental varieties. In addition to the potatoes we have carrots, radishes, cucumbers, green beans, and several kinds of squash and melons. We don't start out with a plan, but add plants as we acquire them, willy-nilly.

At home we have old cartons and egg cups filled with dirt from our backyard (no doubt enriched with chicken droppings) where we nurture tiny seeds, no bigger than specks, until they are strong enough to plant outside.

With nothing new being imported or produced, we're already saving everything—old containers and bags, bits of plastic, twine, anything that might come in handy. Now Mama experiments with a new kind of recycling. Those rare times when we get a vegetable from a honey trade, Mama saves what she can of the growing part and tries to replant it. Already we've had success with onions and garlic, eating the bottom and putting the tops in water until they sprout new roots, though she tells me these will take a long time to mature. She also saves the butts of lettuce, replanting them after we eat most of the leaves. For a while they just look dead, but in a few weeks they are sending out new leaves. Celery re-sprouts too. She hopes that carrot tops might make nutritious new carrots, but they only grow new leaves. "That's okay," she says. "We'll just have carrot leaf salad." It actually doesn't taste half bad.

Davor visits whenever he can. "Your garden is flourishing," he says on his next visit. "I'd rather walk through a beautiful rose garden with you, but this is better than nothing." He shows me the rose he brought from his house, a delicate golden bud that he tucks behind my ear.

"It all looks a little . . . wild," I say, scrutinizing Tata's plot. Vines have taken over the garden, spreading broad leaves and curling tendrils so that I can't tell where one plant ends and another begins. All the foliage looks the same. Is that a squash or a potato? I might dig up the wrong thing.

"But what happened to Omer and Erza's garden?"

Their impeccably neat rows, measured out to precise angles, their seeds planted by scientific theory, have all withered. Their cucumbers have shriveled to the size of shrunken pickles hanging morosely on yellowed vines. Their tomato plants are little more than leafless stalks.

Omer's method made sense when he explained it, but something went wrong. The bean vines didn't use the cornstalks for support—they just oppressed the new corn sprout, weighing it down so it is smothered in the dirt. And the squashes are no better than the cucumbers, dry and wizened.

Just then Omer comes up, surveying his ravaged garden with dismay.

"I think you might have overlooked something," I suggest.

On his next visit, Davor confides that he did some research. "Omer's idea was sound, but he did miss a couple of crucial things. First, the three plants are supposed to be planted in a mound, not on flat earth. And then the corn is supposed to be planted first, so it has time to get strong before the beans weight it down."

"Poor Omer," I say. "A little knowledge is a dangerous thing."

I tell him what Davor discovered, and he replants, but it doesn't help. His crops all look like they're starving, right next to our abundant, leafy-green vegetable jungle.

"I don't understand," Omer mourns, looking at his wasteland. "How could this happen? I used science!"

"And I used heart," Tata tells him, patting him on the back. "Maybe you should love your plants, talk to them?"

Only later do we learn that there's a reason Omer's plot is so perfectly flat. Longer ago than anyone can remember, the military built a secret fuel pipeline that ran through the city and under the Una. The access to that pipeline is right under Omer's garden. Long ago it was sealed, covered in concrete and a layer of sand, then a layer of dirt. Overgrown and neglected, it was forgotten. So poor Omer's crops are grown in a scant few inches of soil, over sand that drains any irrigation away in a heartbeat. And if by chance some struggling plant manages to survive, its roots hit concrete!

Some gardens are so successful that thieves come to steal the produce. After a neighbor's plot is robbed twice, he put out a sign warning: "Caution! This Area Has Been Mined!"

Undeterred, the thief returns the next night, steals more, and leaves a sign of his own:

"All clear. De-mined."

Our garden is never hit. I think it simply looks too wild. No one can believe there might be delicious vegetables hiding under that jungle.

———

As the crops ripen, so does my relationship with Davor. Whenever I see Nura she wants to know all the juicy details . . . and always goes home disappointed. Not that there's anything I won't tell her. It's just that, to teenage ears hoping for a dramatic love story, there's not much to tell.

And yet, I'm happy. For me, it is the perfect love story.

We walk. We sit. We talk. We visit friends. He escorts me to school. Sometimes we go to the river.

I meet his family. I'm shy at first, but they make me feel welcome. Davor's mother is as stylish as Tetka Fatma, with a keen fashion sense and a knack with her foot-powered sewing machine. When we first meet she takes one long disapproving look at me, and I cringe inwardly, thinking she doesn't like me, that I'm not good enough for her son.

Then she says, "That blouse is all wrong for you. Ruffles? No. With your height and bone structure you need sleek lines, spare elegance like Coco Chanel."

"I didn't really pick this out," I tell her. "It came from a pile of donated humanitarian aid." Most of our clothes from before the war are falling apart, and we take what we can get.

"It's bad enough being bombed without having to wear some other country's unfashionable hand-me-downs. When I die, I want to die looking like a fashion model. Here, I have a free moment. Take that off and let me see what I can do with it."

She holds out her hand, and I give Davor a panicked look.

"Er, Mom?"

"Not here, you ninny. Come into my room, Amra, and I'll give you something to wear while you visit."

And so I spend the afternoon chatting with Davor in his mother's silky tunic top, while in the next room her sewing machine whirs and hums. In a little while she calls me in, and I try on the shirt. Its excesses have been pared down, and clever little darts make it hug me around the ribs, emphasizing my chest. The shoulders are slim-fitting and chic.

"Not really your color, though. If only I had some dye. What is your favorite color?"

"Red," I answer at once. A color of life and vitality and strength.

"Yes, that's exactly the color for you!" she says, beaming. I feel like I've passed some test. "Let me see what I can find, and I'll make you a new outfit." She hugs me, and whispers in my ear, "You make my son very happy, Amra. You and that big teddy-bear dog of his are the only things that bring a smile to his face lately. Keep making his eyes light up, and I'll make you a wartime wardrobe like no other!"

Oh, and that dog of his! After my early bad experience with dogs I have no liking for them. Maci is practically a person to me, but everything else with fur and teeth seems dangerous and uncivilized. Mrki is a huge and shaggy Šarplaninac, a kind of dog unique to Bosnia.

When we're introduced, I feel even more timid than when I met Davor's parents. Though he's reassured me over and over that Mrki is gentle and loving, when I finally see him up close I feel like I'm meeting a wild bear. His coat is varying shades of brown, and his muzzle is all black. He stares at me, then gives one deep bark, showing big ivory teeth. I hide behind Davor.

"No, he's just saying hello," Davor reassures me.

I peek from behind him. Sure enough, Mrki is wagging his tail. His bared teeth look like a happy smile.

And when I'm brave enough to pat him, my hand sinks four inches into his fur. There's a lot less of him than I originally thought. He's still a huge dog, but not quite bear size.

"See, he's just a lot of fluff," Davor says, ruffling Mrki's fur.

I'm really won over when I see Mrki looking at him the same way Maci looks at me, with love and patience and deep sympathy.

Soon I realize that despite his fierce appearance, Mrki really is almost as much of a pussycat as Maci. There are a few tense moments when they meet, but after a while they develop an uneasy truce. I think Mrki is more intimidated by Maci than she is by him. As a herding dog, Mrki might be capable of fighting off wolves, but he'd really rather hang out with the sheep.

Even his "guarding" instincts are a little off. One day when we visit some friends, Davor leaves his military boots outside on the stoop, with Mrki snoozing beside them. When we come out an hour later the boots are gone, and Mrki looks happy. A robber had obviously given him his favorite thing—a big belly rub—and made off with the shoes.

But like Maci, Mrki will protect the people (and now cats) he loves. With a big guardian, Maci grows braver about walking past other dogs and will often accompany us on the days Davor walks me to school. One day, we meet a man walking a young German shepherd on a heavy chain. The dog is undisciplined, pulling, and when he sees Maci he lunges for her. His owner—an arrogant man in his twenties— laughs and lets his dog pull him closer.

Suddenly Mrki becomes everything I'm afraid of in dogs—a snarling, slobbering attack dog. With his little friend threatened he knocks the German shepherd to the ground and grabs him by the throat. He gives the other dog one good shake and then holds him there, choking the life out of him, while the owner dances around in a panic screaming that he just got this tough new guard dog and now Mrki is killing him.

With one word from Davor, Mrki lets the other dog go. He's not hurt—I think Mrki just wanted to teach him a lesson—but he slinks off with his tail between his legs. I don't think he'll bother a cat ever again. And I don't think he'll be much of a guard dog!

Davor tells me all sorts of stories about his family, especially his late grandmother who lived next door. Davor's mother is a Croat, his father Muslim, but he was largely raised by his very traditional Muslim grandmother. One day coming back from school he arrived to what looked like white tents in the front of the house, in their shared yard.

"Is there a wedding?" he asked her. Then he realized it wasn't tents, but white bedsheets spread all around the front of the property. When he pushed them aside enough to knock at the door he found his grandmother flustered.

"Did a neighbor complain? I was so sure no one could see me!"

"What's this all about?" Davor asked.

"I wanted to sunbathe, and I needed to make sure no one could spy on me!" She was wearing her traditional outfit of highly decorated full trousers and a tunic. Slyly, she pulled up her pants leg to show Davor her daring tan line—right at midcalf. "You see, I'm moving with the times," she told him.

For a woman who was raised to cover herself up entirely, it must have felt like a big step to expose a small patch of skin. And to think, my own Muslim family prances around braless in thin T-shirts or in skimpy bikinis at the beach!

But that is the beautiful thing about Bosnian Muslims. We accept that we all express our heritage in different ways.

The outsiders, the Serbs, don't see any nuance. To them we are all just Muslim terrorists who need to be killed to make room for the new, ethnically pure Serb homeland.

As we walk home, I wonder, how could anyone think of Davor's sweet, quaint grandmother and start planning genocide?

1993–1994
WINTER

CHAPTER 21

We survive long enough to freeze during one more winter. But this time, we go into it a little healthier from an abundance of summer vegetables and fall cabbages. Now we're in for leaner times, but we've pickled and preserved whatever we can, and I think we might get through the winter without any serious vitamin deficiencies.

Still, vitamins aside, our calorie count is dangerously low. Mama has to add a safety pin to her skirt waistband, and even then it threatens to slip down her narrowing hips.

———

It is strange, though, how much happiness there is in my life. I wonder if people are programmed to look for the best in any situation. We are starving, isolated, without doctors or an infrastructure, at risk of being killed at any moment. Our lives should be no better than a rat or a cockroach, hunted vermin. And yet despite my fear and suffering, my life seems oddly rich.

I have friends. I have love. I have a small furry confidante.

And despite the many obstacles, I have my education.

School is in session again, and we tramp through the snow in our heavy winter coats. We look like fools and harlequins—with hand-me-downs, patched jackets, and mismatched clothes from donations, we are a motley bunch. A friend with too-short sleeves on his coat wears socks on his forearms, with a thumbhole cut to make them double as mittens. Two sisters walk close together with a blanket draped over both of their shoulders.

Many, like me, have shoes with holes in them. Before the war Tetka Fatma used to buy these nubby, hand-woven traditional woolen socks that I absolutely hated. I liked thin, factory-made socks, not ones that look like they were knitted by someone's great-grandmother! Now I'm grateful for them, putting on two layers of these ugly bulky socks to keep my feet almost warm. Still, except when I'm home by the wood stove in our kitchen I can rarely feel my toes. Davor has been hunting for shoes my size, but most of them have to go to the fighting men. My cousin's giant husband, Raja, with his huge size 16 feet is impossible to fit. He has to saw the whole toe off any boot just to get his feet in. Before the war, his shoes were custom made. But the cobbler was a Serb, and he's gone.

"Why don't you wear your volleyball shoes?" Davor asks me.

I bite my lip. "They're too nice," I say at last. "I know that sounds vain of me, and silly, but they're so perfect and clean, white and blue like an alpine lake in the snow, and I just can't stand the thought of them getting all wet and muddy. Someday, when this war is over, I want to have this beautiful pair of shoes waiting for me."

"No, I understand. I have this really nice pair of gloves, thin and stylish, made of the softest leather. The kind of gloves you'd wear out to the theater in the winter. When I work with the horses I wear this old pair with holes in them, thick wool with leather pads, all oiled to keep out the weather. They're so thick I can hardly bend my fingers in them, and I think, You fool, why not just wear your nice gloves? But I feel the same way—when this war is over, I want to take you out on a snowy evening, and I want to wear those fancy, beautiful gloves."

He presses my hand goodbye, and I go into school.

When the war is over . . .

We all say it like that, with a kind of forced certainty. But I for one am not certain. What if it is like the Palestinian and Israeli conflict? I suppose it has to be over someday. Even the Hundred Years War we learned about in history ended eventually.

But I wonder if I'll be here when the war is over.

Maybe it will only be over when all of the Bosnian Muslims are gone.

I shake my head, clearing away the morbid thoughts, and sit next to Nura in our English class. Soon after we returned to school, the English teacher, Lijana, came to our Russian class and asked if anyone would like to switch to English. All her students were gone. It was the first time I realized that only Serb kids were being steered to the more globally significant English. Muslim students had to take Russian. Only the Serbs were being prepared for the world stage, while the Muslims were stifled. It took a war to give us this vital access.

Now, I get a little thrill every time I sit down to study more English. I feel like it is a real victory against Teacher Sava and the entire system that tended to keep Muslims down. English is the most important global language right now. When this war is over . . .

There I go again. But I almost believe it. Even as I sit shivering in this building with its bombed-out windows (it hasn't been hit, but bombs have come close enough to rattle us) I'm thinking about the future.

Thinking about the past—about the things I've lost, the friends I've lost—is just too painful.

Teacher Lijana only has an hour or two with us today, and most of it is spent helping us figure out pronunciation. I can't seem to get my "v" and "w" sounds straight. There's no "w" sound in Bosnian.

Then she asks us what English words we might have heard or read before. When no one raises their hand, mine shoots up and I say, "Even when movies are dubbed, they always leave the English on the titles at the end. So every movie says T-H-E End."

"And what does that mean?" Lijana asks me.

"End means the movie is over. But I don't know what acronym T-H-E stands for."

I can tell she's trying her best not to smile. "They aren't separate letters. They don't stand for anything. Rather, they are a word, pronounced 'the' and used as a definite article, and sometimes as an adverb." She then reads a paragraph, and I'm astonished to realize the word I thought was so special—some kind of Hollywood jargon—is one of the most common words in English.

We hardly have any supplies. There are a couple of English textbooks and a dictionary or two that Teacher Lijana lets some of us borrow. For the most part, we scrounge in our homes and neighborhoods for any books that might be useful. Tata has an old English dictionary from when he was young. He used it in the 1960s to help him pick up girls on the beach in Croatia. A neighbor gives me a paperback book in English. She never learned more than a few words herself, but the cover shows a bosomy, windswept woman and a muscular, bare-chested man, and she admits she kept it mostly for that. I read the story word by word, looking up things like "heaving" and "quivering" and "turgid." I don't think it is very well-written, but it is definitely expanding my vocabulary.

In a later class, our teacher is showing us how both simple and fancy words can be used to say the same things. I think I hear a word I recognize from the trashy book. "I sat at my table to masticate," she says, and I just about sink under my seat! With my face fiery red, I think the world must really be coming to an end if this is what we're going to talk about in school.

Only when she writes it on the board do I realize it is the fancy word for chewing and not the word I thought it was!

We take as many notes as we can in class. Unfortunately there are no more real notebooks or loose-leaf paper. Early in the war we'd bring in whatever spare paper we could find at home: brown paper that used to be used to wrap packages or eggs from the market. By the first winter, though, even that paper is gone, used to kindle fires or cover smashed windowpanes.

Now all we have are tiny, anemic notebooks donated by UNICEF. I fill them up with scrunched writing every day that school is in session. Once I get home I reread it over and over until it is memorized, then erase each page. The next time school meets I fill it up again. Every day I recite as many facts as I can remember in each subject, hoping to keep my knowledge sharp. I write and erase countless words from my English dictionary.

Other students have different methods. Mirza forgets his notebook half the time and mutters to himself throughout the class, trying to force the important information to stay in his brain. Clever Dani, one of the smartest students, who always competed with me for the highest math and physics grades, made the mistake of writing in his notebook in pen, thinking he'd eventually get another one. Dismayed, he had to crisscross every empty space with new notes, until each page looks like a cipher in complex, mysterious code that only he can read, with sentences going in every direction. When there was absolutely no space left he started to write on the blank front pages of novels. Eventually, he started writing on his own arms.

"That's the best method," he jokes with us. "I wish I'd thought of it years ago. I stare at my notes on my own body, and by the time they wear off I'll never forget it. How can someone forget a tattoo?"

Dani has always been one of my favorite classmates, partly because of our friendly competitiveness. Now, everyone in our grade is very protective of him, extra friendly, because he is the only non-Muslim who stayed. His father is a Serb, his mother a Croat who is a friend of Tata's, a woman who was high in the Communist party. Now we applaud his loyalty to our country, and we want to make sure no one treats him badly because of his ethnicity. His presence also gives us hope that maybe not every Serb hates us.

After school lets out, none of us are ready to go home. It is a frigid day, and there's really nothing to do. None of the nearby cafés are open, and none of us have any money for food anyway. I'd like to go to Nura's house, but my parents count the minutes after school lets out, waiting for Dino and me to arrive safely home.

So we all mill around on the grounds just outside the UN headquarters next door, talking, reluctant to go home and lose this shred of normalcy. For all of us, a typical day is staying home, behind shuttered windows, in an ice-cold house, being bored and hungry. And that's a good day. On a bad day, we're starving. On a bad day, we're terrified.

On a good day, some friend of a friend dies.

On a bad day, a relative or close friend dies.

So these moments are precious, and we cling to them. With frozen toes and wind-chapped lips we linger, cracking jokes, trading stories— but only the cheerful ones, when there are any. More often it is the darkly comic or ironic stories.

The UN building next door is surrounded by rolled barbed wire, making it clear that though international protocol makes it necessary that they tolerate our presence, we are by no means welcome. Yet there are people just on the other side, UN officials, going about their business as if there weren't a war going on.

Well, there isn't, not for them. Beyond that barbed wire is another world. That piece of land isn't Bosnia.

I look at them, so plump and sleek and warmly dressed. Several important-looking men are standing near us, talking to each other but pointedly ignoring us. Beyond them are armed peacekeepers—though the only peace they are actually protecting is that which exists inside that compound.

They even have a shopping camp behind the barbed wire, where they can get all the things I used to take for granted—soap and shampoo and toilet paper. I remember how Tata told me that when he went to the orphanage he traded his only pair of shoes for a tube of toothpaste. Now I couldn't get toothpaste to save my life. But there behind the wire is everything the rest of Europe takes for granted.

Looking at them makes me so angry. They should be doing so much more.

While I'm talking to Nura and Mirza, Dani comes over to join us. But he slips on some ice hidden beneath the snow. As he goes down his arms windmill so ridiculously that we can't help but laugh. He looks up with his mouth open in surprise, and I'm immediately sorry.

But before I can ask if he's hurt he cracks a grin, grabs a handful of snow, and hurls it at Mirza's face.

Mirza sputters, then grabs a handful of his own . . . but Dani dodges, and the snowball smacks me full in the face. For a moment I stand there stunned, frost on my lashes. Then with a whoop I join in the snowball fight too. The next thing we know almost all my class is hurling these fun, innocent missiles at each other, laughing, collapsing in the snow, shrieking in a rare moment of glee.

Mirza and Dani have singled each other out, hurling the silliest insults at each other along with snowballs. "Your feet smell like pickled cabbage!" Mirza shouts at him.

Dani ducks behind me as a snowball hurtles past. I squeeze my eyes shut and squeal.

"What does that even mean?" Dani asks with a laugh. "Your breath smells like onions!"

"I wish my breath smelled like onions!" Mirza shouts back. "I wish I had a huge onion right now. I'd eat it like an apple!" He bites into the snowball he was about to throw, chewing the ice with exaggerated gusto.

Since he's distracted, Dani takes this chance to throw a big, tightly packed snowball as hard as he can right at Mirza.

But it goes wide, arcing over the UN's barbed wire like a perfect baseball pitch . . .

And smacks one of the uniformed men right in the butt, perfectly centered. Unfortunately, it is the one with the most medals and ribbons on his chest and sleeves. I think he's a general.

He whirls around, shouting, "Hey!" and some of the guards nearby draw their weapons but don't know where to point them. All they see are a bunch of stunned high school kids in the snow. Our smiles are still frozen on our faces, but none of us can move. We're horrified at what happened, at the drawn guns.

"You! And you! Stay right there!" one of the UN officers snaps, pointing at us.

But we can't tell who he's pointing at, and none of us want to find out, so we scatter like roaches in the bright light, everyone running home.

Dani is running the same way as I am. Only when we're out of sight of the UN building do I stop, leaning against the wall of a building.

"Are you okay?" Dani asks. "Are you crying?"

But the funny noise coming from me is laughter. Panting, near-hysterical laughter. "Did you see the look on his face? Oh, Dani, that's the best thing I've seen in months! Those useless UN officers all deserve a cold, wet butt!"

I think it is over, a minor incident, but it turns into a scandal. When we go into the classroom the next morning—the last expected day of school for a few months, until spring thaw—the UN general Dani hit is there, glowering at us, along with the head of the school and a full UN entourage and security detail.

"I will have answers!" the school head shouts at us. I can see spittle flying from his mouth. "This is an embarrassment, a disgrace. These men, these honorable men, are saving our country, protecting us . . ."

In the back of the room, someone snorts derisively. The school head's eyes dart through the crowd, but he can't find the culprit.

"Yesterday after school there was a vicious attack on the UN general. Some person or persons launched a rock-filled snowball that could have caused serious injury."

I don't know what comes over me. "It didn't have a rock in it!" I say. "It was just a snowball, just fluffy snow!"

"Was it you who threw it, then?" he asks. "I must say, Amra, I'm surprised at you."

"No, I didn't throw it, but . . ."

"But you know who did?"

"N-no. Whoever did it, it was an accident."

He narrows his eyes at me, while behind him the UN officers stand in their uniforms with their square shoulders and expressionless faces. Aren't they ashamed to be interrogating teenagers? Don't they have better things to do? Like, say, negotiating peace?

"Tell me who did it!" the head demands.

It takes all my effort not to let my gaze flick to Dani, who's standing right next to me.

"If you tell, or if the perpetrator confesses, only he or she will be punished. If not, the entire class's discipline grade will be changed from 'exemplary' to 'warning.' After that, as you know, one more infraction means you'll be expelled from school for good. There will be no second chances."

How utterly stupid, I want to rage at him. Here we are braving bullets and bombs to get an education, carrying our books while our starving bodies can barely move, freezing until we have chilblains on

227

our fingers . . . and you want to take away our only chance for a good future over an errant snowball?

We all look at each other. We all know who did it, and even in these abnormal times we all fear punishment.

But as a class we all reach the same unspoken agreement. War has made us loyal to our friends, strong and brave and enduring. What's more, Dani stuck with us when he and his family could have left. We owe him our protection. We will not tell.

The head rants and raves, pacing up and down, but we hold firm. Finally in a fury he slashes our discipline grade and stalks off, the UN staff trailing behind. We breathe a collective sigh of relief when they're gone.

"Thanks," Dani murmurs when it is just us students.

I pat him on the back. "All we have is each other."

CHAPTER 22

It is November 11, just three days before my birthday. Tata, Mama, and I are sitting in the kitchen at the back of the house—a strange kitchen that now has a sofa instead of a refrigerator or stove. The electricity doesn't work, so the appliances have been relegated to another room. This is now our living room, and sometimes our bedroom. It is the only space in the house that ever gets close to warm. We feel snug here, almost safe. The front of the house faces the distant Grabež hill, where the Serbs have mounted their huge launchers and mountain guns. We are like ostriches with our heads in the sand—we feel like if we have those front windows closed and boarded, if we can't see the missiles coming from Grabež, they can't see us. We feel more protected.

Dino is away with Ale and Fatma at the bee farm, helping them out, but mostly getting a bit of a break from the bombing. He should be home this evening.

My parents are drinking their horrible fake coffee. Maci is pawing at my leg, trying to get me to go outside with her, I think, but I'm more comfortable inside. Tata is teasing me about Davor. He knows that Davor is one of the few bright spots in my life, so he likes to bring him up just to see me smile. Now he's talking about love, and surprises for the future. I wonder if he and Davor are dreaming up something for my birthday. I've hardly even thought about it.

We're sitting on a honey-colored velour couch from the 1970s, part of the original furniture from around the time when my parents were newly married. It doesn't quite go with the cabinets, which are bright and clean white and red, but the colors make me happy even if they clash.

The window here isn't boarded up, though we have a piece of wood ready to cover it at a moment's notice. Since we spend most of our time here, we decided to sacrifice a little safety for our sanity. It's too hard to never have natural light, to never see the sky. It is evening now, and when I look out I see an artistic sky, beautiful vivid blotches of red and purple, a bold resistance against the ugliness of war.

"Have some coffee, Amra," Tata says, holding out a cup.

"You know I don't like it."

"Oh, you don't have to drink it. I just want to read your fortune." He pours a scant amount in. The brew is almost gone, so I get mostly the dregs full of grounds—which is actually all you need for fortune-telling. "Go ahead, swirl it around and let me see."

"Tata, you don't know how to tell fortunes!"

"Of course I do. For you, anyway. I can see your future clear as day." I swirl it and tip it into the saucer. He peers into the dregs. "Let's see, I see an excellent job, one that makes you very happy. A job that helps people, lifts them up."

"That's a good start," I say with a laugh. "Though I bet that's more your wishful thinking than the spirits telling you what my future holds."

"Besides," Mama says, "anyone can see that Amra will get a good job. That's not fortune-telling. What else do you see?"

"Hmm . . . love. True love. Lots of it!"

"With who?" I ask, thinking of Davor.

"Oh, everyone. All of your family. A husband. A child. No, children, I think." He squints into the grounds. "A little girl, and . . . another little girl!"

"The coffee tells you all of that?" I ask, hushing Maci, who is

230

meowing insistently at my feet. "Later," I whisper to her. Usually I sit outside with her for a while at this time of day. She walks to the door, then gives me a long look before going outside.

"The coffee is very wise," Tata says with a nod.

"Not bad," Mama admits. "What about me?"

Tata takes her dregs and examines them. "I see a future of peace and tranquility, of calm and quiet. A very quiet life. After decades of listening to chattering children, that sounds like a good future, doesn't it?"

Mama smiles. "I do like peace and quiet. You're a decent fortune-teller, but not as good as Aunt Nure."

That memory is enough to warm me on this chilly day. My mother's aunt Nure was a conservative, covered old lady like my grandmother. She wore white flowery traditional outfits, and we never saw her hair unless she was fixing her head covering. Though old, she loved talking with the younger generations, and my friends and I would gather to listen to her wisdom. She was the favorite grandmother, whether she was someone's actual grandmother or not.

We had big family gatherings every year, with much of the family having houses along the river, all lined up. My close friend and cousin Žana stayed with us, as well as Belma, a blue-eyed blond cousin from Sarajevo, and my friend Samira, whom we adopted each summer when her parents left for the summer. We'd get crushes on boys at the river, and then, over gooey chocolate cake, my mom's aunt Nure would read beans to tell our fortunes. We'd let exactly forty-two beans fall, and she could tell our futures based on how they landed. She always gave us the nicest fortunes, though sprinkled with practical advice. Then we'd run back to the river to see the boys again and check if her fortunes for us came true.

When we didn't have beans handy she'd read coffee grounds. She joked that it was a good thing her husband was no longer alive, because in traditional Islam, telling fortunes is considered a sin. But I think she mostly did it to make us happy.

We talk about those delightful summers, and during the reminiscence, I remember a photo we took with all of my friends and Nure in the middle. I haven't seen that picture in years, and I ask Mama about it.

"It should be in the box in our bedroom," she says. "Wait here, let me see if I can find it."

We very rarely go into the second story or the attic anymore. Sometimes I go up to have a moment alone in my bedroom, or like now, we run up to retrieve something. Now Mama starts up the stairs to the master bedroom. Her knee has been bothering her lately, aching more in the cold, and she takes her time, holding on to the banister. I can hear her slow ascending footsteps.

Just at that moment, something slams into me. I'm vaguely aware of all the windows shattering, the doors blowing inward, a sound like a mountain crumbling, like the earth shattering. It happens all in the space of a second, and I'm thrown to my belly on the floor. Instinctively I curl into a fetal position, hugging myself. There's a loud sound in my ears, an ongoing, single-note roar.

I can barely open my eyes. What I can see seems to be swinging, swaying. Was there an earthquake? I hardly know where I am. I don't remember the war. My brain is trying to make sense of this. The scene keeps going out of focus, fading to black, then reappearing in a flash, like a video put on pause, then fast-forwarded.

Then I feel warm wetness on my back. Oh, that feels nice in the cold weather, I think. Like a summer rain. I almost relax into the feeling, let my eyes close . . .

Then just before they close I see Tata on his hands and knees, crawling toward the stairs. His mouth is open, and I can see his lips move.

He's calling Mama's name, I think. But I can't hear anything, only that maddening one-note droning like a swarm of bees in my brain.

I'm dead. That's why I can't hear my father's voice. That's why the images are jumping around. I'm a spirit, rising above my body, leaving earthly sensations behind.

I see Mama coming carefully down the stairs. The first thing I think is that her hair is a mess. She'll hate that. Will she have to go to the afterlife with messy hair? Tears slide down her face, cutting lines in the dust that coats her cheeks.

Tata is calling for her, but she doesn't respond.

"Am I dead, Mama?" I ask. She doesn't answer this either. I'm not sure if I'm even speaking. "Are we all dead?"

Then the pain comes, and I realize if I'm dead, I'm in hell. My head is throbbing, but worse than that are the lacerations in my back. I struggle to stand, and see pieces of glass sliding off my clothes. Blood drips down my torn and tattered shirt. There's an acrid smell of burning—not wholesome wood smoke but something more sinister.

We find each other, Mama, Tata, and me. We cling to each other like drowning people. Over and over I ask Mama if we're alive. I honestly don't know. I can't tell if the warmth on my cheeks is from her tears or my blood.

I only know I'm alive when I hear Maci calling at the only door that hasn't been destroyed, the back door. Her sweet, plaintive voice is the first sound I've heard since the explosion. I find her on her hind legs begging to come in, the way she did on her first night here. I let her in, and she rubs against me, licking my ankles, my fingers. I scoop her up and hug her to my cheek. Her soft warmth is the only thing that convinces me I'm truly alive.

It was a direct hit into my parents' bedroom, two missiles, one right after the other. Their terrace was struck, and now only one structural support column keeps that side of the house from collapsing. Half of the second story and the attic is gone, and a section of the ground floor is left wide-open with no windows or doors. Everything my parents had sacrificed and saved for is gone in an instant.

I give thanks for Mama's sore knee. If she'd been any faster she would have been blown up. But instead she was in the hallway just about to open the door. All our pictures were burned in that room. When I look later I find that some were blown into the opposite walls, melted and glued by the intensity of the explosion. There are shards of alien metal in the walls and floor. Pieces of bomb. I touch one, and it is still hot enough to burn. The only reason our house isn't on fire is that it's constructed with cement and brick, relatively fireproof.

Half of our house is open to the elements, and it is only November. We have a long, cold winter ahead of us. A long war.

Neighbors come, offering to help but more out of curiosity. There's really nothing they can do. One of Mama's cousins, Galib, comes over and inspects the shells. One exploded as it was meant to. The other is intact. If it hadn't been for that faulty bomb, we would have all been killed. Galib takes the intact one away, saying he'll use it as a vase or umbrella holder.

An hour or two later, still in a daze, I hear screaming outside. It's Dino, Ale, and Fatma in their white Yugo, their last luxury purchase before the war. Someone told them our house was chopped in half. My brother is trembling uncontrollably. I come out with scratches, holes, and blood on my back. I must look like the undead, a walking casualty.

"I can't take it anymore!" Dino says, weeping. "Every day I think I've lost my family. I'm not going to survive this war. The Serbs are killing me. I'm dying more every day." Neither my hugs, nor our parents', nor the gentle love of Maci can calm him down.

I don't feel my wounds anymore. All I feel is his pain. He seems so tender and fragile. I see the teen, almost a young man, tall and strong, but I remember the little boy always calling *Amra, wait for me!* Dino has always had an incredible soul. He was a boy who could never hurt anyone, but also who could not bear to see hurt. So I pretend I'm not hurt.

Lightly, I say, "See, we're all fine. And now our house has more ventilation. So no more black mold in the summer, right? We'll get a nice breeze."

Dino and I had a pact to protect our parents from their worst fears for us. We never talk about what we see on the way to school—the bodies we pass, the bloodstains on the streets. We don't talk about the stories our friends tell us, of women captured by the Serbs, raped and tortured, forcibly impregnated.

Now I know I have to protect Dino too. Whatever happens, I'll shield him as much as possible. I'll laugh off tragedy, find the sunny side of everything. I'll tell him stories of happiness and wonder and blot out the ugly blight of the war.

We are all so vulnerable. What is a human but a soft and tender bit of flesh and a few thoughts, so easily wounded by both bullets and ideas. Tata is old beyond his years, aged by tragedy and stress and his grueling work at the front. Dino, so kind and vital, is repeatedly shell-shocked by reminders of the cruelty of life.

And Mama . . .

My hearing returns quickly, with only a ringing lasting more than a few hours. But Mama's hearing is damaged permanently. She's almost completely deaf. She can hear a little bit if I shout directly into her ear, but for all practical purposes those missiles stole her hearing forever.

It isn't long before I miss my conversations with Mama. So wise, so patient, she was my guidepost, as much my teacher as she was to any of her students. And now even conveying the smallest piece of information is an effort. She's so used to being a strong and competent person that this new weakness frustrates her. Sometimes when I have to repeat myself three or four times, or speak with my lips practically on her ear, she just gives up. Other times she pretends she knows what I'm saying, smiling and nodding to save me from the truth. Even though I can hear her fine, she talks much less herself, annoyed that she can't get any answer. I even lose my temper once or twice after having to repeat the same thing a dozen times.

All of us have lost our spark now. The natural vitality that filled us before the war has dwindled. Maci is the only one untouched by all of this. Her spark remains forever in her bonfire eyes. And whenever it seems like we have too much to bear she will climb into our laps, soothe us with her purr, and keep the internal fires of our own souls warm enough to survive this terrible winter.

CHAPTER 23

There is nothing mediocre in a war, nothing banal. It is all extremes. Either we are starving or every small bite of food is as delicious as a king's banquet. An oversalted, expired lump of feta cheese is the best thing I ever tasted. Our days are endlessly boring . . . until they are much more exciting than we want them to be.

And emotionally, war is either desolation and heartbreak . . . or ecstatic joy.

Davor takes me to the Hatinac coffee shop for a treat. It has been snowing all day, and now the snow lies in tall drifts against the sides of the road. We have no machinery to move the snow, so each resident shovels the street in front of their own house. No cars are coming through now, so only a pedestrian-wide area is cleared. I feel like we're walking through a maze with high sides. The snow muffles sound, covers the worst scars of the war under a virginal blanket. We could be alone in a beautiful alien world, wandering and happy.

Walking into the coffee shop feels almost like old times. They have a generator powering a little stereo, which plays American music from before the war. I wonder what songs have come out since then? I've missed years of global pop culture.

Two small, naked light bulbs burn in the middle of the café, shedding a weak, brownish light that barely penetrates the farthest corners of the room. It is a perfect environment for teens, who like shadowed nooks to hide whatever they are getting up to.

We nod to a few friends but don't join them. We want to be only with each other today. But one person we know comes up to us. Nermin pushes his dark, shiny hair back from his face and leans against our table. "What are you doing now that your school is shut down?" I ask him. He had been studying medicine before the war.

"I'm working as a nurse in a psych ward," he says.

"That must get depressing," Davor says sympathetically.

"We're all nutcases here in Bosnia now. All suffering from post-traumatic stress."

"Post?" I ask. "Is there a diagnosis for current-traumatic stress?"

"Honestly, we could medicate the whole country. Everyone is grieving such terrible losses." He looks pretty cheerful, though. He has a sad history. Before the war he loved a Serb girl, but one day while taking her on a picnic he was hit by a car and paralyzed for almost a year. She didn't stand by him, didn't help him through his recovery. Instead she cheated on him with an arrogant man who just seduced her to prove that he could, and then discarded her. Nermin swore he'd never love another woman. And as far as I know, he hasn't. But it didn't make him bitter. Instead, he has a sort of cheerful nihilism. It seems like he's accepted that the world is a terrible place, that he will never find personal happiness, but having accepted that, he's moved on. He can survive just fine without happiness.

I feel sorry for him. I hope I don't ever come to that point. But he is surviving, and what more can any of us ask?

He leaves us after a few moments, sensing we want to be alone.

Davor has been saving his money for this special treat. He missed my birthday a while ago, and he has been looking forward to doing something special for me. Surprisingly, this place has real coffee, which Davor orders for himself while I have a drink made from a colorful powder that turns plain water a vivid lime color, sweet and tangy. A couple of years ago I would have thought it was disgusting, a drink for a five-year-old, artificially sweet. Now it is a rare treat.

The café also has baklava. Where they got the butter and nuts, I don't know, but I'm willing to bet the honey came from Tetka Fatma's bees in some roundabout way. It is ridiculously expensive, but Davor orders one piece for us to share.

"Since this is a belated birthday dessert, I wish I had a candle for you to blow out," he says. "But I only have the torch in my heart I'm carrying for you—and you can't blow that out! Make a wish anyway."

"I wish . . ." Oh, so many things. Big things. Huge things. How powerful is one little candleless wish? Not strong enough to give me world peace, or health and safety for my family.

This one night, I decide on a small wish. One that is quite achievable. If only I'm brave enough to say it.

Screwing up my courage, I whisper, "Davor, what I really wish is that you would kiss me."

A smile spreads slowly across his face. "You should ask for something harder. When your birthday wish is the same as my fondest dream, there's no way it won't come true." He reaches for my face, stroking my cheek lightly. His fingers play with my hair, grown long by now. I look into his beautiful laughing eyes, but they are more serious now, passionate in the low light. He leans closer . . .

Someone bumps into our table, ruining the moment. "Oh, sorry, lovebirds!" our friend Jasmin says. "Hey, do you want to get in on the betting?"

"What betting?" Davor asks him while I try to collect myself. His lips were so close I could feel his breath on my own.

"Well, Adi didn't have any money for a piece of baklava, so he convinced the owner to have a contest for people to bet on. Everyone puts money into the pot, and if Adi can eat an entire pan of baklava, one of the bettors will win half the money, while the café owner gets the other half. He'll make more than he would have selling the baklava, and most important, Adi will get to satisfy his sweet tooth."

"I wish I'd thought of that," I admit. "I think I could eat an entire pan myself."

"That has to be a hundred-thousand calories," Davor says. "He'll kill himself!"

"Oh, but he'll die a happy man!" Jasmin says, laughing as he departs. He has the most giddy, infectious laugh, and all through the night I hear it across the room. It makes me happy.

"Not here," Davor says when we're alone again. "We'll just get interrupted again, and when I kiss you I want to kiss you slowly, passionately, and for as long as I like."

I'm glad I'm sitting down, because what he's saying makes my knees feel weak.

We stay long enough to watch Adi win his bet, then Davor takes my hand and we leave. Most of our friends stay, but Nermin and Adi leave at the same time. Adi is clutching his bulging stomach. "I'm not going to throw up . . . I'm not going to throw up . . . ," he chants to himself as he walks slowly home. Davor and I look at each other and laugh.

We walk close together, our shoulders brushing, sharing each other's warmth. The snow is a fairy land, sparkling like diamonds, a mirror to the twinkling stars above us. Davor looks so handsome tonight: red jeans, black shirt, his favorite snow-white jacket. And he smells so good! He must have some cologne saved from before the war, a spicy, masculine scent. I lean closer, breathing deeply. I want to savor every sensation of the night.

When we've gone a few blocks back toward my house, we hear an explosion behind us, close enough to make us flinch, but not anywhere near enough to cause damage.

"That sounded like it might be near the . . . ," Davor begins.

I put a finger on his warm lips. "No. I don't want to know. Not tonight."

He nods and pulls me closer. "This has been a perfect night."

"Almost perfect," I murmur, leaning into him. But I pull away just as he realizes what I mean. I want to kiss him, more than anything. My lips, my entire body, yearns for it like a deep hunger.

But I've never kissed anyone before. I'm . . . not afraid, but . . .

Yes, I'm afraid.

And this makes me inexplicably happy, to find myself worried about such a normal thing as a first teenage kiss. What a delight to be scared by first love instead of rape and death and torture.

The moment passed, we walk on. My house is getting closer. I won't dare kiss him on our doorstep. My steps slow, but I don't know how to re-create another perfect moment in time.

We're on my street now. The wind off the river has pushed the snowbanks even higher here, and roofs without enough of a slope have thick snow piles on them. We're only four houses away. Three. Soon I'll have missed my chance for my birthday wish to come true.

Suddenly there's a boom right behind us, and I feel a rush of wind. In an instant Davor flings me down into the nearest deep snowdrift and throws his body on top of me, protecting me from what we're both momentarily sure is a bomb.

But there's no fire, no explosion, no shards of metal. Only a cloud of swirling snow.

A pile of snow just slid dramatically off the neighbor's roof, making a sound that, to our taut and primed nerves, sounded like a bomb.

Davor lies on top of me, breathing hard. "I thought we were going to die," he says softly to me.

"You tried to save me," I whisper wonderingly.

The stars are behind him, winking down at me.

I tilt my chin, bringing us closer . . .

Then his lips are on mine, soft and hard all at once, kissing me slowly, telling me unequivocally that I am alive and loved. I yield to his kiss, return it, feeling a warm tingling through my body. Even the snow doesn't feel cold. It is a cushion of pure white, and a tent to keep us safe from the outside world. For the first time in almost two years, I feel safe.

Then Davor says, "Oof!" And then, "Hey, stop that!"

Thinking I've done something wrong—is there some kissing protocol I'm unaware of?—I bite my lip. Then I hear an adamant meow from Davor's back. Maci, hearing the commotion, has come to investigate. She's jumped onto his back and is now pressing her paws rhythmically into him as she settles down to join us. Her claws prick him here and there as she kneads him.

"Maci, go away!" I laugh.

"No, that's okay," Davor says. "I don't mind. Now, if Mrki tried it . . ."

I dissolve into helpless laughter. "Can you imagine? What if Mrki accidentally crushed us as we kissed?"

"There are worse ways to go," Davor murmurs, silencing my laughter in the best possible way.

———————————

That night I go to bed so giddy with happiness that I can scarcely sleep. The next morning, though, Tata says I must have slept very well indeed, because I'm glowing.

The glow lasts until afternoon, when Dino comes home from visiting friends.

"Did you hear? Last night a missile hit the Hatinac Café. I don't think anyone was killed, but some of our friends were badly hurt. You know Jasmin, right? He was hit in the throat by some shrapnel. They say he'll never talk again."

And just last night I heard him laughing so joyfully, probably the last sound he'll ever make.

1994
SUMMER

CHAPTER 24

Summer has come again, and we are still alive. We, my family and closest friends, and we, the Bosnian Muslims. Somehow we've held on against a stronger force. Little things have turned the tide slightly. There is more coordination with the Croats, who are also hated by the Serbs (though not so fiercely as they hate the Muslims). And some nation has defied the arms ban and secretly flown guns and missiles in for our side. It is common knowledge that a Russian-made helicopter routinely sneaks in on moonless nights, bringing guns to help the Bosnian Muslims. Who is behind it, I have no idea. Some say Pakistan, others claim it is the United States.

We're still running our little store just to get by. Some beer, some honey, a bit of oil, scrounged and scavenged by whatever means we can. The barter system is alive and well, and Mama has traded some of her nicest clothes for things we can sell.

Maci is the store's bodyguard or bouncer, sitting in the threshold during most of the day, greeting customers and following them inside if they seem friendly. Though we don't have much to sell, some people come into our store just to see Maci. She's becoming famous throughout the neighborhood for her gracious ways. There are several stray cats in the area, and a couple of pets, but none of them are as loved as Maci. She is the star of the store.

Everyone is trying to sell something. There's an elderly woman who haunts every funeral, hawking her stakes used to tie up tomato plants. They're hardly more than sticks—just almost-straight pieces of wood she's whittled a bit—but they're all she has to sell. And funerals are the only places where people gather in large numbers these days.

But commerce in war is difficult. Everyone needs things, but no one has money. We have a collection of foreign currency—German marks, Swiss francs, and even a few American dollars. The old money is useless now, backed by nothing, good for nothing except kindling. Things of value as currency are cigarettes, real coffee, and arable land, as well as small valuables that can be used to bribe Serb soldiers or cross a border.

But here is the good news! I'm a graduate!

It's official: I've finished high school. It's not quite what I once looked forward to, but I get a certificate of graduation, and a list of my grades. All fives. Even my conduct grade has been raised back to exemplary. I think maybe the school head was putting on a show to appease the UN soldiers. Later, when it was all forgotten about, he took away our demerit.

Even though we only met perhaps six weeks out of the last year, when school is officially over I miss it intensely. It was a little bastion of normalcy, where I could both be with my friends and indulge my intensely nerdy side. It is true that I learned more from independent study over these last two years, but my teachers offered the kind of guidance that I don't think I could do without.

More than that, they reaffirmed every day class was in session that there were people who cared about me, about my future. *We are paving the way for a better world for you, Amra,* they seemed to say, simply by showing up to teach us. Their dedication inspired me.

Our class even manages a party to celebrate our graduation. Mama gives me an old black dress with flowery details along the edges. Davor's mother alters it to fit my body type and update the style. Tetka Fatma gives me bright-red lipstick, the most darling little woven black evening bag . . . and high heels! I feel so elegant as I slip on those

Italian heels. I've never worn high heels before, and at first I totter, feeling like a skyscraper. But soon I learn how to walk in them, and head to the party at a small hotel near the teacher's college.

We party like there's no tomorrow! In that dark dance hall, lit by one or two generator-powered light bulbs, we have a live local band that plays so loudly we can't hear any gunshots or explosions outside. That one night we are happy teens.

Halfway home I take off my beautiful high heels to save them from wear and tear. Barefoot at three in the morning, I'm still singing with my friends. We sang and shouted until I lost my voice!

When they turn off to go to their own homes and I'm all alone in the night, I feel a sudden nervousness. Somewhere, a single shot rings out. What if this moment of happiness and normalcy is the moment it all ends with a single bullet in my head? I let my guard down—I forgot the war for a night. Will I pay the price?

Running on my bare feet, I try to sing to comfort myself, but my voice is ragged and breathless. As soon as I get on my own street, though, Maci runs up to me.

As soon as she's with me, I feel like I'm in the safest place on Earth. Together we walk home. I tell her about my wonderful night and sink into a blissful sleep, my red lipstick still on, staining the pillow.

But the next morning—what to do now, today and for the rest of my life? I'd always assumed I'd go on to college, get an advanced degree. I hadn't decided in what, but I knew without a doubt I'd be continuing my education. Maybe I'd be an engineer, or a physicist, or a doctor.

But now there's no way to access any of the universities. They did open a sort of stop-gap teachers college, so I go to see the administrator, a man named Ahmet who knows me from math and physics competitions. He has dark circles under his eyes and hair so thin you could see if a mosquito landed between the strands. I wonder if the war made him look so tired or if he was just born tired. He gives a weary sigh and says, "So, what subject would you like to teach? Our roster of instructors is full now, but we can add you to the wait list in case there are any openings."

"I don't want to teach—I want to learn!"

He looks over my records again. "I'm afraid this school is not for you, Amra," he says. I realize the school is makeshift at best, giving students some opportunity, but nothing like what they can get at a real university. They'll have nothing to teach me.

And even if I could find a school that would challenge me, my parents need me.

When someone comes into our store—walking through our front door—they are treated like a guest, welcomed in our friendly, open Bosnian style. But when a customer asks for something, Mama can't hear what they're saying. When they've shouted it a couple of times Tata comes to the rescue. But now his untreated diabetes is making his eyes bad, and he can't see well enough to make change. Here Mama takes over, counting out coins and bills. He is her ears, she is his eyes.

They're a good team, but still it is painful to watch them. I always thought of my parents as superheroes, capable of anything. Now they are weak, and it scares me to death. Big, tall Tata is all gray now, stooped and shuffling. Mama is gaunt and worried. She's lost her usual stoic self-confidence.

With no chance of college, and my parents to help, it is imperative that I find work.

I have been tutoring for a while now, students here and there. Now I have a job teaching in the K–8 school where Mama teaches. It doesn't pay, except for a rare box of humanitarian aid, but so many of the teachers are gone or fighting, and there are so many displaced students in addition to our own, that I know people like me are the last hope for that generation getting any education. Classes are still very sporadic, but every now and then, for a few weeks at a time, Mama and I walk to her school and spend the day reminding young people that there is a world beyond Bosnia, a world where a person can look forward to more than mere survival.

Mama teaches them this in a more literal sense, continuing to expand their horizons through geography and history. (Of course, her teaching style has changed. Once she was very interactive, encouraging questions and discussion. Now she lectures them, trapped in her own silent world, telling stories to her lost and shocked students.)

I give my students the world in a more metaphorical sense. To my astonishment, I've been asked to teach English.

"But I'm still a student myself!" I object when the school head informs me. As a perfectionist, I can't imagine teaching something I haven't mastered myself. "I've hardly been studying it more than a year. I know a lot of words, but the grammar barely makes any sense."

Truly, it seemed a ridiculous language when I first started learning it, full of contradictions and rules that are no sooner learned than broken. Yet the more I studied English, the more I began to appreciate the mongrel elegance of it. The language, like the people, first overwhelmed then absorbed the best of other languages and cultures. Now it is a unique and expressive global language: a bit smug, but mostly welcoming.

The school head pooh-poohs my objections. "You've been studying longer than any of these students. Just make sure you keep one step ahead of them and you'll be fine."

And so I wind up teaching a language I barely know to students who are no more than a few years younger than I am. When I first walk into the class, I worry that I'll have no authority. At first I'm reserved and formal, thinking that if I'm too friendly they won't take me seriously. But my reputation has preceded me. Someone (maybe my mother) told them I was one of the best students in my year, and my new students treat me with the same respect as they would any other teacher. Maybe even more, because they are very eager to learn English.

Increasingly as the war progresses, leaving Bosnia seems like the only guaranteed way to survive. And in much of the world, English is the language that will get you ahead. We'd been held back by having Russian forced on us.

But teaching there, and sometimes at an engineering high school, only takes a few weeks out of the year. Private tutoring fills the other days. I discover my most profitable niche teaching the children of a seedy bar owner.

A friend of mine, Sara—who went to my high school but focused on the humanities while I took the math and science track—had been tutoring the three children, but one day she comes to me and throws up her hands.

"I can't take it, Amra. I just can't do it anymore!"

"What happened?" I ask her. "Isn't he paying you?"

"No, it's not that," she says. "The pay is better than anything else I can get."

"What, then? Are the children monsters?"

"Well, they're arrogant and not very bright, but they're not bad kids overall. No, it's . . . what goes on there."

She won't tell me any more, and she has to hurry to another job interview, so I'm left wondering what it could be. Is it because it's located in a bar? Maybe the patrons get too rowdy and say lewd things to her as she's leaving. Maybe the owner is hitting on her?

When I think of the things that are happening to other girls and women all around Bosnia, I think I can tolerate these kinds of verbal assaults for the sake of steady work. It might be unpleasant, but if letting someone wolf-whistle and ask me out is the price of feeding my family, I'll pay it. It won't be pleasant, but these are Muslims, my people. They might be harassing, but I'll be able to say no.

So without telling anyone I head to the bar my friend mentioned. In the middle of the day, it isn't very busy. A couple of men sit at the bar, and check me out as I enter, but then they resume their conversation with a woman sitting on a stool. All I can see are legs in fishnet tights and a black skirt that's barely there. I was all braced to give the men a stern look and a cold rebuff, so I'm thrown, and even more off balance when the bar owner greets me politely as an uncle and asks if he can help me with anything.

"I've heard you're looking for someone to tutor your children," I say boldly.

I tell him my qualifications, and he asks a few sharp questions about my education and experience managing children. His wife comes out, a plump and friendly person who chides her husband for not offering me a drink. Finally we agree that I'll teach his children three days a week.

As I leave, I see the rest of the woman in fishnet stockings. I smile at her but am taken aback when I see her blackened eyes. No, not bruises, but very heavy eyeliner. It's smudged like she's been crying. She looks away from me, reaching up a hand to fix her blond hair.

Well, I think, most people have something to cry about these days. I feel sorry for her, but don't worry about her.

I come to find out that it is a mark of pride that the bar owners—an uneducated, lower-status family—have hired me—an educated girl from a good family—to teach their children. I hear them bragging to anyone who will listen. "Oh, those government people and intellectuals, not as clever as they think they are. Look what her family is reduced to. If not for us, she'd starve!"

There isn't even a set payment. At the end of each lesson they'll give me some food to take home in a basket, always reminding me to return the basket next time.

I don't meet the children that day—they're with a cousin—but so far I don't see anything wrong with this arrangement. I can't let my pride get in the way of survival.

When I meet the children they are a little bratty and rambunctious, but nothing worth quitting over. I can tell they're used to being left on their own all the time. The mother is soft and indulgent, calling the children pet names—*my three little plums, my sweet sugar cubes*—before leaving to spend the day gossiping with friends.

Their father is strict but always busy. Before class he'll frown and shake his finger at them and promise horrible consequences if they don't behave and master their lessons. Then he'll vanish, chatting with patrons at the bar and then disappearing on various errands. There's usually a man with a rifle somewhere in the room, occasionally standing guard by the door but more often lounging around, at the bar chatting with the owner or sitting and eating ćevapi. I suppose since this is one of the few places with food and beer the owner wants to protect his investment. But the gun in plain sight doesn't make me feel safer.

I always bypass the guard, but make sure I say hello to the waitress. She looks so stressed and unhappy, glancing at the owner or the guard as if for permission before meeting my eyes. It is only after a few weeks that I realize she's not Bosnian but Ukrainian, and barely speaks any of our language. When I say hello in Russian she answers with just a few words and then bends her head to her task.

"Poor thing, was she trapped here when the war started?" I ask the mother.

"Oh, no, she came quite recently," the mother says, waving her hand dismissively.

That strikes me as strange. Who would come into a war zone?

Surely she could get a job as a waitress in Ukraine. And there are certainly plenty of local people who need work. Whose lives, in fact, depend on it.

I see other women, too, but they come and go. The blonde in the fishnets is almost always there. Sometimes she's animated, smiling at the men in the bar. Sometimes she looks like she's been crying. One day I see bruises on her legs in the gaps of her fishnet.

After some initial conflicts the rowdy children settle down and let me teach them. They aren't model students, but they have endearing, funny ways. Once the youngest brings me a wilted bouquet of yellow flowers. "I stole them from the neighbor's yard!" she whispers loudly in my ear. The two boys are always poking each other whenever my back is turned, but once I beat them both in a staring contest they behave better.

So what could it be that upset my friend?

The bar is big, and surprisingly crowded every evening. The owner seems to have plenty of beer and food too. The family lives upstairs, and in the back of the large property are other buildings whose purpose I don't know. There's a scraggly, unkempt garden in the courtyard between, and a high fence around the entire property.

Usually we work upstairs, but one day we go out into the courtyard to study the parts of plants. While I'm telling them about pistils and stamens, xylem and phloem, I see a man saunter out from the back buildings, adjusting his belt.

I shrink behind the children, but he walks by without acknowledging me, looking smug and satisfied.

"What are those buildings for?" I ask the kids later as they clumsily dissect a flower.

"Oh, that's the inn," the oldest says knowingly. "Kind of an unofficial hotel. Sometimes travelers don't know where to stay, or someone at the bar has too much to drink and can't go home."

"Dad used to rent it out as storage space for a couple of factories, but now each room has a bed."

"We're not allowed in there," the girl confides.

"I don't care about that!" the older boy says with a laugh. "When Dad wasn't looking I went in and bounced on one of the beds, but it was too hard. No bounce! If Dad wants to make money he should put in better mattresses."

"Dad has plenty of money," the younger boy says defensively. "He said since the UN came he makes twice what he did before the war."

When we go back inside, we run into the children's mother. "Oh, don't go into that nasty courtyard," she chides, handing us a plate of snacks. "There's broken glass out there. You have to be careful! Here, take these upstairs and do your lessons up there from now on. Then I don't have to worry about you running into something you shouldn't."

She looks perfectly cheerful, her moon-round face guileless and innocent.

"That's what Dad says too," the girl tells me. "There are all kinds of dirty things out there that aren't good for children."

I don't ask any more questions—I feel guilty interrogating children—but between that and the foreign women who come and go I have a bad feeling about this place. I don't feel comfortable or safe here, though I don't really know why. Finally, I tell the mother that I can't tutor her children anymore.

"Do you know anyone else who can take your place?" the mother asks, wringing her hands anxiously. "Another nice, smart girl like you?"

"I'll ask my friends," I tell her. But I never do. I don't want anyone I care about working here.

1994
AUTUMN

CHAPTER 25

It is autumn now, and the linden trees along the Blue Bridge are dressed in russet and copper, their dry leaves rustling in the breeze. The oppressive heat of summer has passed, and we enjoy these days of briskness, deliberately not yet thinking about the harsh winter to come. I once thought we lived in an age where people no longer died of starvation or cold, but my classmates' dreams of universities are gone. Those who can have found work, but there are few jobs even for adults. Some of the males have been conscripted into military service, in order of birthdate. Some who were supposed to serve are excused because of family connections. There is a saying: The rich give bulls, the poor give boys. Wealthy people can always make a donation, get a fake diagnosis, or bribe to keep their sons from the army.

I learn from Nura that within a day of enlisting, sweet and funny Mirza, along with another classmate, were captured.

"He never should have been in the army!" I say, horrified at the thought of this mischievous but gentle boy in the middle of blood and violence and death. "He never even held a gun before."

"At least he wasn't killed," Nura points out.

But this is a small comfort. We know that Serb soldiers have routinely gone through villages, massacring every male over twelve and under eighty. Why would they treat prisoners any differently?

"The Geneva Convention," Mama says when I tell her what happened. "And because we no doubt have captured some of their soldiers too. They'll keep our boys to trade, I'm sure."

She says it with confidence, but I know her well enough to see the bleak despair in her eyes. Already she's gotten word about many of her own students who have been killed or captured fighting for Bosnia. I know she hasn't heard from any of those who have been taken prisoner.

Poor Tata is still sent to the front lines, working for days at a stretch. This war has been going on so long, how many more ditches could they possibly need?

I tell Tata he should try to find some of his old friends in the government. Maybe one of them would see how ridiculous it is that Tata is wading through mud with a shovel three days out of seven. But Tata refuses. He is stubborn in his pride. He doesn't want to admit weakness or ask for any favors.

He hides his injuries and sickness as best he can. He does it so well that when I take his socks to wash them, and find them covered in blood, I'm utterly shocked.

"Tata, let me see your feet!"

"Oh, it's nothing. I had a wrinkle in my sock, and that made a blister, which burst."

But I know it's not nothing. His shoes are ill-fitting, ragged, and full of holes. That's bad enough, but the poor circulation that comes with his untreated diabetes means that he's getting open wounds on his feet, sores that never heal. His feet look like ants have been eating them. His legs have become misshapen.

"Tata, you should be putting your feet up, having your legs massaged. If you don't stop marching and digging, your feet are only going to get worse!"

But he won't let me see the injuries, and only assures me that they are healing well.

I don't believe him.

The next time he comes home, his shoes are full of blood.

"You can't go back, Tata!" I insist, beseeching him to stay. What can they do? Shoot him as a deserter?

I gulp, suddenly afraid. Actually, who's to say they wouldn't do exactly that? The very thing that makes our volunteer army so dedicated is also what makes it unpredictable. Made up of everything from criminals to martial arts teachers to farmers to shopkeepers, it makes its own rules as it goes along. This helps it fight the Serbs, but what does it mean for military justice? A desperate civilian army wouldn't have time or resources to try or imprison a deserter. No one can quit, or everyone might quit. I think they wouldn't hesitate to make an example of poor Tata.

Alone in my upstairs room for a few minutes where I can rant and rave and cry without upsetting my family any further, I wrack my brains for some way to help him. Maybe if I seek out the government or army officials myself? Would they listen to a teenage girl, a concerned daughter? Or would they only say, "Everyone's father is in danger. What makes yours so special that we should save him while another takes his place and dies?"

Despairing, I close my eyes.

When I open them, they alight on the box holding my volleyball shoes.

Some of my happiest memories from before the war are of playing volleyball. Even in a nation of traditionally tall people, I am exceptionally tall for a woman. I reached my full height of six feet by the end of fifth grade. I grew so fast then that I still have stretch marks on my back. My skin simply could not keep up with the phenomenal growth of my bones.

So of course I was perfect for volleyball. I played either side or mid spiker, leaping for the ball while it was still high over everyone else's heads and slamming it down on the opposing side's court so fast and so hard that they didn't have a chance of stopping it. That physical exhilaration was such a change from my usual mental exertions. Both gave me pleasure, but leaping up to intercept that ball was thrilling, liberating. It was, in its own way, something pure and absolute, like mathematics.

The summer before the war began I was in pre-training before the regular season. My coach, pushing me hard, told me to run around the soccer stadium until he said I could stop. I was wearing cheap Converse-type sneakers (but not Converse, of course) that weren't meant for real running. At first my feet hurt. But then, by the time my coach told me to stop, they started feeling so warm and lovely. It was only when I stopped and they cooled down that they started to hurt again. I saw my coach looking in shock at my feet. My dirty white sneakers were red and wet with blood! I was in bed with my feet up for days after that. That's what prompted Mama to splurge on new volleyball sneakers, too big in case my feet kept growing.

I haven't played since the war began. All this time, even when my regular shoes had practically disintegrated, I've kept these shoes pristine. It always gives me pleasure to think that when the world is normal again, kind and gentle enough for such innocent things as sports, they will be waiting for me.

Now when I think of poor Tata's feet, I have another idea. If they could save my feet from bleeding, can't they save Tata's?

We're different shoe sizes, of course. Tata's feet are at least an inch longer than mine. He could never fit in these shoes as they are. But maybe with a little modification . . .

That day, I begin my secret project.

Without telling Mama, I sneak into her sewing kit and get the stoutest needle I can find. She doesn't have any heavy-duty thread—I think I really need something like high-test fishing line—but regular thread will have to do. Besides that I just need scissors . . . and another pair of my old shoes that are so hopelessly broken and worn down that they're beyond repair.

All this time Maci is with me, nosing the sewing basket, trying to play with bits of string. She follows me back upstairs and leaps onto my bed, looking at me with curiosity. She can tell something important and exciting is happening, but since it clearly doesn't involve food or Davor (one of her favorite people) she is puzzled.

These supplies in hand, I sit with my precious volleyball shoes on my lap. They are so beautiful, pure arctic white and vivid blue. They've never touched dirt. The few times I used them before the war, it was only on a well-polished indoor court.

Now I hover over them with my scissors. I never dreamed it would hurt so much, but when I make the first cut in the toes my heart gives a painful wrench.

"It's for Tata," I tell Maci, but I feel like I'm cutting up all my hopes for a decent, peaceful future.

For three days I work in secret, strategically slicing my sneakers and patching them with pieces from other shoes to make a new Frankenstein monster pair that will fit Tata.

When I present them to Tata, he beams and tells me they're the most beautiful things he's ever seen.

"Well, they don't have to be beautiful," I say. Truthfully, they are more thread than sneaker. They have a higher thread count than some carpets. "As long as they protect your poor feet."

I'm so proud of myself for my genius idea, and I think that at least these splendid shoes will allow Tata's feet to heal, even if he is still digging ditches. The next day he sets off, wearing his new makeshift shoes.

He comes home with the shoes falling completely apart, filled with blood.

"Oh, Tata, I'm so sorry!" I whisk them away and spend the rest of the day washing and repairing them. But I'm less hopeful this time.

Over and over he comes home limping and bloody. And every time I fix his shoes as best I can.

One day he doesn't come home.

I find out when I get home from a tutoring job. Mama has just come from the hospital. A nurse friend of ours sent word that he'd been admitted.

"He finished his shift, the stubborn man, and then walked halfway back before collapsing. They say he lost so much blood . . ." She covers her mouth with her hand and tries to be strong.

Dino is at school, so I set off to visit Tata alone. It's been a bad week. Worse than normal, anyway. I was supposed to be paid in food aid from my job at the high school, but the shipments never came. They were either stopped by the Serbs or even stolen by corrupt Bosnians who took it for themselves.

Last night we had beans, hard to digest.

This morning, nothing.

I'm feeling faint when I set out, but that's nothing new. I have low blood pressure, and my height sometimes makes it hard for my blood to reach my brain effectively. If I bend down the world sways when I stand straight again. If I kneel down for any length of time, trapping my blood in my legs, I pass out.

And that's during normal times, with plenty to eat. Now, starving, it is even worse.

The world swims in and out as I walk, my vision clouding and then clearing. The air seems thick and hazy, and I move in slow motion. I cross the bridge, almost vomiting when I see the holes and missing chunks, remembering the carnage that came at that bombing. But there's nothing in my stomach to throw up, and I only taste bitter bile.

Then, a few blocks from the hospital, the streets around me go gray, then black . . . then there's nothing . . .

I open my eyes to a kindly face. "There you are, back with us," the middle-aged woman says. I look around and realize I'm sprawled on the ground. I've fainted. "Can you stand? Best to get out of the road. Come, my house is right here."

She's forty years older than me, but I lean on her with all my weight just to walk the few steps to her door. I hobble into the kitchen and collapse while she makes tea.

"Do you like rose tea, my dear? It's about all I can get these days." She hands me a cup, and I start to cry quietly, unobtrusively. The smell of the tea reminds me of better times, when Mama would make us rose tea and I'd sit on Tata's lap while we watched TV. And more recently, Davor's rose tea, his love, his kindness. I haven't seen him for weeks. He's with our army, and who knows whether he's alive or dead?

"There, there, dear. Life goes on, doesn't it?" She pats my hand and leaves me to my tea and grief.

When I'm ready to walk again I thank her. "No need," she says. "We all need to help each other. Else what's the point of being here?"

Only when I'm half a block away do I realize I never even asked her name.

Hospitals used to be places of hope and healing. Now they are where people go to die. Against international conventions, the Serbs deliberately target the hospital. The windows are all blown out, and as I walk up I can see plastic sheeting covering gaping holes. Patients line the hallways. There are hardly any doctors, hardly any supplies. People with minor injuries are dying from infection. People are having their limbs sawed off because we don't have surgeons to save them.

Tata is in a room with at least ten other people. I slip between cots, past people who seem almost moments away from death, and stand at his bedside.

"Amra, my love!" he says, looking up at me with his widest smile. "Did you walk all this way to see me? You didn't have to. I'll be home before you know it."

But his skin has a deathly pallor, and his eyes are yellowed. I don't believe his optimism.

"And I know that winter will be here soon, so I want to make sure you know I'll be taking care of the firewood as soon as I get out of here. We want to be prepared, don't we?" He is doing his best to look cheerful, but I can't keep it up.

"I . . . I have to go to the restroom, Tata. I'll be right back."

I run out of the room and collapse in the corridor outside. Tata might not be here this winter, and he's thinking about getting wood for us? My heart is breaking for my family.

When the doctor comes by I ask him, "Tell me the truth, how is he?"

"It's very likely he'll lose his leg. Maybe the other foot too. Only time will tell. I'm very sorry."

Tata is in the hospital for two weeks. He doesn't die, he doesn't lose his leg or foot. But it is clear that his strength has left him permanently.

On the way home from visiting Tata in the hospital a day before he is due to be released, I see a familiar face walking along the boulevard.

"Mirza!" I cry, and run to hug him. "I heard you'd been captured. Was I wrong?"

No, I can see in his face even before he answers that something terrible has happened. His once-merry eyes are haunted. The happy child I knew for years is gone, replaced by a cynical, jaded, suffering man.

"I was in a concentration camp," he tells me. I bet the world thinks the last concentration camp closed at the end of World War II, but what else can you call these places they force Muslims to go, where they torture and kill them. "There was disease in the camp. People started getting diarrhea, vomiting, even before they had us registered. A lot of people died almost as soon as they got there. They took our

IDs but hadn't matched us up yet, because they didn't know who was alive and who was dead.

"Our friend, son of a Muslim widow, had a Serb father and a Serb last name, so when he was called out of the list they let him go. Then they called another name. Mirza Jević." Mirza's last name is not Jević. "That's a Serb last name. When they called it, no one answered. So I took a chance. I figured maybe that other Mirza had died in the camp. I put up my hand, marched forward, and said it was me. One of the guards had been friendly with me. He liked my jokes. He knew my name was Mirza, never heard my last name, so he confirmed it and they let me go."

I can see Mirza doing his best to joke even in the worst situations. Even with the guards who were dehumanizing him. This time it paid off.

But there is a new restraint to this former jokester. I think there is much more that happened to him with the Serbs that he's not telling me, and might never tell anyone. For as long as I know Mirza after this, there is always a wry cynical twist to his jokes. His carefree innocence is gone forever.

1995
SPRING

CHAPTER 26

We've run out of things to sell. And we're running out of things to eat.

The war has entered its fourth year, and we are still alive. But for how much longer?

The long, bitter winter has taken all we have, every last bit of produce harvested the summer and autumn before, and every last bit of fat stored in our bodies. I look one step up from a skeleton. My hair is the only thick thing about me. Long and Amazonian, untouched by any chemical or dye or even shampoo, it is in its wild and natural state. I'm sure some women in peaceful countries would envy this bounty of hair, the only healthy thing about me. But what I wouldn't give for red hair dye or a curling iron!

Isn't it ridiculous to think of those things when survival is on the line? But we all fantasize about those kinds of silly luxuries. Fatma told me she dreams of travel. She wants to go back to Greece with Ale and have more lunches on the beach. Carts drawn by soft-nosed mules would drive by with baskets of peaches and oranges, and you could pick whatever fruit you wanted to finish your meal of pasta with truffles.

All of us daydream about food—and not just filling, healthy, nourishing food, the kind we actually need. We talk about fluffy white bread, freshly baked, or sticky baklava. We even fantasize about exotic foods like pineapples.

We'd be better off with bags of rice and beans, but a girl can dream, can't she? And so along with that, I might as well dream of having exotic bright-red hair and big movie-star curls.

I might as well dream about peace or a doctorate degree. All the dreams seem equally impossible.

Now our store stands empty, as empty as our bellies. No humanitarian aid has come in at least a week. We have to get something to eat or sell, and fast.

The black market in the city is so overpriced that it would take wheelbarrows of foreign currency to buy what we need—if we can even find it. Even the greediest black marketeers are running low on supplies.

"There's one other possibility," Mama tells me when I'm sitting at the table, studying English, with Maci on my lap. No one else is home. She can't hear herself, so she tends to speak louder than necessary. And of course I have to shout back to make myself heard at all. So for this conversation she makes sure neither Tata nor Dino can overhear us. She knows they'd stop her if they found out what she's planning. "We can cut out the middleman."

At first I don't know what she means. Then with shock I understand.

"No, we can't! It's too dangerous."

"Who said anything about 'we,'" Mom asks. "I'll go on my own, and . . ."

But that's impossible. Mom won't be able to hear commands or warnings. She won't be able to bargain. And a woman alone . . .

"I'll go with you," I tell her.

This she forbids. "It's too dangerous for you. An old woman like me they won't bother with."

What she says simply isn't true.

"I won't let you go alone," I tell her staunchly. She tries to argue, but it is too frustrating for her to have long conversations anymore. Finally, she agrees that we'll go together.

And so the next morning we tell Tata and Dino that we're visiting Tetka Fatma. In reality, we are taking a bus to the Croatian border, to the no-man's-land between the Bosnian self-organized army and the

Serb army's front lines. The bus runs very irregularly, and it is filled with a mix of shady characters and desperate people like us. Everyone is nervous. Just last week, one passenger tells me, someone got off the bus and was blown up by a land mine not a hundred meters away.

The bus stops near a desolate village at the border. Most of the residents have left. From there we walk a kilometer or more until we reach a field of tall, waving grass.

"Well, this doesn't look so bad," Mama says too loudly. I shush her, because I notice things she hasn't seen yet.

Places where the tall grass lies flattened in an irregular circle.

A smell of smoke and char.

An ominous silence, not even a bird singing or a cricket chirping.

And then there's a sound after all. The harsh sound of drunken men laughing. I can't see anyone yet, but the sound is coming from the forest just beyond the grassy field.

There are no guards, no fences. Someone from either side would have to be crazy to cross this field. Crazy . . . or desperate.

Those flattened patches? Those are places where a land mine exploded. The smell is from burned grass. Or burned flesh. This is a field of death, booby-trapped.

But the supplies we need are right on the other side. We have to cross to a dried-up streambed where the Serbs have a bunker.

Mama starts right off, but I hold her back. "Look, see those places where the grass looks a lighter green?" She can't hear me, for I dare not shout, but her eyes follow where I point. In places the grass looks slightly different, like something bent it slightly and it hasn't quite regrown to its normal sun-following straightness. When the sun hits these places the grass shows a slightly different color from the exposed undersides. Some of these variations seem to be in a line. A trail.

I think these may be the marks showing where someone else passed before, probably within a day or two ago. One of the paths leads to one of the circular, flattened patches and stops. I know what that means. But another leads all the way across the field.

"There," I tell Mama. "We go this way."

Taking her hand, I lead her along the path I've picked out. It was easier to see from far away. In the middle of it, though, it is almost impossible to tell the bent grass from the straight. Over and over I lose my way.

What makes me think this is safe? I wonder. One step to the left or right can make the difference. Even on this path, if my foot falls just a little differently than the last person, I might hit a land mine they missed.

Halfway through another terrible thought enters my head: What if this path was left by a Serb laying new mines? The path of safety could in fact be the path of doom.

Our route takes us very close to one of the flattened patches where another mine went off. As we pass, I can't help but look. Then I have to look away quickly. The grass is covered in a rust color and . . . Oh God, there's a foot! A severed foot, in a neat woman's boot, with fleshless bone protruding . . .

I learned only one prayer ever, and it was in the war. Once when I thought the Serbs were about to enter the city I found Tetak Ale's tiny book with a few prayers, written in Bosnian and also in Arabic. While bombs were whistling overhead I read one in fear and never forgot it. In the grimmest moments I say it sometimes:

Auzubillahi Minash Shaitan ir Rajeem.
Bismillah ir Rahman ir Rahim:
I seek refuge in Allah from Satan.
In the Name of Allah, the Most Gracious, the Most Merciful.
Rabbi yassir wa la Tua'ssir:
O God, make it easy and don't make it difficult.

Rabbi tammim bil khayr:
O God, complete this with the good.

I say this now under my breath. I'm going to die. Right here, in the middle of the field, and Tata and Dino will never know what happened to us. My heart is racing wildly, and the only reason I don't fall apart is so that Mama is less afraid. I want to run away, back across the field, back home, but I know that would be suicidal. Going forward is our best chance.

Finally, impossibly, we are across the field and at the verge of the forest. Now I almost wish for the minefield again. At least an explosion would be quick and impersonal. For now I see the Serbs, camped deeper in the woods, laughing and watching us.

These men would be happy to kill us, but they'd rather have our money. And they know they can always kill us tomorrow. They have nothing to fear from our side now. Bosnian soldiers won't fire the first shot. We don't have enough ammunition.

I can't go on. I can't get closer to these men. They're like the ones on the train, the Četniks, with shaggy beards and loud, cruel voices.

But I know that they are like predators, and running now will only stimulate them to hunt. If we are bringing money we are valuable to them. If we accomplish a trade we might come back with more money so they'll let us live, and leave. But if we run we are just Muslims, just vermin, free for them to shoot at or capture. Theirs to use.

So I swallow hard, grit my teeth, and pull Mama forward. There's no going back now.

"Welcome to Greater Serbia, balije," one of them sneers, stepping unsteadily forward. He stumbles over a tree root and I think he's lunging for us, but I realize he's just terribly drunk. My heart sinks to my feet, and my courage flies away. There's nothing a drunk man won't do.

His friends laugh behind him, and he grins an evil smile and makes

273

an obscene gesture at them. They pass a bottle around, each taking long swigs. Several other bottles lie around them, some smashed to shards.

I give him a courteous greeting in a shaky voice, and say, "We would like to buy some food." Then I add, "Please."

"Oh, we have some food for you!" a drunken man behind him shouts to us, and makes a suggestive motion with his hips. "We have plenty of cucumbers for both of you." I'm only thankful that Mama can't hear what they're saying.

The man in front, though, seems eager for money, and this gives me hope. "Do you have any food?" I ask him. "Anything? Or cooking oil?"

"No, but we have some lovely soaps." He pulls a little bar out of his pocket, elegantly wrapped in purple paper. I catch a whiff of lavender. It is so incongruous in this vile, dangerous setting that I almost laugh. To think that we would risk all this for scented soap!

"We can't afford that. No one can. We don't need luxury. We need food!" I'm angry as well as scared. I want to tell him what he's doing to us. Killing us, starving us, and then extorting us. But survival instinct holds my tongue.

"If you don't have food we'll go," I say, taking Mama's arm again.

"What did he say, Amra?" she whispers loudly.

I don't answer. I just want to get out of here.

The Serb grabs me by the arm. "Hold on, balije, we're not through yet." I shake his hand off. I can feel the impression of his fingers still on my skin. I know it will leave bruises.

"Let us go, please!"

He makes another grab for my hand, and I can smell his breath, rank and sour. Mama pulls one arm, he pulls the other, and for a moment it is a tug of war with me as the rope. My hands are sweating so much with fear that his grip slips off again and, unbalanced, he falls headlong into the dead leaves.

His friends get hysterical at this. "What's the matter, Đorđe, aren't you man enough for two balije? Let us help you!"

But they're so drunk they get tangled in each other's legs. The Serb who grabbed me insults them, one takes offense, and a second later they're rolling on the ground in a drunken brawl, punching each other over who is more capable of raping Muslims.

We don't wait around any longer. Running as fast as we can, we retrace our path through the field. I don't even think about being blown up. Anything is better than those leering, drunken, cruel men.

We hear a shot from our side, one brave Muslim soldier who wants to cover our escape. The Serbs shoot back. Their gunfire is like music with rapid beats, they have so many bullets they can spray as many as they want, waste them. We don't know if they're shooting at us or our soldier or into the air. I think they are too drunk to hit anything.

On the bus ride home I just stare out the window, hiding my tears so that Mama doesn't get more upset. She's mostly unhappy that we didn't get anything to sell in our store. But she didn't hear what they said, their lascivious, violent comments. She doesn't know how close we came to being raped in that forest. Only their intoxication saved us.

I cry on that bus back, realizing that my life is miserable and will never get any better. I am disgusted at life, at us, at our desperation, at the world, at everything around us. So long I've struggled to hold on to decency, to believe that there is hope in the world. Now I know: Nothing can be good and pure in this world. Not my love for Davor. Not even Maci. All of humanity is infected.

In this moment I don't even try to search for light or hope. I am like an addict, addicted to misery, to inhumanity.

And all this because I am a Muslim. A Muslim who never prayed, just a Muslim by birth and blood. For that I am marked.

CHAPTER 27

I think Mama was more aware of the exact nature of those Serbs' threats than I wanted to admit, because since that moment Mama and Tata make a concerted effort to get both Dino and me out of the country. I think their efforts are concentrated on me, though. As the older one I'm more ready to take on responsibility. Maybe if I get out, I can eventually pull the others out behind me.

Every night as I try to sleep, Maci lies with me, comforting me as a mother comforts her child before bed. But as I stroke her softness I'm not thinking gentle thoughts. I'm conditioning myself, as I conditioned my body for volleyball, as I conditioned my brain for math. These nights, I condition my resilience. I imagine being raped so that when it actually happens I can survive it. Trembling with fear and rage, I imagine Dino being killed. But this I cannot bear. I would rather take anything on myself than see those I love suffer. But I try to make myself strong to bear whatever is coming.

Then Maci leaves for her nightly rounds outside, thinking I'm soothed. I look out through the crack in the boarded-up window and see a sliver of moon. Other teenage girls are looking at that same moon, thinking of parties and boys, of college and careers. They are American girls in my mind, because the best things, the freest things, are all in America. Don't they know what's happening here? Don't they think about the suffering in the rest of the world as they lie in their soft, safe beds?

Then, as my last thought before I fall asleep, I think of a piece of freshly baked white bread, warm and soft . . .

Some people escape. A few planes and even helicopters manage to enter Bosnian air space. Weapons are brought in the middle of the night. Fighters too—young men who were trapped away from their families, in school or the military, when the war started and have returned to defend their home. A few people even manage to get out, but this is very rare. There's an air strip—hardly more than a level field cleared of debris—at Ćoralići.

One day in May my parents receive word that a cousin, the gynecologist named Mensur who managed to leave early in the war to become a diplomat, has returned to Bihać in the company of a Bosnian foreign minister. They flew in late at night for some secret meeting. When he finds this out, Tata contacts him and begs him to take me out of Bosnia. I'd have to go to Slovenia, snuck in clandestinely. I'd be an illegal refugee.

Mensur wants to help, but says it will be almost impossible. "This is a diplomatic mission to end the war, not a tourist plane," he says. "They won't just smuggle civilians out. I'd have to come up with some cover story. They wouldn't let a random teenage girl out on a flight like this."

At first he refuses outright, but my father calls and pleads with him so often, so piteously, that he finally relents.

"Okay, I'll figure something out," Mensur promises. "I have an idea that might work. But I can't give you a day or a time. You understand how tight security is. She'll have to be ready to leave at a moment's notice. No time for packing or goodbyes. When I call, she goes, just like that. There are no second chances."

When my parents tell me, I start to cry. "I don't want to leave you!" Maci, immediately sensing my distress, climbs into my lap and pats my wet cheek with her paw.

But they don't give me a choice. Before the war when they wanted me to leave, they respected my refusal. Back then, they were innocent. We all were. We never knew it would come to this.

"You have no future here," Mama says shortly. "You have to leave."

I spend the next two days trapped in the house, waiting. I'd only traveled out of the country once before, to Switzerland to play volleyball in seventh grade. On that trip I bought the only two brand-new shirts I'd ever owned, one red, the other orange. And of course I bought chocolate too. I try to reassure myself with happy memories of that trip as I pack Tata's old army duffel bag. It's half-empty because I hardly have any clothes. Tata waits by the phone.

I wonder how Mensur is going to get me on the plane. Will he say I'm the secret mistress of an important official? Maybe he'll bandage my face like a burn victim and say I'm one of his patients, a very important person's child. I have no passport, except an invalid one from when I was very young, so I'd have to be snuck out with no documentation.

Twice I call up Davor where he's stationed in the barracks near the front. Once when I get him on the line, I don't have the courage to tell him I'm leaving. The next time I try, he's not there.

"Get off the phone, Amra," Mama tells me. "Mensur could call any minute."

I find myself half hoping he doesn't. Terrible as it is, this is my life now. I want to live it with my family. If I leave, who will I become? Who will want me? Here, I am a hardworking, commendable student who does everything right. In another country I will be a despised refugee, someone's stereotype.

The next morning the air is heavy and muggy. Clouds on the horizon presage a day of spring rains. Still Mensur hasn't called. I'm going stir-crazy waiting.

"Tata, I'm just going to go outside for a while," I tell him. "Just a little walk around the neighborhood."

I can tell he's not thrilled by the idea, but he consents. "Just stay close enough to hear if I call."

Maci and I go outside, and for a while I sit under the peony bush watching the billowing clouds get closer. "Maci, you don't want me to go, do you?"

She meows at me, then looks down the road at the coming storm. "You should go inside," I tell her. "We don't want to be caught in that." But she doesn't move, not even when there's a bolt of lightning quickly followed by an explosive boom of thunder. Neither do I. The danger is coming, and neither of us will run away from it.

Somehow, Maci always tells me what I need to hear.

"But I have to go with Mensur," I whisper into her soft fur. "My parents arranged it all, and he went through so much trouble. I wish I could bring you. I wish I could bring everyone—Mama and Tata and Dino. Davor too. Oh!" I bury my face in her fur. "I wish I could see him one last time. Just to tell him goodbye."

I have butterflies in my stomach, a mixture of panic, love, nervousness, a fear that I won't ever kiss or hug him again. I love him, and I don't know if anyone else will ever again understand me. Some other boy in some other country can't understand a girl who starved, thought she would be killed or raped, ate cow's udder and alien chicken-foot soup to survive. No other world will understand me. I imagine how lonely I'll feel far away from anyone who has shared these experiences.

As I listen to the deep rumble of her purr I make a sudden, rash decision. "Maci, stay here," I say as I start to run to a neighbor's house. I feel as if there's someone else inside me, making this decision for me.

Maci tries to follow me as always. I stop her and look her right in the eyes. "No, you have to stay here. If Tata looks out and sees you on the lawn, he'll think I'm still close. He knows you follow me everywhere. But if you're gone, he'll know I'm gone too. I don't want him to try to stop me or come after me."

She meows at me, concerned. Her ears lie down flat, as they always do when I have a serious tone. "I won't be gone long, Maci. I promise."

With that I kiss her nose and dash off to borrow a bike from my neighbor. A moment later I'm pedaling as hard as I can toward the barracks.

Once I clear the main city it is a long straight road to the barracks. It's crazy of me, suicidal. The road runs right below the hills for a few kilometers where the Serbs have encampments and heavy artillery mounted. Any time they wanted they could shoot this insane girl pedaling for all she's worth in plain sight. And they probably would. But the moment I hit that road, the heavens open up in a torrential downpour. I'm skidding all along the slick pavement. The wind pushes me so hard I feel like no matter how vigorously I pedal I'm almost standing still. I can barely see where I am. But then, neither can the Serbs. I manage to make it to Davor's barracks, sopping wet. The perimeter guard lets me in and sends someone to get him, and a moment later we're in each other's arms, kissing each other in the rain.

"Oh, Davor, I hope I'm not going to get you in trouble. I had to see you!"

"Is everything okay? Your family . . ."

"Yes, everyone's fine. It's just . . ." And then I simply kiss him again, laughing. His hair, in a short military cut, is spiked with the rain. His neck is suntanned against an olive-green shirt and his military pants hug his hips and rear in the most distracting way. Water droplets dot his eyelashes like diamonds, and his eyes sparkle with surprise and love as he looks at me. He thinks I had a crazy romantic inspiration just to find him and kiss him. The other soldiers and his commander make fun of him, whistling and joking with me about how in love he is. I've never seen him happier. Just the sight of him, the touch, the taste revives me. I want to hold on to this moment forever.

I don't want to ruin it by telling him I'm leaving.

So I only say, "I missed you so much, I had to see you." And he accepts that.

He takes me around the barracks, introduces me to a few people, and then we go to the stables to meet some of the mules and cows he's taking care of. As I stroke their soft noses we talk about unimportant things—when he's going to have leave, my tutoring work, whether the Una is warm enough to swim in yet.

I leave while it's still raining, kissing him passionately. The rain hides my tears as I tell him goodbye.

When I get home I'm still crying, guilty at not telling Davor the truth and wretched at the thought of leaving him. Before I can reach the door Tata flings it open and shouts, "Where were you?" loud enough for the whole neighborhood to hear. He's furious. I don't think I've ever seen Tata this mad, and certainly not at me.

"I was just . . ." I gesture helplessly down the road.

"You snuck off without permission, when I specifically told you to stay near. How dare you! Where did you go?"

I open my mouth to answer, but suddenly he seems to crumple.

"No, never mind. It doesn't matter anymore." He takes me in his arms, the anger gone. "He called. Mensur called. He said the plane was leaving in sixty minutes, that we had to be there in half an hour if there was any hope of you being on it." He looks at his watch. "That was two hours ago. Oh, my precious girl, you missed your only chance!"

I feel a strange sense of calm about this, almost as though it were fated to turn out this way. After all, the life of a refugee—illegal, hunted, without ID or paperwork, always in danger of deportation, always hiding—is not exactly a dream come true. Maci rubs against my ankles as I enter the house, sharing a conspiratorial look.

Still, only think, if I hadn't gone to see Davor, then it would just be a short plane ride, no more than thirty minutes, to a whole new world.

Mama and Tata stay mad at me for the rest of the day, hardly speaking to me. Maci is the only one who will interact with me. She sits on my lap as I write in my diary. Later, when the rain clears, we walk in silence to Tetka Fatma's house. Maci comes with us, as always. Tetka Fatma has electricity tonight, so we plan to listen to the radio or, hopefully, watch television to get a little news of the outside world. Of course only biased Serb news will be broadcast, but it is better than nothing. We can pick through the skewed reporting and find some grains of truth.

The Serb announcer reports about some gymnast the Serbs are proud of, and then a story about their supposedly stellar educational system. That makes me burn with jealousy. How am I ever supposed to get a real education now?

Then the news anchor gets more serious. A plane was shot down today trying to fly through restricted airspace from Bihać to Croatia. There is no word of its purpose or passengers, but one unnamed source believes that the plane carried terrorists and weapons that would be used against the Serb people. They show footage of charred bodies and wreckage. The anchor says that more information will be revealed as it comes in.

My entire family falls silent.

There could only be one plane leaving Bihać today.

If I hadn't gone to see Davor one last time I would have been on that plane.

My parents don't say anything, but they never try to evacuate me from Bihać again.

As for me, I realize that this city is my destiny. I am fated to be with my family, with Maci, no matter what. I will be here for the duration of the war, however long that lasts. I'll stick it through until the end, whatever end that might be. I believe it is my fate: If I leave, I will die. If I stay, I will die. At least if I stay, I'll have love while I live.

That night Maci walks home proudly beside us, like our guardian, better than any guard dog. A dog may have teeth, but Maci has a more profound way of protecting the people she loves.

"I went to see Davor because of Maci," I tell my parents on the way home. "I was talking to her, patting her, and she reminded me of how important love is. As good as if she told me with words, she convinced me to go see Davor. She's the reason I'm alive."

How many times has this benevolent spirit, this loving soul, helped my family now?

Where would we be without our Maci? We owe her our lives.

CHAPTER 28

Some time after I graduate, I find out the results of my math and physics competitions and overall scholastic ranking. To my astonishment, I came in first in physics in my region, and third in mathematics. We are told in a letter faxed to the local Ministry of Education from our government in Sarajevo that this places me in the top ten of all students in Bosnia.

I'm proud, but I don't really know what it means for me. With no real opportunity for higher education here in Bosnia it is an empty honor. If anything, it is a mockery, a slap in the face. Here, it seems to say—*Look what you are capable of! Now we forbid you to do anything with it.*

But later there is more news. Amateur radio operators connect Tata with the Bosnian embassy in Turkey. Scholarship documentation and funding will be routed first to the Bosnian embassy in Croatia, and from there to the besieged Bihać pocket. Go to the local minister of education, we are told, and there you will receive your scholarship.

"Scholarship to where?" I ask. There's a university in Sarajevo, but the trip there would be next to impossible, and it is at least as dangerous there as in Bihać.

Mama and Tata shrug, but we go into town to meet with the minister of education, who, it turns out, is a high school classmate of my father's named Mustafa. He welcomes us warmly, but he seems to take a back seat to his assistant, a woman named Ilma.

I dislike her right away. When she first sees me she looks me up and down, smirks, then cuts her eyes away dismissively. I am beneath her notice. I see her glance over my mother the same way. Then her eyes settle on Tata, still handsome despite his hardships.

I don't think Ilma cares what any man looks like, though. She is only determined that they find her alluring.

She's slim and witchy, with huge blue eyes ringed with purple eyeliner and aqua eyeshadow straight out of the 1980s. Her hair is teased up high. And she's smoking—a real Marlboro cigarette! How is she getting real Marlboro cigarettes in the middle of a war? Tata doesn't even notice her looks. He's just beaming with joy at the fact that his little girl is getting a scholarship.

"The government of Egypt has sponsored this scholarship for Bosnia's best and brightest," Ilma tells us, her smile too bright, her eyes flicking from Tata to Mustafa. If they are not competing with her, women don't exist for her. "You can study anywhere in the world, you lucky girl! Very soon you'll get a passport, and then it is just a matter of waiting for the documents and money to come through. We'll contact you as soon as everything is ready!"

"How long do you think it will be?" Tata asks, smiling briefly at Ilma but turning to his old friend Mustafa. Mustafa opens his mouth to answer, but Ilma jumps in. "Oh, who can say, things being what they are. You just sit back and wait, and we'll let you know." Mustafa shakes my hand, and then we go home, all of us in a sort of daze. It happened so fast! I'm going to leave, to study, to make something of myself! I don't think of it in terms of my own success, but only as far as what I do might help my family. I would never leave them just for my own safety, but this is completely different.

Over dinner (beans and the ever-present onions) we all chatter excitedly over my prospects. "Where are you going to go?" Dino asks.

"They say I can go anywhere!" I answer. It is like a dream, too good to be real.

Tata wants me to go to Malaysia. His good friend is a high-ranking Bosnian executive who runs the Malaysian outpost of Energoinvest, a huge exporter in the former Yugoslavia.

"You should go to the United States," Dino says decisively.

"They do have very good schools there," I say. "But so do Germany and England, and who knows, maybe Egypt wants me to go there."

"No," Dino says, "you should definitely go to the US. They have the best basketball teams. You can introduce me to Michael Jordan!"

We all laugh, and for the first time in ages I go to bed thinking about the future.

But what if it isn't real, I ask myself over the next days and weeks. Something this good can't be happening to me.

No matter how much I try to prepare myself for the worst, I find I'm walking around with a big grin on my face. Maci catches my mood and capers around me like a new kitten, full of manic energy. I pick her up and rub my nose against hers. "I think it might really be real!" I whisper to her as she nuzzles me back.

Then, oh miracle! I get a passport!

There it is, a little book with my photo in it. I show it to everyone. It's me! It's mine! It hardly looks like me, though. With no way to take new pictures in the official size, I have to use my old passport picture, taken when I went to the volleyball competition in Switzerland in seventh grade. It is black and white, and my hair is short and cut like a boy's. Still, it has all the right signatures and stamps to make it official. With this, I can legally go anywhere in the world!

Now we just have to wait for the documents and funding to arrive.

We wait.

And wait.

And wait.

Tata and I go to see Mustafa, but we are met by the 1980s peacock Ilma and her saccharine smile. "Oh, it hasn't come in yet. It won't be much longer, I'm sure." She sends us on our way.

Again and again we check. Days. Weeks. Finally months pass, and each time she tells us to be patient, it will come.

I notice that every time we see her, she has newer, finer clothes. Her hair is freshly dyed, her nails impeccably painted blood-red. She chats about her new apartment.

Finally, after checking every day for thirty days, I ask her point-blank who stole my scholarship. Her eyes widen, then she composes her face in a fake smile and says, "Oh, don't be so dramatic! Do you think it is easy to get anything in or out of Bihać these days? People are risking their lives to bring you these documents. Do you expect someone to die just to hurry your paperwork through?"

We leave, but we go back the next day. This time Ilma isn't there to greet us or fend us off, and we find Mustafa.

"Have Amra's scholarship documents arrived?" Tata asks the minister.

"If they have, I haven't seen them," he confesses. "I usually leave all the paperwork to Ilma. She's so efficient at that sort of thing."

"Where is she?" I ask.

"Oh, she said she wasn't feeling well yesterday around noon." That was right after we were there. "She left and didn't come to work this morning. I'll send someone to check on her. I hope she's not very sick. I don't know how this place would run without her!" Ilma stays away from the office for a long time, and before she returns we realize the futility of chasing after this dream any longer. Though we never get the full story, details gradually emerge about the apartment she has, the furs and food and cigarettes.

"I'll tell you how someone might pay for that," I say to Tata. "The kind of money one might get from selling one girl's documents and scholarship money to some other family, to a rich family desperate to evacuate their daughter to another country!"

"No, I can't believe anyone would do something so underhanded," Tata says. He's always loath to believe the worst of anyone.

We don't know for sure what happened. All we know is that I never get the scholarship I won, and Ilma became suddenly wealthy.

"It was too good to be true," I tell Maci when at last I accept that I'm stuck in Bihać with no chance of an education.

I feel my brain darken as if in a fog. I feel my body start to get heavy, weighted down, as I begin the slide into depression again. I creep to my mattress and crumple up. I want to lie here and never move again. I don't care if I live or die . . .

Meow.

Maci butts at my face with her head.

"Leave me alone, Maci," I snap at her. "What does it matter?"

Meow!

She won't let me lie down, won't let me rest. She pokes me in the face with her cold nose, sits on my chest and stares in my eyes. She'll give me no peace until I finally jump up and say, "Fine, have it your way!"

I grab a pile of books and head out on my tutoring rounds just as if all my dreams hadn't just been smashed. I stomp and storm, but it is better than inaction. It's only once I'm out in the sunshine that I realize what Maci did for me. She won't allow me to feel sorry for myself. She won't let me sink into a depression again.

I smile grimly, sigh, and continue the arduous task of survival.

CHAPTER 29

Tutoring jobs start to dry up. No one has any money or food to pay with, so education falls by the wayside. One by one I lose my students, and start asking my friends for any leads to a new job. "Anything!" I tell them. "I'm desperate!"

But everyone is desperate, and for a long time I can't find work.

I remember when I was a little girl in my father's home village of Šumatac, I saw so many wild animals—all the birds and bunnies and voles and deer—but I never once saw a dead wild animal. Not so much as a sparrow. When I asked my parents they told me that wild animals, when they feel the end is near, find some peaceful, out-of-the-way place. They hide their sickness, their illness, as long as possible and then they find a quiet place to die.

I feel like all Bihać is like that now. We struggled. We hid our pain and suffering, tried to appear strong. But now, for me at least, the end feels very near, and all I want to do is curl up in some still place, under a flowering hedge, and surrender.

I never imagined we could suffer so long. How is it that no one has helped us?

I am at the end of my rope when finally my friend Ifeta tells me she heard a rumor—just a whisper, no more than that—about the International Rescue Committee needing a translator. But she has no idea which government office might be coordinating it, or indeed if the job is still open.

So I begin what I'm sure must be a wild-goose chase, going from building to building, asking if anyone knows about the position. My best bet is in the government building, but there are so many offices there and no one knows what is going on. The government is in a constant state of disorder and confusion. We are forced to operate as a stand-alone entity. Bihać is cut off from Sarajevo, and it is one of a few cities that haven't fallen into Serbs' hands, yet. Even in the best times there is a massive bureaucracy. It is a Bosnian joke that if you shout out, "Excuse me, Minister!" on any public street at least half of the people will turn around, thinking you are calling them.

I find the office of the Minister of Health, which seems like a possible option. I poke my head into an open door with a friendly smile on my face and say, "Good afternoon!" to the man sitting behind the desk.

He scowls at me and barks, "It's salam alejkum or you leave."

I'm so taken aback that I lose the politeness I usually show my seniors and snap back, "It is good afternoon or nothing, so I'll leave!"

Outside in the corridor I'm trembling with agitation. Our country is not supposed to be like this. We're Muslims, yes, but we have always been free to personally decide the extent of our religiosity. We define ourselves as Bosnians first, Muslims second.

But the Serbs don't. To them, we are Muslims first, last, always. And now my own people are responding by behaving exactly as the Serbs expect us to. In a way it is understandable—we want to embrace our religious identity now that we can. But our identity as Muslims was always flexible. The Serbs think we are all one kind of backward Muslims. This man trying to force me to be overtly religious feels like playing right into Serb propaganda.

(I do think it's funny, though, that our Fifth Corps soldiers will leverage Serb fear of Muslims to use against them. The soldiers may be non-practicing Muslims, but that doesn't stop commanders from shouting, "Tekbir!" and soldiers all screaming, "Allahu Akbar!" when they charge into battle, because they've seen how it frightens the Serbs!)

Never, never in my life did a fellow Muslim judge me for my faith or how I expressed it. Now this man is telling me I can't speak to him unless I begin with a traditional religious greeting? What's next? Is he going to make me cover my face and hair?

This is not what we're fighting for.

Torn between tears and fury, I'm thinking about going home when I hear the most beautiful sound—someone speaking English down the hallway!

I run toward them and burst into the room they've just entered. "Do you need a translator?" I ask the two men breathlessly, then smile when I realize I'm speaking Bosnian. Not a very good way to show off my skills! I switch to English, and though my speech is halting I choose the simplest sentences and get my point across.

These two men, young and strong, their faces ruddy with health, are a reminder of how people should be. They are well-fed. Their faces aren't lined with constant worry.

"I'm Wayne," the shorter one says, holding out his hand. He looks like a hippie, or the way I imagine a hippie looks. Another era, another country. He has a long black beard, but somehow it doesn't remind me of a Četnik beard at all. Wayne's beard looks like it should have flowers woven through it.

"I'm Amra," I say, feeling a little giddy, a little dizzy, though this might be more from lack of food than from meeting Americans.

The other man introduces himself as Drew. He's tall and nerdy with blond hair. I can't help thinking what a nice, sweet boyfriend he would make for some intellectual American girl.

"We're child psychologists," Wayne says. "We're trying to see what the war is doing to kids, to their education, to their emotions and brains."

"Well," Drew breaks in, "we know what it does, really. Who doesn't? But we have to document it, prove it. Once we take what we find back to the IRC, they'll be more willing to help after the war is over."

"If the war is ever over," I say in English.

They look sadly at each other. "I don't know why NATO hasn't done anything," Wayne says. "I'm sorry."

"It's not your fault," I tell him. "Maybe once you tell them what the children are suffering it will make a difference."

They hire me, just for the few days they'll be in Bihać, but for more money than anyone local can pay. A fortune that will get us through a few weeks if we're lucky. They want to visit schools first, so I take them to my old school. My former teachers are welcoming and helpful, though a little confused about what these two kind, soft American men can do to help them. The students answer their questions, but there is an air of hopelessness to everything they say. I translate as best I can, but I know my rudimentary English is only catching half of the disappointment and fear and desperation the younger students feel.

At last, toward the end of the day, we pay a final visit to Teacher Živko, my science teacher. He looks the same, with his puff of unruly hair, but he's thin as a matchstick now. He answers some of their questions, then breaks off almost angrily.

"You can't save them!" he says. "This whole generation—it's broken, ruined. What is there for them?" He pushes up his spectacles and wipes his eyes. "Their world is ended."

Then he points to me. "You can't save them, but you can save her."

Drew and Wayne look at me.

"She is one of the best and brightest. The most clever student I ever had the pleasure of teaching. She should be in medical school or winning a Nobel Prize in physics. Do you know, she came in first in physics in the entire region? First! And third in math. She is in the top ten of all students in the country!"

I stumble over the words and blush as Živko heaps this praise on me.

"And yet she may very well die of starvation or infection," he goes on. "Is this the Middle Ages? Or at any moment a bomb might drop on her head. She is one of the people who can change the world, and yet she has nothing but death to look forward to!"

The Americans scribble frantic notes, then we leave.

"Would you like to go to America to study?" Wayne asks me before we part for the day.

I just laugh. "What I'd really like is bright-red hair dye!" I say. "Why wish for the impossible? America is impossible. Well, red hair dye is impossible. I'd settle for blond, or pink, or blue—anything dramatic and exciting. Though honestly I'd be happy just to have a nice shampoo."

I'm making conversation, not asking for anything. These are kids from America, privileged and well-meaning, but what can they do? They are like tourists. They can glimpse our misery and then head home to their safe, comfortable lives.

"Why don't you give us your transcripts anyway," Wayne says casually. I bring them my only copies. After all, they're not doing me any good here. I know there's nothing they can do. They're just being nice.

I work with them for several days. When they leave to visit another part of Bosnia they want to take me, but it is too dangerous. They can pass Serb checkpoints, but if I tried that I'd just disappear.

They pay me with a hundred German marks—the first such bill I've earned, or seen. When I take it home that night my family and I sit and stare at that magic money, that can buy us things like oil or salt. Not much of either—perhaps a bottle of oil or a kilo of salt. But still, it is more than I've earned since the war began. Even Maci comes to sniff the exotic bill. I wonder if her sensitive nose can smell all the hands this money has passed through on its long, strange journey to us?

When Drew and Wayne say goodbye at their hotel, they give me a newspaper from Croatia. I haven't seen a newspaper in four years! But when I skim the front page, I read about our war from an outsider's eyes. We are not in our own bubble. The world sees it. They could pop that bubble at any time. But they don't.

Their next farewell gift saves me from the tears of self-pity I'm about to shed. With amazement, I accept a bright-pink bottle. Shampoo! I open it and take a deep sniff. Coconut!

"We can't take you, but we can make introductions," Wayne says as they're leaving. Then they take me to another room in the hotel where a new foreigner has just arrived—a Colombian doctor who is spearheading a medical and immunization program. They praise my work as a translator and my cleverness and initiative. The jet-lagged doctor agrees to hire me on the spot, I think more from tiredness than anything else. In the face of these exuberant Americans it is easiest to say yes.

I hug Drew and Wayne goodbye, thinking that though I'll never see or hear from them again, they are another bright spot in my life.

As soon as I get home I shampoo my hair. I smell so sweet I'm surprised all the bees in Bihać aren't following me!

1995
SUMMER

CHAPTER 30

My new job with the International Medical Corps is a godsend. It pays well, and is steady, reliable work. The doctor coordinating medical relief for children is amiable and earnest, with a real desire to help. He's a young doctor, too, and I think he had an idea that it would be a glamorous, exciting adventure to work in a war zone. He's quickly disabused of that notion. One day I catch him weeping silently, and when I ask what's wrong he tells me about a child brought into the clinic. He's mostly there to train local nurses to give vaccinations. Any person brought to the field clinics is supposed to be sent on to a hospital. But it was too late for this little girl. She had minor shrapnel wounds from a mine—a mine that killed her mother and older brother. With no medical aid, her wounds became infected and she died too, in horrible agony, right before his eyes. There was nothing he could do to save her.

But he wipes his tears and carries on, just like the rest of us.

The only difference is, when it gets to be too much for him, he can quit. He can leave.

But he doesn't, and I help him coordinate a vaccination program for children throughout the Bihać pocket. There are many areas we can't reach, those in Serb control, but we go where we can.

After working with the IMC team for several weeks, I find myself alone in the office early one morning. The pre-dawn hours are often the safest. Even hateful enemy soldiers don't like waking up early to start their artillery attacks. Mostly they wait for later morning or early evening, when more people are going to work, school (though few are doing either), or leaving the relative safety of their homes or basements to socialize before they go stir-crazy.

I'm catching up on some paperwork, tidying when suddenly the doors fly open as violently as if they were blown open by an explosion. Two soldiers come in, their guns out. When they point them at me I'm sure they are Serbs. This is it! They've broken through our defenses and now they're swarming through the city. I'll be sent to a rape camp. My family will be killed . . .

I think this all in an instant as I cringe in the corner behind my desk. Then I see the winged stallion emblem on their uniforms. These men are in the Fifth Corps—our own soldiers!

"What do you want? I'm Bosnian—I'm Muslim!" I tell them.

"Give us your pink pens!" one of them barks.

I swear I almost laugh. Am I dreaming?

I just stare at them in disbelief.

"Pink pens, yellow pens!" he says. "Any highlighter markers you have."

Is he insane? Drunk? He doesn't look it. He looks deadly serious.

"I can't give you any office supplies because they aren't mine to give," I tell them as calmly as I can. I feel like if I can maintain my composure this surreal scene might start to make sense. "Everything here belongs to the International Medical Corps and UNICEF."

He points his handgun in my face, just as if I were an enemy Serb soldier. "You don't need to give us anything. You have no choice, we're commandeering them." He holds me at bay—as if I were going to resist him—while the other soldier rifles through the drawers until he finds a few bright highlighters. He pockets the pens, and both of them holster their handguns.

"Thank you for your contribution to the war effort," he says sardonically as they back out, keeping their eyes on me all the time. What do they expect me to do, tackle armed soldiers to wrestle the pens back?

When they leave, I sit down heavily in a swivel chair. I don't move until the first medical worker comes in a quarter hour later. I don't even tell him what happened. I don't know if I believe it myself.

Was it a joke? Are our soldiers having a scavenger hunt to pass the time?

How could a highlighter pen possibly help fight a war?

I don't tell my family about it when I get home either. They don't need to worry anymore. We enjoy a nice meal of green beans and tomatoes from our garden, and some kind of salty canned meat from an aid delivery. Dino tells a tragicomic story of how his day of swimming was cut short. He has a pair of Hugo Boss swimming trunks that our cousin Žana gave him before the war. We never have brand-name things, so these trunks, black with bright green lettering, make him feel like Superman, the envy of every other teen boy, admired by every teen girl.

Today, he was showing off with an impressive jackknife dive, where he leaps high in the air, folds his body quickly in half, then straightens out for the dive.

"As I folded, my bathing suit unfolded behind me," he says, blushing. "Everything I have was on display!"

"Oh, you have nothing to be embarrassed about," our straightforward Mama tells him. "If anything, I'm sure you gave those girls a treat."

After dinner she takes up her sewing kit and tries to repair the precious swim trunks, but the material is too worn. They are another casualty of the war.

I'm sitting up late by a kerosene lantern, looking up medical words in English to help with my work, when there's a knock at the door.

"I'll get it!" I call, assuming it is a neighbor who needs to borrow something, or who is passing on some news. Secretly in my heart I hope it is Davor, whom I haven't seen for a few weeks. He's managed to send me a note twice, delivered by a friend. Maybe even if this isn't Davor, at least it is a message of love from him.

I fling open the door, and find two soldiers. They're not the same ones that came to the office this morning, but they too have the Fifth Corps flying horse on their jackets.

"What do you want this time, my paper clips?" I ask them.

They ignore my quip and ask, "Are you Amra Šabić?"

I nod, wondering what this could possibly be about. I've done nothing wrong, but seeing these soldiers here makes me think I'm about to be dragged away.

Tata comes up behind me. "What's this all about, soldiers?"

"We understand you were recently issued a passport." The soldier holds out his hand. "We need it. Now."

At least he's not pointing a gun in my face. Yet.

Tata isn't going to let them get away with it that easily. "Which unit are you with? You have no reason to confiscate my daughter's passport. She's done nothing wrong! In fact, she was selected for a scholarship. It has been, er, delayed, but she'll need her passport to continue her studies."

The soldiers are polite but adamant. "Go get her passport, sir. We won't leave without it."

I don't want this to get any worse, so I run up to my room, where I have my passport tucked away in a drawer.

"How could they do that?" Tata asks after they leave.

"What does it matter, Tata?" I say. "I was never going to be able to use it anyway. It was a souvenir of a dream."

All the same, I go to bed deeply troubled. With soldiers in my office and in my very home, this horrible war seems closer than ever.

Early the next morning we hear a frantic shouting from the street.

Sure of disaster, we all run out. Our neighbor Binka is running through the streets, shouting something about Grabež.

"Not again," Tata sighs. At least five times in the last year Binka has heard or dreamed some false story of good news. Each time she says the war is over. Each time she has been wrong.

I go out to talk with her, and she grabs me by the arms, looking at me through her huge glasses. "The siege is over! The siege is over!" She's dancing, shaking my arms up and down.

I smile weakly. Another false report. What she says is impossible. The Serbs have a stronghold above the city. It's fortified with many guns and soldiers. So many of our own boys have lost their lives there. It's too well defended for us to have a hope of capturing. All we can do is harry and harass them.

I tell my parents, who sigh and shake their heads. But to humor her, Dino hooks up our radio to the car battery.

First there is nothing but static. Then we find the right frequency.

The siege is over! Or in any event, close enough! Our fighters are punching through on all sides, sending the Serbs scattering, and now they're pushing on toward Banja Luka, the Serb stronghold where their leaders are orchestrating our genocide. They're also moving into the Serb-controlled areas of Croatia.

It makes sense now. The surreal demand for highlighter markers? Surely they were used in the war room as our generals marked maps, highlighting routes of our Fifth Corps' planned assault. In this besieged area the army wouldn't have something as simple and vital as office supplies, so they had to raid international aid organizations.

And as for my passport, of course if we have pushed through there will be Serbs now trapped on our side, war criminals who might try to flee under a stolen or purchased Bosnian Muslim passport. It makes complete sense that they would collect every passport right before launching such an all-out attack.

Those encounters that frightened me so much yesterday were the signs of something marvelous if only I'd been able to read the clues!

I have to shout the news to Mama. She staggers into the other room, and I hear such a terrible cry. It sounds like it is torn from her lips, like some clawed hand has reached deep inside of her and ripped that savage sound out. She made a sound like that when Amar died. Maci runs in, sure that her beloved family is under attack.

But this sound is not grief. It is an uncontrollable, animalistic release of years of accumulated pain. Everything she had been holding in so stoically for four years—all that suffering and fury and frustration—is released into the universe.

And when she is quiet again, I can see the light of hope in her eyes.

CHAPTER 31

There is a new air of enthusiasm in Bihać. Before we were like dogs clinging to a dried bone, snarling and determined to hold on to the barest scraps. Now we have real hope. We are fighters with a real chance at freedom.

There's a new flurry of activity in the city. We're not safe yet, but with the siege broken, most of the mountainside artillery fire has ceased. Suddenly the streets are filled with people eager for sunshine and gossip. There is a sense of anticipation. Will Bosnia be Bosnia again? Will we be free? Is it possible to ever again have peace? Can we forget? Should we forgive but never forget?

It is full summer, and the weather seems to be giving us a special blessing. Under cloudless skies we gather by the banks of the Una while a seemingly benevolent sun watches over us.

The happiness is premature, I know. Horrible things are still happening. But with the tides of war turning and a bit of money coming in, my whole family is more sanguine.

And our little store is thriving! I laugh to say this, comparing it with even the most meager markets before the war. But all three of our shelves are filled with merchandise. And people are more willing to spend. Just a few weeks ago everyone in Bihać had been wondering how we'd ever survive one more winter.

Now, with an end in sight, people are more willing to spend their carefully hoarded money. Even better, money can come in from other countries. Nearly everyone in Bosnia has a relative who left to work in

Germany or Austria before the war. People had tried to send money before, but of course the Serbs intercepted it. Now money is flowing in. People aren't hoarding it either. Once, they'd believed it might have to last for another year or two. Now, maybe, the war could be over in months.

And then our hopes rise even higher. NATO has begun air strikes against the Serbs.

My cynical friend Nura says that NATO didn't care how long the war lasted as long as the Serbs were winning. But once there is a chance that Muslims might win, they step right in with their planes and missiles.

"They see that the Serbs are monsters," Nura says. "All the same, the idea of Muslims taking more territory in Europe terrifies them. They will graciously allow us to live, and have a bit of territory, but isn't it suspicious that they step in right when there's a danger we actually drive the Serbs completely back and might even claim more land?"

I don't know if she has a point. I'm just glad that the world has finally stepped in to end the atrocities.

But wars aren't over in a day.

I wind up working with my friend Samir. He went to my high school, but was a first-year engineering student when the war started. He drives the jeep while I act as interpreter and general facilitator to foreign doctors trying to understand our ways. After the Muslim victories and the NATO intervention, we start traveling farther and farther from Bihać. As we move into newly liberated areas we see frightful things. The refuse of human lives is strewn along the roadside. Shoes and clothes are tumbled and muddy, making me wonder what happened to the owners. Then, as we drive on, I have to turn my head away. What I first think is another pile of clothes is actually a body curled in the weeds. I can't tell if it is a man or a woman; the darkened flesh has shrunken, clinging to the bones.

When I see things like this, my optimism ends. Maybe the war will end for me (though there are still snipers and mines all along our route), but for that person abandoned in the weeds and dust no cease-fire will ever matter.

When we come into the town of Sanski Most we find burned-out cars, demolished houses. Those that still stand bear spray paint signs that make me know how much I am hated. Left for any traumatized survivors is yet another trauma. Scribbled by Serbs as they retreated are threats of death and rape. They call us Turks—referring to our origins when Turks brought Islam here centuries ago. "Get out of Greater Serbia, balije!" those signs shout.

To my amazement, there are people in these devastated little villages. They must have been hiding in the countryside all this time. Now there are hollow-eyed children peeking from the doorways. They are gaunt and scabbed. Some of the tiniest haven't seen a doctor their entire lives. The Colombian doctor with us says that as an intern he saw terrible things in the ravaged villages of his home country, victims of drug wars. But never had he imagined anything like this.

He gives a shot to a little boy about four, the age when a child should wail at a sudden jab. But the boy just looks at him with stoic, enduring eyes, and I realize that this tiny pain is probably the least traumatic of his life. Compared to what he has suffered, it doesn't even register. The doctor touches his head, asks if he's all right. The boy says nothing, but chunks of his hair fall out under the doctor's fingers. Malnutrition, the doctor tells me.

———————

Back at home I bask in my family, so grateful that we've survived this long. There are many cousins we haven't heard from. Maybe soon when more roads open up, more telephone lines are connected, we'll get some news of them. For now I'm just glad that Tata, Mama, and Dino are still with me.

And of course Maci!

Everyone for blocks around comes in to buy something, even if it is just a bit of honey or a scoop of flour out of our bag. Maci greets each person as if she is the ambassador.

"Good morning, little Maci," Erza says as she comes in for a handful of beans to eke out their dinner. "Have you been keeping the mice away, you good little kitty?" Maci mews in answer, and allows Erza to pat her before continuing her rounds of the yard.

"She's such a polite creature," Erza says admiringly to Mama (who nods as if she understands, but though she can't hear she catches Erza's meaning). "Other cats I know would knock all the merchandise off and sleep on the shelves."

"Not our Maci," Tata says proudly. "She comes and goes just like a person. And like a person, she's completely respectful. She never bothers the food." Of course we don't have an actual separate shop, but we have that section divided from the rest of the house. Maci understands that area is not where she should play. She is just the soft and friendly ambassador.

Children come specifically to visit her. People without money to spend stop in to peruse our merchandise but mostly, I think, for a chance to see Maci. Before long everyone in the neighborhood is getting comfort from our little cat friend.

She has become a symbol of normal life for all of us.

Davor manages to pay me a flying visit, turning up covered in dirt and mud but with a special chocolate bar for me. I can't believe it. I haven't seen chocolate in years! I remember diving, racing after that candy wrapper in the Una. That was the last time I had any hopes of chocolate. I want to gobble it up, but I save it to share with my family. (Realistically, only with Dino. I'll offer some to Mama and Tata, but even if their mouths water, they'll turn it down. That's how parents are.)

"We're not just moving into the Serb side," Davor tells me after sneaking a kiss. "The Fifth Corps is taking land that the Serbs had held on the Croat side." The Croats have been fighting the Serbs too. "We met up with some of the Croat soldiers, and our commander told our cooks to make the very best bean stew to impress them, so they'd know we are powerful and not starved. Well, these Croats come over with these high-calorie MREs—meals ready to eat, you know—and they look like buff models compared to our army full of scarecrows. They even had dessert with every meal!"

We share stories of the devastated villages we've seen. "I was busy with all the animals that were left behind. Cows, sheep, dogs, just abandoned. Once we made headway the Serbs were desperate to escape. They are afraid of what we'll do to them in revenge for genocide. They left cars full of petrol, even tanks, still armed! The Fifth Corps just climbs in and takes them over."

One day, his group found a pig foraging through the refuse of an abandoned town. "We had many Croat soldiers with us, who of course eat pork, and many of the others do too—especially when there's not much else to eat." Davor himself is half Croatian with a Catholic mother. We celebrated Christmas and all her holidays throughout the war. "Since I'm the animal expert I was charged with slaughtering the pig, something I never, ever want to do again. It is like a doctor being put in charge of a firing squad, just because he knows where the vital organs are!"

"It must have been horrible," I say with sympathy.

"You don't know the half of it! When we butchered the pig to roast it, we found . . ." He gulps hard. "We found human fingers in its stomach. One of them was wearing a gold wedding band. None of us could eat. I don't think I'll ever eat pork again. We buried the fingers, and because we weren't sure what else to do, we buried the pig too. The ring we wrapped in a piece of paper, marked with the name of the village where we found it. Maybe someday we can find family of whoever . . ."

He breaks down then, and I just hold him.

It would be nice if we could just flip a switch and end this war. But even as we start to win, even as NATO helps defeat the Serbs, people are still getting shot, massacred. Along the outskirts of the Bihać pocket, and in places where the Serbs still hold territory, we are always at risk. Bombs still fall occasionally near Bihać, launched from some last Serb stronghold.

In early fall, though, I get a surprise. A UN soldier comes into my office, asking for me by name. He slips me a big unmarked envelope that is stuffed with something lumpy and rectangular, and he leaves before I can ask any questions. Curious and more than a little nervous, I carefully open the envelope (thinking I might reuse it later, paper still being so scarce).

Inside I find a cheerful neon green and pink postcard with a picture of Barbie on it. "What color hair should I have?" she asks in a speech bubble.

I reach into the envelope again and pull out a box of the brightest red hair dye I can imagine!

Within an hour of getting home, I'm sashaying down the street so all the neighbors can see my wild scarlet hair. Mama and my aunts are redheads, but what really inspired me was Julia Roberts in *Pretty Woman*. I watched it at Tetka Fatma's house on the rare days she had electricity.

Now I finally have red hair myself. Even if the Serbs kill me, at least I'll die with dye!

———

You would think that once things got just a little better, just a little safer, that people would breathe a sigh of relief and focus on rebuilding their lives. There are many who are still starving, sick. The infrastructure is in shambles, the education system at a virtual standstill. There is so much to do.

And yet, the first thing to rebuild out of the wreckage is the bureaucracy.

Stuck here, with only the dimmest light in the future, my family is trying to make the best of a bad situation. With all other prospects gone, we try at least to make a success of our little store. It is the only thing we have left, so we put all our energy into it.

Then very early one morning, while Dino is still sleeping and Mama and Tata have gone out to tend the garden, someone barges into the house. At first I think he's a burglar, because he starts to go through the rooms like he owns the place.

Maci, who is at my feet as I rearrange small bags of flour on the store shelves, feels my fear and stands between us, hissing at him as he comes near.

"This is the store?" he asks, looking around. We've expanded from three shelves to three shelves and a table. "Not much."

"We're not open yet, sir," I tell him, resenting his rudeness. "You can come back in an hour." For a neighbor we'd open at any time if they needed something, but not for this man.

"What is that dirty animal doing in here?"

"She's not dirty!" I object.

He ignores me, looking over the meager—but gradually increasing—store of goods we have for sale. "Where is this honey from? Is it pasteurized?"

"Honey doesn't need to be," I tell him. "It's pure sugar, no bacteria can grow in it."

"Hmm," he says, and pulls out a notebook.

"May I ask who you are?" I stand with my arms crossed, glaring at him.

"I'm the Deputy Inspector of Commerce, here to inspect your store. I've counted three violations so far. Improper labeling for one. Each item must be clearly labeled, with a description and price. Otherwise you will take advantage of customers, charging whatever you like."

"We would never!" We charge less than things are worth half the time, because Tata is soft, and because most of the customers are our friends. Maci makes a low yowling sound, baring her teeth at the intruder. He kicks in her direction, but she's out of reach. I pick her up, soothing her as she wiggles and tries to escape. I'm afraid she'll attack him. Little Maci, who loves everyone, clearly despises this man.

"And then where are your receipts of purchase?" he asks. "How can I know that you didn't steal these goods from a relief convoy, or trade with the enemy?"

I would like to tell him that trading with the enemy is the only thing that kept Bihać from starving all these years. Shut off completely from the outside world, where else were we to get our food except from our enemies, who not only killed us but got rich from our desperation? Did this man just fall from the moon? How could he not know how we all survived? Does he think I went to the magical warehouse and bought all these things?

But before I can answer he says, "And the last thing, the worst thing—this dirty cat right here in the same room where you have all your foodstuffs. Do you realize how many diseases this mangy animal might be carrying? You could start an epidemic!"

"This cat is cleaner than you!" I snap. It's true. This supposed deputy inspector has dirt under his fingernails and in the creases of his neck. Maci cleans herself fastidiously many times each day, and even in the worst of the war her fur is always impeccable.

He scowls at me, then tears off a sheet of paper. "This is the preliminary report. I advise you to address these issues before my next inspection or you'll be charged a considerable fine. If you get cited three times, I'll close your shop down for good!"

He slaps his notebook closed and turns on his heel. Maci glares after him, lashing her tail.

I'm still shaking and indignant when Tata and Mama come home. When I show them the warning they exchange looks. "I know this man," Tata says, reading the inspector's signature. "He was a low-level worker when I was with the party. I remember he got expelled for corruption."

"And you probably testified against him?" Mama guesses.

"What could I do? They asked how much money should be in the account, who had access to it. I didn't turn him in, I only answered questions in the investigation. But I'm sure he knows I had a part in his firing."

"And now he's hired again," Mama says. "Now the rats have power while lions like you suffer. I don't think we've seen the last of this inspector."

We do what we can to correct the supposed violations. We create makeshift labels with prices. Tata dons glasses that no longer do him any good and painfully records every purchase.

And we tell Maci that she can no longer come in the store at all.

But the store is just a corner of the living room. Maci has had the run of the inside and the outside since she moved here. The door is always open—and the windows are blown open by bombs! She can get into the house through any balcony, and she always goes wherever she likes. She never jumps on any shelf or table. She never bothers the food. She's such a perfect lady that no matter how hungry she gets, she would never steal food. She'll only take it if we deliberately offer it to her.

We try to keep her out, but she loves meeting the customers so much that she follows them in, greeting them with her pretty meows as if she's making suggestions about what to buy. No one has complained—everyone loves her!

No cat hair has even gotten in any of the food. And even if it did, we had to worry about Serbs lacing our food with rat poison! I don't think anyone would care at all about a cat hair in their beans. We're just happy to have food at all.

When the inspector comes again, he's on the heels of Erza, one of Maci's favorite customers. We've kept Maci out when we can, but of course now she's rubbing affectionately against Erza's ankles as she picks out a small jar of honey.

"Did you think I was joking?" he fumes at Tata. "Do you think I'll let this disgusting place stay open a minute longer with that cat in here? I'm fining you a thousand German marks and shutting down your store for a week."

He scribbles out a citation and slams it on the table, then storms out before Tata can object, before Mama has even figured out what is going on. When we shout the news to her she says that Tata can go to the Ministry of Commerce and get it fixed. But when he does, he comes back dejected. The fine has been waived, but they won't let him reopen the shop, and they won't assign a different inspector. With no real laws post-war, these petty bureaucrats can use any excuse to get a little extra money in the form of fines or bribes.

"Just get rid of the cat," they say, as if it is nothing, as if Maci isn't a member of the family.

"We have no choice," Tata says as the week of punishment draws to a close. "Our family can't survive without the store. We have to get rid of Maci."

"Tata, no! She's more than just a cat! You say we can't survive without the store? Well, we wouldn't have survived the war without Maci! You know that! She saved Dino from the bomb, she saved me from certain death. I would have died of depression if not for her. You can no more get rid of Maci than you can get rid of me!"

Tata doesn't argue. But when I get up the next morning he's gone. So is Maci.

"Where are they?" I demand angrily of Mama. This time I'd be shouting anyway, even if she weren't nearly deaf.

"Your father is driving Maci to the bee farm," she says. She sounds as stoic as ever, but I can see the pain in her eyes. The woman who hates mess, who never wanted a pet, has grown to love our Maci as much as the rest of us. "We have no other choice."

"There is always another choice!" I rage.

But it is too late. My Maci is gone.

CHAPTER 32

I never should have worried. How could I have doubted my Maci? She is the most brilliant, resourceful cat on the planet. She knows the route home from the bee farm now, and she comes back in half the time. She's thinner and footsore, but when she comes to the door just a couple of mornings later meowing for me, she acts like there's nothing unusual. I squeeze her in such a tight hug that she wiggles away and jumps down. But as soon as I sit she's snuggled in my lap.

"What must you think of us, Maci, taking you so far away and leaving you all alone!" I weep tears of joy into her fur. And I wonder, does she really understand? Maybe she just thinks that we're very careless, leaving her at the bee farm twice.

"I owe you an explanation, Maci," I tell her as I stroke her under the chin. She raises her head to better enjoy it, her eyes closed in bliss. "You're part of the family, and you need to know why Tata took you away. You need to know how serious this is."

And so I explain it to her as if she were a person—how important the store is to us, how the petty bureaucrat's inspections put our livelihood in peril. "You can stay. Of course you can stay. I promise I won't let Tata take you away again. But you have to stay out of the store!"

In all ways she is a perfectly behaved cat. The only problem is, she loves us and thinks she's a person. Where we go, she wants to go. If we had a separate store we could keep her away, but with the store right in the living room, there's no real way to keep her permanently out. Even if we banish her outside she'll wait by the door and slip in with each customer. Then she'll sit politely beside Mama or Tata like she is a little inspector herself, making sure everything runs smoothly. She never touches the merchandise, never bothers customers if they don't make eye contact and smile at her.

Word soon gets out about the neighborhood mascot's return, and the neighbors flock by to welcome her, to praise her . . . and to buy a little something while they're here. Her return inspires a neighborhood celebration, an impromptu party. After our dark years we are all ready to embrace happiness. Neighbors and customers come with coffee, desserts, all the little delectables we've been deprived of for so long. Children are singing, calling out to Maci with meows. She answers them all lovingly, knowing she's the center of attention.

The only customer who frowns at her isn't really a customer at all. Our neighbor Zumra has a store, too. Zumra's store, which is the entire first floor of her home, has expanded, and almost as soon as the bombing stopped she not only repaired her shattered windows but even began improvements, replacing the roof, adding a room out back. I see trucks bring her new appliances as soon as the electricity is back on. Zumra had been one of the people in charge of distributing humanitarian aid during the war. Our family only ever got two or three boxes of aid throughout the entire war. I'd assumed most of it was stopped and confiscated by Serbs, but now that I see Zumra's apparent post-war wealth I wonder if she wasn't doing the same as Ilma—selling the help meant for others. One spoonful of flour for humanitarian aid, one spoonful for herself to sell on the black market.

Her shop looks like an actual store, well stocked and neat.

And yet, people love visiting our tiny store much more. Part of that is because we are frankly nicer people. We are family to everyone who comes.

Part of the reason is Maci.

If people came to see her before the inspector banished her, now they flock to visit her even after her homecoming day. Children grab their mothers' hands and drag them away from Zumra's shop. "I want the kitty store!" they shriek, and they won't be satisfied until they can see Maci pounce on a piece of string or gingerly touch her soft belly while she stretches.

Zumra sometimes walks by our shop with one of her cronies named Šefika. Mama invites them in, but they turn up their noses. Šefika is always critical of Mama and Tata's loving relationship. When she sees them holding hands, she'll sneeringly ask, "Are you teenagers?" I remember Šefika once saying she and her husband have separate bedrooms. This astonishes me. One of my earliest memories is of running into my parents' bedroom and seeing them resting on the bed, Mama's head on Tata's shoulder, reading the same book.

We're pleasant to Zumra. I know she resents that we take any of her customers away, even if she's making far more money than we are.

Once, coming in without us noticing, she finds Maci snoozing on the orange-and-white-swirled carpet. "Ugh, what is that thing doing so near the food?" Her lip curls, and before anyone can stop her, she kicks Maci!

Luckily Maci was only half asleep. She leaps away at the last second and runs to the corner, arching her back and hissing, puffed up to twice her normal size. "It should be put down! Stray cats are a menace."

"If you're not going to buy anything, make room for paying customers," I snap at her.

Tata frowns at me in disapproval.

"I know, be courteous to everyone," I sigh when she leaves. "But not everyone deserves courtesy!"

Our store flourishes. Money is flowing freely into the city now, and everyone has German marks to spend. The inspector comes back twice, but luckily Maci is out by the river hunting.

"I know that animal is back," he growls at Tata. "You're fined fifty marks for inadequate recordkeeping. But if I catch that vermin in the store I'm fining you a thousand marks and shutting you down!"

He takes his fine and leaves in a huff. I wonder if his office is ever going to see those fifty marks or if they will just live in his own pocket.

We risked our lives for years, I think as I watch him leave. Many of us gave our lives. Many who survived are so broken in body or in mind that they might just as well be dead. And yet in war or in peace there will always be people like the inspector or Zumra, thinking only of themselves, who put profit before people.

Just then, as if she were waiting for him to leave (and I wouldn't put it past her) Maci saunters out from under the peony bush. I sit down beside her.

"I need to do something," I tell her as she looks at me with her bonfire eyes. "Tata and Mama . . . they've gotten so old! They were a young, happy couple when the war began. They had their sorrows, their struggles, but they were strong. Now they are barely holding on. Mama is deaf, Tata is so ill, though he tries to hide it. Dino is just a boy, though he pretends to be a man." I sigh, stroking her rhythmically. "There's just me."

Only today at work I heard from Samir that the first bus from Bihać to Sarajevo would be running soon. His cousin is the bus owner and driver. There aren't public buses, city buses—rather they are private companies that run whenever they can get petrol, and when they calculate that the risk will be worth the reward. Now that NATO air strikes and strong Fifth Corps resistance has quelled the Serbs in most regions, the roads are opening up.

But it won't be safe. Oh, nothing like safe! There are still pockets of Serbs, holdouts bent on slaughter, all the more vicious for being beaten and desperate. There are mines on the roads, snipers hidden in the tree line. A trip to the newly liberated Sarajevo will be twenty-four hours, maybe more, of constant danger.

But I decide that when that first bus departs, I'll be on it.

Sarajevo is the capital, with more schools, more jobs, more opportunities. There's a medical school there. I love math and science, but I don't want to do anything that's purely scholarly. I don't want to be alone in a room thinking for a living, even if I'm thinking about equations that explain the universe. I need to do something that helps people. After working with the doctor and nurses on the immunization project, I think I see a clear path ahead of me.

I'll go to Sarajevo and become a doctor. That will give me a reliable way to support my family and also help my country. And if we should ever have to leave Bosnia, the skills I learn will be just as vital elsewhere. Doctors are needed everywhere.

Of course, going to medical school takes money. "But I'll find a job there," I tell Maci. "I can tutor or work with aid agencies—anything! There are many more opportunities in Sarajevo, so I can pay for my schooling and send money home."

Maci looks up at me questioningly.

"No, I haven't gotten accepted yet. I'll be going there blind, throwing myself on the college steps and asking them to take me in." She purrs and rolls trustingly on her back in my lap so I can tickle the white fluff of her tummy.

I don't want to sound arrogant or too confident, but I think with my grades and experience I have a good chance of getting into the medical school. Once my cousin Azra thought about going to medical school and was working on the practice test for the entrance exam. I helped her, and found I could do all of the math and science questions in my head. I think with a little review I could breeze through it now. Even if I don't this year, there's next year, and in the meantime I can work in Sarajevo and send money home. Then Tata and Mama won't have to rely on the store. Dino can focus on finishing school instead of working to help make ends meet.

And my darling Maci will never have to be sent away again.

Maybe I can even take her with me to Sarajevo! I think if she's with me she won't try to go back to Bihać.

I go to work that next day with renewed vigor, noticing everything the medical staff is doing, asking more questions than ever. And I ask Samir to let me know the moment the bus to Sarajevo is scheduled. I'll only have a day's warning at best.

"It's for a friend," I tell him. I don't want it getting back to my parents that I'm planning to leave. They'll worry about my safety, they'll try to talk me out of it. I want to tell them one day and leave the next.

I go home so happy with my new plan. I'm nervous but excited too. I'd always rather be doing something, even if it is scary, than doing nothing. This gives me a project, a prospect—something to hope and plan for. I think more and more about taking Maci with me. Not only will that keep her safe from the inspector, but that way I'll have my best friend with me.

I'm singing as I walk down my block. "Maci!" I call between verses, thinking she'll come bounding out of the grass. But she must be closer to the house, or inside.

My smile fades when I find a sign posted on the front door: Closed By Order of the Ministry of Commerce.

Mama and Dino sit at the dining table with sorrowful faces.

"The inspector came again," Mama says. "Someone reported that Maci had been in the store. They said she was . . . defecating."

"That's nonsense. Why, in all the time I've known Maci I've never once seen her go to the bathroom! She goes far from the house to do that. Who said it?"

Mama can't quite hear me, but Dino answers. "He wouldn't say, but I bet it was Zumra."

"Where is Tata? I have an idea how to fix the Maci problem." I didn't want to tell them about my plans for Sarajevo, but if I can let Tata know that I can take Maci away within a few days, maybe he can tell them at the ministry and open the store again.

But Dino looks up at me with red eyes, and I realize he's been crying. Through the whole war he only cried when he'd thought one of us had been killed—the bridge bombing, and the day the bomb hit our house.

"There is no more Maci problem," Dino says as my heart sinks. "Tata took her away again, this time to Šumatac."

Šumatac is Tata's home village. It is nearly a three-hour car ride away. Maci will never find her way back.

The tears start to flow, and I want to scream at someone, to hit someone. But it isn't Dino's fault, and it isn't really Mama's either. I know Tata was the one who made the decision.

He's the one I'm shouting at before he even parks the car in the garage. For all the neighbors to hear I scream, "How could you? How could you dare take my Maci away without talking to me? Would you drive me away if I became inconvenient? You welcomed her, you told me she needed us! Well, I need her too. Get back in the car, go get her."

I stand with my arms defiantly folded, glaring at him, not even noticing his pallor, the tremor in his hands.

"If you don't go, I will," I threaten, though I barely know how to drive. "How could you take her from me? How could you leave her all alone?"

"She's not alone," Tata says weakly, not rising to an argument with me. "I left her with Aunt Rahima. She's been through so much, I thought a creature as loving as Maci might comfort her. And Maci will have the other animals as companions too." A few years ago we brought Rahima a huge black-and-white rabbit that someone had given us, and it is still living happily on her farm. And as rabbits do, it multiplied into many rabbits currently hopping around her house.

Tata's words give me pause. Aunt Rahima has had so many losses in her family and among friends in the village. Two sons were killed in the war, and the beautiful, gentle Lejla has been missing for more than a year. She was in a village that was overrun by Serbs, and her body was never found. Someone who escaped reported that she was taken away with other women on a bus. I remember the list with my name on it, the fate the Serbs had planned for every Bosnian Muslim girl and woman. It might have been better if they'd found Lejla's body.

Is it selfish of me to want Maci back when she might be able to provide some solace for Rahima, who has lost so much? Rahima is a sweet and giving person who smiled all her life. She's beloved by all who know her. Usually she is the one providing quiet comfort to other people. In a way she reminds me of Maci. Maybe it is fitting that Maci is now her kitty.

Maci will be happy there, I think. Rahima will spoil her, giving her milk fresh from the cow, giving her tidbits of rabbit and chicken. Maci will love the other farm animals and the beautiful flowery hillsides around the house. With a new loving friend there, Maci won't have any desire to leave. Her love for us is strong, but once Rahima has her cozied in a basket beside the fireplace, Maci will be content. It's a better place for a cat than the city, I tell myself.

But I cry the whole night, and the next day I won't talk to Tata at all. I go to work, and decide to proceed with my plan. Once I get established in Sarajevo I can go get Maci.

I work grimly and stoically, waiting for word of the bus to Sarajevo. Finally one day Samir tells me that he heard from his cousin the bus driver—the bus will be running tomorrow. I quit my job that very day. Samir has to leave early, so it turns out that I'm the last one left in the office on my last day.

I straighten things up slowly, making sure all the files are neatly put away, adding supplies to the drawers. I'll miss this office, and I'll even miss the dangerous yet rewarding trips out to the newly liberated countryside with Samir and the doctor. This job has helped my family a lot, and it inspired me to my new career choice. But now it is time to move on.

As my hand is on the doorknob to leave, the huge satellite phone rings. It is one of the few such phones in Bihać, capable of receiving international calls. I don't feel like answering it, but it might be something about the doctor's family back in Colombia. I know his mother recently broke her hip. So though I'm now anxious to leave, I pick up the receiver and say, "Hello, IMC Bihać headquarters, Amra speaking. How may I help you?"

The voice on the other end is a bit garbled. "This is Davorka Sabljak from the World University Service. Did you say this is Amra? Perfect. We've been trying to reach you for six months! We want to let you know your scholarship to the United States has come through. You have to come here to get your visa, and then you can leave for the US right away. Hello? Hello?"

That's the last thing I hear from her before I hang up.

Because it has to be a prank. I got my hopes up about a scholarship once before, and the disappointment crushed me.

I stand frozen until the phone rings again. "Hello, Amra?"

"Who is this? It isn't very nice to joke with me like that."

The woman laughs but says, "I'm not joking, I promise! I have it right here, for Amra Šabić." She recites my address and my birthday. "Your application was submitted by . . . let's see, someone named Wayne through the Community of Bosnia organization, which wants to bring Bosnians to study in the US. It is all very official, and very wonderful for you. Congratulations. Amra, are you there?"

I don't know if I'm here! I feel numb, in too much shock to even be happy. Drew and Wayne hadn't forgotten me!

"Amra, listen to me—pick up a pencil and write all this down. I'm not sure if I'll be able to get through again, and you don't want to miss the deadline. You must go to the office of . . ."

In a trance I write it all down, but if someone put a gun to my head I couldn't tell them what she said a moment later. Somehow I mutter a "thank you" and walk like a zombie out the door, clutching my instructions in my hand.

At home I open the door in a fog to find Tata and Mama and Dino sitting around the table. "I got a scholarship to go to the United States of America," I blurt out, loudly enough for Mama to hear. And then I start weeping like a child.

They glance at each other. Then Mama jumps up, looking really worried. She hugs me, patting my hair. "It's okay, baby," she murmurs into my ear. Then she starts weeping too. "It's okay, the war is ending. You'll go to America someday, I just know you will." She strokes my hair the way I pat Maci when she's agitated by something.

"She's so upset from missing Maci that she's lost her mind," Mama says over her shoulder in what she thinks is a whisper.

"Mama, I'm not crazy," I say, disengaging myself. "Look!" I thrust out the paper, but my agitated scribbles are impossible for anyone but me to read.

Mama starts to cry. "We'll get you help, baby. Don't you worry about America, don't even think about college. The war has been too much for you. You can go somewhere quiet for a while. The mind is a very fragile thing, and . . ." She breaks down, crying loudly now.

I'm baffled.

"You think I'm crazy?" I ask them. "I'm really going to America."

"Yes," Tata says. "America, Malaysia, England . . . wherever you like."

Finally it is Dino who suggests calling Tata's friend in Zagreb and confirming the scholarship. A few phone calls later on the pay-per-minute satellite phone in the post office and it is verified.

I'm going to the United States.

"Can you bring Maci home now, please, Tata?" I beg of him. "I'll work while I'm in school in America. I'll send every penny I make to you, only please bring Maci back home! Maybe there's a way I can take her with me." I have no idea if animals can travel, but if any cat could fly, it would be well-behaved Maci. But even if this is impossible, at least I can return in the summers to see her. Maci belongs with my family. She's our luck, our benevolent spirit.

"We don't have any gasoline left," Tata says. "And besides . . ." He swallows hard and looks away. "I got a call from Aunt Rahima. Maci is gone."

She left the very same day that Tata dropped her off. Rahima said Maci didn't even have a sip of water. As soon as Rahima opened the back door Maci slipped out and ran down the hillside into the forest.

That was many days ago. The way home is much worse than from the bee farm. There are mountains and wolves, wild forests, fields seeded with deadly land mines. It is nearly fifty kilometers away. How can a gentle little kitty travel such a dangerous route?

My heart breaks as it never had before. Because I now know that I've lost my dear little friend. No cat could make that journey. There are packs of wild dogs. There are wide rivers to cross. A human would be hard-pressed to make the journey on foot.

What chance does an elegant, soft calico cat have?

I mourn her as Rahima mourns the loved ones she lost. I will never know for sure if Maci is dead, but logic tells me there is no other option. I should be celebrating my accomplishment, looking toward a bright future. The war is over, and I have a chance that is a dream come true.

But I am leaving everything I love behind.

I understand now how Tata felt compelled to give up Maci. We will do anything to save the ones we love, make any sacrifice, give up any precious thing held dear. Tata loves his family, and he made what must have been an impossible choice. He loved Maci too. He knows what she's done for us. I wouldn't be here if not for Maci. Neither would Dino. She saved our lives, and more than that she saved our minds, our souls. Whenever things were at their bleakest, she was the shining beacon that guided us.

And Tata gave her up, to save the rest of us, as a surgeon might have to cut off a limb to save the patient.

I don't know if I'd have had the strength to do what Tata did. I'm sorry that I hated him for a few days. As I get ready to leave my family behind so I can help them survive, I understand a little better the choice he had to make.

And now I have to say goodbye to Davor.

I call his house, knowing he's been released from military duties, but he's not home. I tell his parents my news and ask them to have Davor call me back. When he never calls, I visit the next day.

But he won't see me.

"He's unhappy, Amra dear, and can you blame him?" his mother tells me. "He loves you. He doesn't want to say goodbye."

"It won't be forever!" I promise.

"Oh, child, you can make all the promises you like, but the world doesn't work that way. You'll come back, but you'll be a different person. You'll have friends in America, boys you meet and like, and no matter how much you love him now, that love will fade."

"Never!" I say.

She hugs me. "It's not a crime to change. I know you love my son. I even thought that maybe, one day . . ." She wipes away a tear and smiles at me. "Your future is waiting, Amra. Go and catch it before it runs away!"

And so I say goodbye to Davor's parents, and to big slobbering Mrki, but not to the man I love.

I leave his house heartsick. I'm supposed to be happy to be going to America, but I am devastated by the lives broken by this war. I feel as much to blame as the war itself. I let Davor love me, and now I'm making him miserable. I think of Mama and Tata's broken life. If they didn't have me and Dino, maybe they would have easily escaped. Should have I escaped when my uncle offered at the start of the war? Would our lives have been better?

And Maci. If I'd never found her she might have found a different home, a better home. Someone who wouldn't drive her away . . .

Tomorrow I catch a bus to Zagreb to begin my new life. That night, I cry myself to sleep for all I have lost. The war is over, but everything still feels broken.

The next morning I wake up to Mama shrieking! Half awake, I think the Serbs are here, and my heart flutters as I steel myself for the coming horror. Then I remember: The war is over. We're safe.

I run downstairs to find Mama babbling.

"I opened the door . . . I almost fell . . . she was there! She's here! It's a miracle!"

She points to the corner where I see a dirty little lump of fur. My hands fly to my mouth as I gasp. She looks dead, so still, her chest not moving.

Then her golden, bonfire eyes open and look at me with undying love.

"Maci! Oh my Maci!"

I cover her exhausted, emaciated body with kisses.

Sleepy Tata comes out, followed by Dino, rubbing his eyes. When Tata sees Maci, he falls to his knees. My father, who once seemed invincible, looks like a broken man. All he believed in and tried to do, all his optimism and enthusiasm he had even during the worst moments in the war has evaporated.

"You can't send her away again, Tata," I say as I clutch her to me like I'll never let her go. "Please, Tata, you just can't. Not after she worked so hard to come back. Hasn't she proved her love for us? Don't we owe her our protection?"

Tata doesn't answer, but he looks at Maci like he's seeing a ghost.

In the brief time before I have to leave I feed her milk from a spoon. She's panting, her little sides heaving. She barely opens her eyes, but the whole time she rumbles her wonderful purr.

My Maci is home!

Oh, how my heart wrenches to leave her. "I'll come back again, Maci—I promise. Just like you did. I'm going far away, but I'll always come back to my family." I press my face into her fur, wetting her with my tears.

After she eats a little more, I sling Tata's duffel bag over my shoulder and then cradle her in my arms as my family walks with me to the bus.

"Remember, find Michael Jordan as soon as you can," Dino tells me as he hugs me. "Tell him to visit his biggest fan in Bosnia."

"Study hard," Mama tells me as she pushes my hair away from my face and looks at me like she's memorizing me. "Don't let yourself get distracted by boys and parties. But," she adds in a sly afterthought, "don't forget to have a little fun."

Tata just looks at me for a long time with tears streaming freely down his face. Again and again his mouth opens to say something, but each time he's overwhelmed with emotion. Finally he gasps out, "My baby girl!" and smothers me in a hug. It is one of our family's signature hugs, what other people call "no-breathing hugs." Under his breath he sings the little song we'd always croon to each other: "Đule rumeni volimo se mi!" *My red rose, how we love each other.*

327

I curl against my Tata, clinging to him, remembering how when I was a little girl he used to make me feel so safe. My big strong Tata! Now he's stooped and fragile, with failing eyesight. Yet somehow he still makes me feel safe. His body might be growing frail, but his love is more powerful than ever. It sustains me.

I pick up Maci for a last goodbye.

"You be good, Maci," I tell her, though she always is. "I hope you catch many fish in the Una while I'm gone. Take care of Dino for me. Cheer him up. And spend a lot of time with Mama. She needs someone who can listen to her without talking back. And oh, keep Tata safe, Maci! Make him strong and healthy again. I know you can do it. You can do anything, my magical cat. Oh, Maci, I never would have survived this war without you."

I rest my forehead against hers as the bus starts its engine. As soon as it warms up I'll be on my way. I'd have stayed like that, hugging Maci, until the end, except a voice behind me says, "Hi, Amra."

I whirl around, and there is Davor, his cheeks flushed with cold, his eyes bright with tears. I see their silver traces down his cheeks.

"I couldn't let you leave without saying goodbye." And then he's kissing me, with Maci between us, as the snow starts to swirl around us and the bus driver honks his horn. In that moment the rest of the world doesn't exist. There is only Davor and me, with the happy, purring Maci between us.

"Everyone on board!" the driver shouts, breaking the spell.

Davor takes Maci from my arms and folds her against his chest beneath his coat. I look at my family, my loved ones gathered around me. I think of those who are lost, those who are missing.

And I think of the love that holds us together, the love that endures though death and distance.

I'm so full of love that I give in to a sudden impulse. I have a little money saved to take to the US, about 1,000 US dollars. Without pausing to think I take it from my pocket, reserving only a single bill, and thrust it into Davor's hand. I feel guilty for leaving him, for having this wonderful opportunity. He needs all the help he can get to go back to veterinarian school. He needs the money more than I do. I'll get by on 100 US dollars somehow. I just need some money for food while waiting for my visa in Croatia, and I will figure out the rest once I make it to America. I love him so much at this moment I'm leaving him.

Just as I board, Davor hands me a card. He's painted a red rose on one side.

The other side I read as the bus pulls away. It is a sevdalinka, one of our emotional, tragic love songs.

> Here, this red rose
> from my humble quarters
> as the gift to you, my soul, I am sending it
> her name is my love.
> If you like its scent
> and its pure color
> you receive it with respect
> and decorate yourself.
> If you do not like it
> Throw it on the fire alive,
> let it burn, let it be created into ash . . .

My heart is dissolving. I'm torn in two. I know that staying would be the wrong decision. But leaving home is terrifyingly painful. How can I live when I'm broken in two pieces?

CHAPTER 33

The heavy snow that blankets the city and surrounding hills looks so clean, so innocent. You might almost think the war had never happened. But I know the snow hides bombed buildings and cratered roads. It covers mass graves. There is blood in the earth, beneath all that frozen beauty. You can hide the past, cover it up with snow or lies or years, but those who were there do not forget.

From my seat in the back I see narrow shoulders, wisps of gray hair from under dark head scarves. They are all in black, as if in mourning, as the older Croat women here dress. There are a few men, too, all middle aged or older. I allow myself a tiny sigh of relief. There's no one here whom soldiers of any side might take a special interest in.

No one except me, a teenage Muslim girl traveling alone across the border into Croatia.

I feel so alone. For the first time in my life I don't have my family around me. In front of these strangers there is no need to keep up a brave front. As soon as we pull away, I burst into uncontrollable tears.

But amid the sorrow is a spark of eager anticipation. As the bus rumbles on I eventually let myself think about the future, a thing I hardly dared to do over the last four years. As I stare out the window, I think of the United States I know from movies, from stories. A place so big, so rich that no tragedy can truly touch it. A safe place that has opened its arms to immigrants since its founding. It is a miracle that I'm going there.

But on the flip side of the coin are other things I've heard about the

United States. There is an ugly side too, I think: guns, drugs, racism. Are people really any different there?

On the other side of the rutted road I see an old man driving a horse-drawn cart full of firewood. The man is lean, the horse is gaunt, but they plod on. When they come to a muddy, slushy depression the man climbs down and leads his horse. I see him stroke the beast's neck, whisper words of encouragement into his ear as they struggle through the mud. Behind them, the laden fir trees droop under blankets of snow.

For a while we roll and judder along past the Croatian border without incident. At first, every bump, every backfiring car makes me tense up. But eventually the hypnotic gray-and-white scenery flashing by lulls me, and I settle back in the seat. Some of the old women strike up a friendship, comparing ailments. One opens up a newspaper-wrapped masnica—a pie of phyllo dough with a jar of plum jam on the side. But no one talks to me, and I'm glad of it. Eventually, I feel secure enough to take out a book and start reading.

And so I'm dwelling not on the past, not on the future, but on a fictional character's problems when the bus suddenly brakes and we pull over to the side of the road. I have to tear my mind away from the adventures in the novel, blinking hard to reconnect with reality.

My current reality is about as bad as it could be.

Militia members, men with guns, are blockading the road. I can't even tell who they are, probably Croatian soldiers who want to make sure no Serb war criminals are escaping. Even so, it's not looking good for the one Muslim girl on the bus. I hunker down in the seat and keep my eyes downcast, trying to make myself as small and unnoticeable as possible.

I hear the stomp of their boots, the rough, harsh voices as they go down the aisle. The small noises of protest the passengers make sound like squeaks, small and powerless. I sneak a peek over the seat in front of me. The men wear mismatched military clothes and balaclavas or fur hats, no two alike. Yet they all carry guns, and that in itself is a kind of uniform. I think as soon as a man picks up a gun he has to find himself an enemy.

They're demanding passports from each passenger. The first few pass whatever they are checking for. Then they get to one of the younger old women, a stout lady in her fifties with a defiant set to her mouth. The men growl something at her and then drag her off the bus. She doesn't seem surprised, but she resists on general principle. I see one of them cuff the back of her head, this woman who could be their mother. She seems to shrink under the blow.

They go down the line, barking interrogations at each passenger. When they get to another middle-aged woman she hands over her passport with resignation and stands almost before they can pull her away. I can see a resemblance between the two women. Sisters? They sat apart to avoid suspicion, but it did them no good. I sink lower in my seat.

I hear the men talking about lunch. One wants sausages. Another says only beef stew with noodles can satisfy on a winter day. We fear for our lives, and they think only of their stomachs.

Finally they get to me. The one who holds out his hand for my passport seems a little taken aback. Trying not to shake, I hand it over. They don't bother to tell me who they are or what they are looking for.

He opens the little book and stares at the photo. Stares at me. At the photo again.

"It was before the war," I say in a small voice.

With a snort he shows his comrade. The passport photo shows an innocent little girl with an impish, chubby-cheeked face and short, boyish hair.

Now, at twenty, I am six feet tall with wild, Amazonian red hair down to my waist. It hasn't been cut since the war began. And I am beyond skinny. I'm gaunt, bony, hollow-cheeked. I look like a strange Balinese puppet, all limbs and joints. And though I look like an adult I still feel in many ways a child. Four years of my childhood were excised from my life, leaving me with a strange mix of innocence and experience.

"Where do you think you're going?" asks the man holding my passport.

I gulp before I answer. I know what can happen here. Angry, hateful men, with unlimited power in their small sphere and no real laws to control them, do things to girls. It happened to my cousin. It happened to thousands of women and girls in my country. They could take me off this bus and do anything they wanted to me. Who could stop them? Who would even know what happened to me? I could disappear . . .

"A-America," I manage to say.

He looks surprised, and I wonder if that word, "America," might have some magic power that will protect me. "What would America want with you?"

"I have a scholarship, to study . . ."

He turns to his friend and repeats my words. For a moment they stare at me. Then they both break into belly laughs.

"Did you hear her? America! Crazy girl, you might not even make it to Zagreb alive. America is for rich and beautiful people. Look at you!" He slaps his thigh with the hand that doesn't hold his gun, and his face turns red. "America, she says. Look around you." He gestures to the bleak, desolate landscape. "Do you think anyone from here would make it to America? Do you think they would accept you, looking like that?"

I am frozen with fear, certain that I'll be pulled off the bus. But the man only spits out another incredulous "America!" and throws my

333

passport disdainfully on the floor before they stomp out, talking about lunch again.

I don't take another breath until the bus is in motion.

And I realize, as my heart continues to pound wildly in my chest and my body seems to burn with fever, that they let me go because they think I'm crazy. Too scrawny and outlandish looking to molest, too deluded to bother with. Who wants to deal with an insane girl babbling about her crazed visions of a future in America? Lunch seemed more important to them than interrogating or violating me.

Luck, I think. How many times has luck saved me? How many times has bad luck doomed other people?

I turn my head to look after the militia men. The two middle-aged women stand by the roadside, looking more sullen than scared as the men march off, abandoning them. Why did they take them in the first place? Fake passports? Why not just leave them alone? Nothing makes sense.

As we drive closer to Zagreb, to the free part of Croatia that was never occupied by Serbs, I realize that sometimes even people on different sides can think alike. Both the militia men and I think that studying in America is an impossible dream. The only difference is, I am willing to try the impossible.

———————

For a few days I stay with a family friend in Zagreb, getting my visa, buying a cheap winter coat. Then almost before I know it I'm on a plane for the first time in my life. As we rise I look down at the forests, bare and sleeping through the winter, and then at the Adriatic Sea below. It is lapis, the color of ancient mosaic tiles, and looks so vital after the cold grays of winter. We would go there, my family and I—aunts and cousins, my two brothers—and romp in the waves every holiday.

Then we are above Italy, far from everything I've known my whole life.

Then we are above the clouds, so high that the borders between countries, between almost-identical groups of humans seem arbitrary.

Somewhere over the Atlantic I fall asleep. When I wake, I look down to see a million winking lights. It is a country of stars! A moment later we descend for landing, and now it looks like the sky is on fire. So many lights, so much never-ending power coursing through the country! How can any land be so rich? With so much, surely there must be a little bit extra for me. For the first time I feel like maybe I can make my way in this new country.

We make a bumpy landing and taxi across the tarmac as a voice comes over the intercom. This staticky, garbled voice is nothing like the clipped, studied English phrases I learned in the classroom. Now people are dragging their carry-ons from overhead storage, bleary-eyed and weary. I follow them.

For just a second as I step off the plane I feel relieved. I feel safe and free. I can't believe I made it! After all that happened . . . what if I fail? My family is counting on me. Maci is counting on me.

Then the breath I am just exhaling in a relieved sign catches in my throat. There's a stocky, muscular woman in a uniform, with black military boots, her hair in a severe knot at the back of her neck. She's heading right toward me, being half pulled by a terrifying German shepherd, its sharp ears pointed forward, at me.

"Give me your passport and ticket," she says, while her terrifying dog sniffs my knees.

It was too good to be true. I knew I'd never make it.

"You have to return to the plane," the woman says.

I bow my head, fighting tears. They're sending me back to Bosnia . . .

"Go, hurry, before the plane leaves," she says with the stressed, tight smile of the overworked and underappreciated.

I'm several words behind in understanding her. My brain is still catching up when I ask, "What?"

"Your ticket is to Philadelphia. This is Boston. They're holding the plane for you." She hands me back my ticket and passport, and before I can stammer a word of thanks I'm running back to the plane. I barely notice the angry voices, the curses from people whose comfortable lives have been disrupted and delayed by a confused immigrant girl.

The confrontation ended well, but now I'm spooked. After the next short leg of the flight I exit with trepidation, certain that something will go wrong.

I'm sweating and shaking as I walk up to the customs desk. Something will go wrong. I'll be sent back to the war-torn land I came from, where more militia men will be waiting for me . . .

I hand over my passport and say in my hesitant English, "I am here on scholarship, to go to Chestnut Hill College."

The customs agent stares at my passport in heavy silence. What is he thinking? There is something wrong with my visa, with my passport. He sees the picture of the child and thinks it cannot be the gaunt young woman with the frightened, hollow eyes standing before him.

Without taking his eyes from the passport he reaches for a stamp and smashes it onto a page. I cannot read what it says, but I know it must say REJECTED or DEPORT.

Then he looks up with kind brown eyes and says, "I've never seen a Bosnian passport before." He slides it to me through the little gap at the bottom of the window. "I'm sorry for what's happened to your country. You're safe now, ma'am. Welcome to the United States of America."

I look at the official stamp. In a bright-red oval it says ADMITTED with today's date. January 17, 1996.

All I can do in response is sob. He has paralyzed me with his humanity. This, I think, is what America is. With his welcome, he reinstated my belief that there is good in the world.

With a heart that feels so light it might float away, if it weren't weighed down by so many memories, I head toward my new life.

EPILOGUE

Dear Dino,

I'm coming to visit again next summer! Can you imagine, two summers in a row? And no, I won't be bringing Michael Jordan with me. Have you heard anything about your own scholarship yet? Before you know it, you'll be able to meet him yourself. Who would have guessed that my little brother might get to the USA on a basketball scholarship! I'm keeping my fingers crossed for you every moment of every day. Which makes taking notes in class very hard—but I'll do it for you!

I enjoyed the job working with the Organization for Security and Cooperation in Europe, educating people on their right to return back to their homes now that the war is over. It was nice being based in Bihać, and to be able to make enough to leave with Mama and Tata before I went back to school. That way you can go off to school yourself without worrying about helping them with the store.

I set my pen down and gaze out the window of my dorm room at the huge magnolia trees that dot the campus. I remember before the war Mama and Tata saved to buy one tiny magnolia tree, and they nurtured it until it was strong enough to stand without stakes. The bomb that hit our house killed our magnolia. But here on the green, tree-filled grounds of Brown University I can be reminded of home whenever I see the dark glossy leaves and creamy white flowers.

After spending some time at Chestnut Hill College I transferred to Brown last year, with a summer at home between. This school is a perfect fit. Everyone around me seems to have such an intense intellectual curiosity. They don't live in an academic bubble either. The students and faculty alike seem to be global citizens, aware of problems outside their own sphere. Now at the beginning of my second year, I feel comfortable here.

I have an idea, Dino, and I'm going to need your help to make it happen. I want Mama and Tata to move to the US eventually. After I graduate, I want to get a good job, something in a big banking firm, I'm not sure yet, but something so we never have to worry again. I want to take care of all of you. I need you to start planting the idea in their heads. I know they're set in their ways and don't want to uproot their lives, but after living in America I think they will be so much happier here. I love Bosnia, but when I am there visiting every moment is full of such painful memories. Everywhere I look I think, oh, Uncle died there or that's where a friend got blown up. Surely they must feel the same way. Our home is like a wound that never quite heals. Maybe we should make a new home.

I think of the story I heard of an old friend, a beautiful young woman who was taken by the Serbs. For a long time her family thought she was dead. Then one day she was discovered among a group of refugees, ill and out of her mind after the torments she endured.

Her family never discovered exactly what happened to her. When she's on medication it is like none of it ever happened—blank, like nothing ever happened or will again. Her eyes are dead, but at least she's not screaming like she was when they first found her. When she goes off her medication she reenacts the horrors she experienced, taking the part of her tormenters and herself, changing voices, shouting profanities.

This is the beautiful, happy, innocent girl I used to collect flowers with.

The Serbs broke her.

I turn back to my letter, searching my brain for happy words to clear away painful memories.

> I miss you all so much. Is Zuhra's pastry shop still thriving? Will she make me a chocolate nut cake when I return? Start planting that hint too! I can't wait to see you all! Can we have a big reunion, and can I see Fatma and Ale, and all my friends? Tell them I'm coming home! Tell Nura and Samira and Asmira and . . .

Automatically, I want to add Davor to that list. Davor, my first love, my handsome, funny young man who made me believe in the future all through the war, who, along with Maci, brought the only true lightness and hope to my dark world. When I left, Davor was so heartbroken. I promised him that I'd be back, and for the first few months in the US I was still basking in the glow of his love. I was sure that one day we'd be together again. After all his tears and sentiment I was sure he loved me with a deep and eternal love.

Then one day, after I'd only been gone a few months, I called him in Sarajevo, where he'd gone back to school, using some of my money to help pay for his apartment. He couldn't talk long, he said.

That's okay, I told him—the call was costing two dollars a minute! I just wanted to tell him that I was thinking about him. Then he had to go abruptly, and I heard a click. But he must not have disconnected the phone, for a moment later I heard a woman's voice.

"Who is it?" the woman asked.

"No one, just a friend of my cousin."

Then I heard endearments that were impossible not to recognize.

I listened for a moment, my face burning, then very softly set the receiver down.

The pain of this encounter still aches.

I started dating the most American boy I could find—tall, blond, blue eyed, a sweet and simple young man. I liked him, but he didn't really understand my past. How could he, living his safe, coddled American life? Only someone deeper than him could really understand what it meant to live every day with the certainty of death, and worse. My boyfriend was a creature of sunshine who had never lived in darkness. And though I enjoyed being in the sun with him, there was always a distance between us because he couldn't truly see my shadows.

> Take care of yourself, little brother, and give everyone
> big kisses from me. Do you remember how . . .

I stop and scratch out the last four words, because I'm about to talk about Maci and I can't. I just can't. I make myself keep this whole letter light and happy. No mention of Maci, no questions about Tata's health, or my heart will break.

> I'll see you next summer!
> I love you, Dino, more than anyone in the world!
> Your seka Amra

I address an envelope and slip a twenty-dollar bill in between the pages, hoping this one will make it through. Some do, some don't, but I always send what I can. Then I seal the letter, planting a kiss on the pointed closure. We all write to each other regularly, and call when we can, though calls are so expensive. But it's not the same as being in the warm, glowing, loving presence of my family. I'm glad I'll be able to combine a summer visit with a good job.

Here's the thing I don't let myself think: Will Tata be there next summer? This past summer was blissful until the very end. Maybe there were signs I missed—I don't know. Maci was there, the inspector stayed away, Dino was excelling in his studies, and Mama and Tata were keeping our little store afloat. There were scars on our city, and on our memories and hearts, but I got together with friends and everything felt almost good again.

But, Tata didn't tell me that the inspector came back.

Mama didn't tell me that this was our last chance to save the store.

My flight back to the US, to my third semester at Brown, left at five a.m. on a Sunday. On Saturday, Tata said he was leaving to buy some eggs for the store from a farmer he knew outside of town. I kissed his cheek and went to see a friend before he left. When I came home for lunch he was still out. I didn't think anything of it until . . .

"Dino, where's Maci?" I asked. He didn't know. Neither did Mama.

Even then I didn't worry too much. Maci still liked to go on adventures in the tall grass by the river, hunting or basking in the sun.

When Tata drove home at nightfall he could hardly get out of the car. There was a new dent in the fender, and a headlight was shattered. And in the back seat all the eggs were smashed, dozens and dozens of them. When Tata stood up he was swaying and his speech was slurred. He sounded like he was drunk, almost.

"Tata, what happened?" I cried.

I couldn't understand what he was saying, but I heard the word *Maci*. The word *gone*.

He didn't want to go to the hospital, but we made him go. He was in bad shape. It wasn't until later that we got the story from him. He'd taken Maci past the Croatian border, almost a three-hour drive away. Not to a friend or relative's house this time, but to a village we always stopped in on the way to Zagreb. Every house has a flowerbox in the window, and it looks like a scene on a postcard. Tata thought it was such a pretty, prosperous place that someone would take in a sweet cat like Maci.

So he left her there, without a friend in the world.

Mama told me later what happened with the inspector. When he came, he yelled at Tata. Yelled at him! There were customers inside, and this little ignorant man came in and spoke to Tata like he was a peon. He fined Tata two thousand marks and said if Maci even crossed the doorstep one more time he would have Tata thrown in prison. For endangering human life through disease, he said. You'd think Maci was sitting on the sausages!

Tata didn't know what to do. Plenty of people would have taken Maci in—everyone loves her—but she'd always come back. A neighbor tried to make her an indoor cat when the inspector came another time, but she yowled nonstop and finally knocked out a windowpane to escape and come home to us. She came home from the bee farm, from Šumatac. Nothing would keep her away from us.

I knew Tata was heartbroken. I think that's why he crashed. He stopped at a farm on the way back and picked up a bunch of eggs, and later he ran off the road and into a tree. I think he must have been crying and couldn't see the road . . .

At the hospital, I badgered every doctor, every nurse, but I found no sympathy. No one would tell me that my Tata would get better. No one comforted me in my grief. When I tracked down the nurses' private room I collapsed on the ground in tears but one of them just walked me out. I thought she was going to tell me something, whisper words of comfort or even hard truth. But no, she just shut the door and left me alone in the hall.

I dried my tears and went back to Tata's room.

He was sitting stiffly on the edge of the bed. "Don't you want to lie down?" I asked him.

"No, I'm comfortable like this," he said in his slurred voice. I didn't realize until later that he didn't have complete control over one side of his body, and he didn't want me to see how hard it was for him to move. He was trying to look alert and healthy.

So I would leave him.

"I'm perfectly fine," he insisted. "I don't need to be here taking up space. I only agreed to come to keep your mother happy. Of course you're still leaving tomorrow. Don't be ridiculous! There's nothing wrong with me a good night's sleep won't fix. You women are a bunch of worriers!" He looked from me to Mama and back, and I tried not to stare at the way one side of his face was drooping.

When I told him again that I couldn't get on the plane, he got very stern. "You're going for all of us, Amra. It would be selfish to stay."

I hugged him and kissed him like it was the last time.

We didn't talk about Maci. How could I blame him when he's in a hospital half paralyzed, so powerless? But later, after midnight when Dino and Mama and I were home for an hour or two of sleep before I left, Mama touched my cheek and said, "He could have waited until you left but he didn't want to lie or sneak. He wanted to look you in the eye and tell you he did what had to be done. Your father saved our family. He did the impossible thing that needed to be done. Now you will do the same thing by leaving."

I closed my eyes but said nothing. My heart was too full. Love for Tata. Worry for Tata. And resentment for sending Maci away.

Understanding something doesn't make it hurt any less.

My heart was so heavy I'm surprised the plane could take off.

Now, some time later, Tata is home and getting better. At least, that's what Mama and Dino have been telling me. I'm still so scared for him. But—and I can't help this—I'm still furious at him for taking Maci away. She's alone, scared, maybe dead. She's family. You don't do that to family.

I walk to the basement mail room of a building at the Main Green, drop my letter in the general mailbox, then check my own mail. To my delight there's a letter from Dino.

I take it outside and sit under a tree to read it. Around me, students are playing Frisbee, or walking in groups of two or three, laughing, or else talking earnestly with their heads bent. I love the way frivolity and serious academics exist so easily side by side here.

I see one of my favorite people, a man I hardly know but who fills me with joy whenever I see him. He's a tall man with locs who has such an open smile. He greets everyone he sees as if they were his best friend. And he likes to entertain himself by walking in interesting ways. Sometimes he'll hop, sometimes he'll dance, without any self-consciousness. He makes me realize that I can do pretty much anything in America. He reminds me that I don't have to be afraid.

Still smiling after greeting him, I open Dino's letter.

Dear Seka,

Is fall there as beautiful as fall here? It is still warm, and the bees on Tetka Fatma's farm are going crazy, flying from flower to flower like they can't make up their minds. They're like you on your ninth birthday, remember? When you had Zuhra's cake, but then Fatma brought a cake too, and one of the cousins brought cookies, and a neighbor brought almond pastries. You were running from table to table, not knowing which sweet to eat first, and in the end you were crying because you couldn't eat them all at once! It was the first time I'd ever seen my big sister out of control, and it gave me hope that maybe you weren't perfect after all. Do you know how hard it is having a perfect big sister? Then I remember Amar made you a plate with a little of everything on it, and you calmed down. I think about Amar so much now. I didn't during the war. I think with everything so hard for us I was almost grateful he didn't have to be there to suffer too. But now that things are a little better I keep wishing he were here.

I felt the same way about my older brother. The war deadened the missing a bit. Now every time I learn something new in school, I think about how much Amar would have liked being in an American university. His mind was so open and expansive, even when his body failed him. If he were alive today, maybe American doctors could have helped him.

I wipe away a tear and turn Dino's letter over.

I saved this for the second page, Seka, because I wanted you to think of something nice first to soften the blow.

I close my eyes quickly, tightly, feeling a sickening flutter in my belly. That old feeling from the war comes back, where I was braced for the most terrible things. I have to force myself to open my eyes and read on.

Tata isn't doing well. I think he had another small stroke but he won't go to the hospital this time. He's been talking a lot about people we lost during the war . . . and about Maci. The other day he pulled a piece of unraveling yarn from his sweater and I heard him call her. Maci's gone, I had to remind him. Then he started to cry. I took her away, he said. She was our luck and I took her away. Amra, I know there's no way you can come home soon, but he's getting worse every day. He won't admit it, and Mama helps him hide it, but . . .

Oh, Seka, I'm scared for him!

I'm crying now, wrenching sobs that blur my sight and make the ink on Dino's letter swirl. I shove the letter away, crumpling it into the grass. I don't want to read any more. Since the moment I left in August, I've been dreaming of the day when we can all be together again, locked in one fierce and never-ending hug. Tata, Mama, Dino, me . . . and I even have hope that Maci might still come home again. We're a family, and I thank whatever powers exist in the universe that we were all spared, that we came through the war not unscathed but at least alive.

Everything I've done has been for them, for my family, for that moment when we can be together and whole again. Together for the summer in eight or nine months, but beyond that, when I have a good job, together forever. Always in that image are Dino, Tata, and Mama, with Maci on my lap, purring her delightful rumble, looking at me with her serene and loving bonfire eyes. I know she's gone, but she's still part of my dreams of happiness.

Now Tata is dangerously ill, and my world, which I had so carefully pieced back together after the war, shatters again.

Maybe Tata will get better. Maybe Maci will find her way back even after a few weeks had passed. I tell myself that, and try to believe it.

But I don't really believe either one is possible. Tata aged so terribly during the war, with diabetes and starvation, stress and fear and loss. Now with two strokes I know there's not much hope. And I know Maci will never come back to us. Nearly fifty kilometers was a miracle. The Croatian village must be close to a hundred, across rough, winding roads, through areas that are still mined, devoid of people who might help her. She's a miracle cat, but she's still just a cat. A small, soft, mortal cat.

And why would she want to come back? Even her love and loyalty must have evaporated by now. Her trust in us is broken.

She's found another home, another family.

Or—and I see this as clearly as if it is happening before my eyes—Maci gave in to despair. She sat down in that bread loaf shape of hers with her paws tucked in and never ate, never drank, never moved. She gave up. She let herself die.

It's what I would do if my family abandoned me.

I pick up Dino's letter again and read the rest through tear-blurred eyes.

> I know it's impossible, I know it would ruin the store, but I wish Maci would come home one more time. I feel like if she did, she'd give Tata the will to live. Every night I start to pray for her return, but then I stop myself. If she comes home, the shop will be closed, and she'll just be sent away again, or worse. Amra, I miss her so much! Especially now. We need her luck. Do you remember when she saved my life? I would have been blown up if not for her. And all those years when I thought I'd die every day, when life didn't seem worth living, I would have died if not for Maci, I just know it. She kept us safe, and she kept us sane. And now, with Maci gone, we've lost our luck. Tata needs luck right now.

I love you, Seka, and I'm so proud of you. Tata talks
about you all the time. I only hope the summer comes soon.
I love you most in the entire world!
Your buraz Dino

Around me, the campus is as beautiful as ever. The trees are red
and gold, and already leaves are blowing in the crisp wind, crunching
underfoot. The students are fresh from break, excited to learn, their
faces fresh and full of eagerness for life.

But for me the world is desolate and dark.

I should be used to this by now—the sorrow, the certainty of loss.
Every Bosnian has lived with it. Members of my extended family have
suffered horribly. And my own core, my parents and brother, have been
hurt and sick and tormented. But we got through it together. We
stayed together.

I'd let my guard down. I thought we were safe.

I thought the war was over.

But the war has claimed two more victims: first my Maci, now my
Tata. The arbitrary cruelty of humankind and the stupidity of states
has won again, and I'm faced with more loss.

I have a paper due tomorrow, and some tough equations to solve. I
have to read a chapter about post–World War I Europe. But I know
I can't do any of that. What does it matter? I'd finally let myself
believe that education could keep the people I love safe, that bettering
myself was the key to a good future. Now I think I was wrong. I feel
the crushing darkness of depression settle over me as I walk heavily
upstairs to my dorm room.

For a long time I lie on my bed, staring blankly at the ceiling.
A nonstop flow of tears falls from each corner of my eyes, wetting my
pillow, but they are silent tears. I feel like they will flow forever.

Finally, I reach for the phone by my bedside. Only local calls are free, but I have a phone card with a few dollars left on it. I press the numbers to home, misdialing twice before I hear it ring.

As it rings, I think about what I'm going to say. Depression, like a stone on my chest, makes me want to say drastic things. I'm quitting school, I want to say. I'll come home to take care of you. Why did you send Maci away? Why do I have to lose her and you both? I feel like I can't forgive him for both sending her away, and now trying to leave me himself.

But when I hear Tata's voice say hello from the other side of the world, everything melts away except for pure love.

"Tata, it's me—Amra!" I say.

"My darling girl!" he answers, and his voice is incandescent. Does he slur his words? I don't even know, I'm just so happy to hear his voice.

And I know, with absolute certainty, that he's not going to talk about his health, or about Maci. He'd be mad at Dino if he knew he wrote to me about his illness. Tata wants to protect me.

I think of my father as he was before the war, movie-star handsome, Cary Grant or Henry Fonda, with his impeccable suits and pomaded silver hair. Then I remember the last time I saw him, bent with suffering and illness until he was the same height as I am. His wrists were like bird bones, and his skin looked like bruised crepe paper.

I decide then and there that I must swallow my pain. I'll protect him by letting him protect me. I'll pretend I don't know about his illness. I'll pretend I don't miss Maci.

"Why are you calling, my darling? Is everything okay?"

"Of course, Tata, I just wanted to hear your voice."

"You should be saving your money," he cautions. "These international calls are expensive."

"Oh, books cost less than usual this term, and I hardly have any expenses. We can talk for a little while. How are you doing, Tata?"

"I can't complain," he says. "I was a little achy, but I'm feeling much better now. In fact I'm in top shape! Did I tell you we've started the community garden up again? If the weather holds I might go and plant some late cabbages tomorrow. Which reminds me, are they feeding you well there? You looked so skinny when you were here this summer."

I can't help smiling. I must weigh twenty pounds more than I did at the end of the war. After years of the blockade, we were all nearly starving. I had to learn how to eat right, how to think about nutrients, instead of simply getting enough food. What I don't tell Tata is that my scholarship meal plan only allows for ten meals a week. So I have to plan things very carefully, eating a wide variety of foods at seven dinners a week, and calculating how best to divide the other three meals. There's so much bounty here that I manage, with the help of bananas and oranges we're allowed to take from the dining hall, and the occasional dinner date with my boyfriend.

"They're feeding me enough, Tata. Blame my genes if I don't get fat, not the school dining hall. How is the shop doing?"

He's silent for a moment, then says brightly, "Oh, very well! We got some excellent cheeses in last week."

"And Mama, is she still teaching?" Of course I know the answer. She taught when she lost her hearing. She taught when they couldn't even pay her. Teaching is a love and a duty.

"Yes, and she brought one of the children home last night, just like she used to. I think he got more of the new cheese than any of the customers did, the cute little guy. Your Mama says he's a natural storyteller, if only he'll stay in school long enough to learn how to write."

There's a whole generation of Bosnian children with brighter futures because of Mama.

Somehow, I keep my voice from shaking. It's the hardest thing I've ever had to do, keeping Tata from knowing that I know how sick he is. Harder than walking back over the Blue Bridge after it was bombed. Harder than crossing the mined field to try to buy food from Serb soldiers. I want to seek explanations or comfort. I want to cry, to yell, to be reassured that he'll get better.

But that is what a child would do. Instead, I keep my hurt in my heart, and I spare my father from more pain. I let him think that I am happy, because it is what he wants most in the world. I spare him the way that he always tried to spare me from the worst.

Somehow, my parents kept me alive through the war, and thanks to them I have at this exact moment fully become an adult.

I tell him about the interview I just did for a job with an investment bank. They seem interested in hiring me next summer or after I graduate. Banking isn't what I'd first set out to do, but it is a reliable job, a way to take care of my family. Then I tell him about the paper I'm writing on international trade.

"Tata, are you crying?" I gasp.

"No, no. These aren't real tears. Just the emotions of an old tata who is so very proud of his little girl. Oh how I love you, my sweet Amra. Can you ever forgive me?"

"For what?" I ask with a catch in my throat.

"For . . . for not being a better father to you."

"Oh, Tata, you are the best father! There's no one better. Everything I am today is because of you. Tata, I love you so much. I can't wait to see you next summer. It's not too far away. I wish you were here with me now, sitting beside me, helping me with my homework."

I hear him sniff. "Here we are, saying such silly things at such expense. You better go before this phone call costs as much as your scholarship. You go, sweetheart. And always remember that I'm so proud of y—"

Then the money on the phone card runs out, and I hear nothing but a dial tone.

As soon as he can't hear me I break down. The sobs shake me until my sides ache, until I think I'll never be able to breathe again. My lungs seem to lock up before I can finally draw in a ragged, hiccupping breath.

But at last there comes a calm, settling on my chest with a tangible presence. A familiar weight. The same weight of the soft furry being who would come and comfort me when things were at their darkest, when I would lie on my mattress on the floor of our bombed-out home and feel so dead inside that I never wanted to get up again.

"Maci?" I whisper, opening my burning eyes.

There are no bonfire eyes staring back at me. I know Maci is gone.

But I feel her. I feel her love for me, her gentle support, her encouragement, the loving softness that reminded me there is always some good in the world.

Maci is proof that some love never dies. It withstands distance and time. It even conquers death.

Davor's love didn't last through the slightest trial of time. But now I know that the love of Mama, Tata, Dino, Tetka Fatma, and some of my other relatives is a different kind of love. Amar, too, though he died so many years ago. Just like Maci's—eternal. It will be with me all my life. Even if the ones I love are gone.

I blink slowly, as Maci would blink at me, with that look of absolute trust.

Then with a sigh I rise from bed and go to my desk. I have homework to finish. I have a future to plan for.

All my life, in the darkest moments I will sometimes feel a brush of the softest fur against my leg. And in the times of greatest joy, years from now, when I hold my newborn daughters in my arms, I will think I hear a low, rumbling purr. And I will know my protective kitty spirit is with me always.

ACKNOWLEDGMENTS

The Cat I Never Named has been in me for years. I would share stories about Maci with Dinah and Jannah, my two daughters, as I would put them to bed. They knew what genocide was early on because those stories are my life. They are now young women whose dedication to social justice was born out of the kinds of stories I tell in this book. Still, many elements of the emotional complexity of my experience came to life only during the writing process.

At first, I didn't know where this deep excavation and return to my war life, day after day, would take me. I feared falling into the darkest whirlpools that I resided in during the war. Could I, at will, pull myself out of them? The longer I was there, the more broken I felt, and the harder the reconstruction was. I often struggled to find the light to return. While writing, I would play sevdalinke, Bosnian music, and transport myself deeply into the scenes, to relive them; to fully visualize every movement; to feel every emotion and smell every scent. Sometimes tears rolled down my face as stories came to life. But, after each story was written down, I felt heard in ways I never could have been during the war. My hands were no longer tied. My mouth was no longer taped. Each page memorialized my voice. I no longer needed any acknowledgment from Serbia or Bosnian Serbs for what they did to me, for the crimes and killings they had committed against my family, friends, and my country. The more I wrote, the more I shed the painful layers, and the more skilled I became in rebuilding my broken self into one.

The Cat I Never Named demanded this emotional journey by me, but I could have taken it only with love in my life. To overcome hatred and trauma, love is a prerequisite.

In 2017, Dinah, my younger daughter, asked me: "Mom, what will happen to children like me if Muslims are rounded up in America?

Will I be left alone without you? And Mom, what will happen to all children whose parents are immigrants like you?" On another day, Jannah, my older daughter, came home from school and shared that one of her closest friends at that time advised Jannah during school lunch to never marry a Muslim because Muslims are terrorists. She responded: "My dad is the greatest dad ever. He is not a terrorist. My mom, too, has never done anything to anyone but has suffered all her life for simply being a Muslim." These moments changed my children, making them acutely aware of the stereotypes now attached to them, too. After what I had survived, I had hoped this would never happen to my daughters, but it did, and it still does. These kinds of biases about other-ed people, Muslims or not, percolate through ordinary American conversations every day. These labels do not reflect who we are, the labeled and stereotyped. But they do reflect the harmful narratives told about Muslims as an other-ed group. This hurts. It hurts my children. It hurts me, but it also hurts the future of America as a diverse nation.

At the time, I was already working on a different book manuscript about Islam, but as an educator, a mom, and a genocide survivor, I realized I was abdicating my responsibilities by not sharing my own story and lending it to educators around the world to aid in dismantling stereotypes. My love for Jannah and Dinah gave me the courage to begin writing *The Cat I Never Named*. Throughout the process, Dinah in particular played a critical role. She has read every chapter, published and unpublished, along with each revision, and she never settled on changes I had made until each chapter delivered the same emotional effect she felt when I would tell her my war stories. Dinah's exceptional intellectual maturity and depth have produced invaluable feedback that has made this book what it is today.

The Cat I Never Named became a reality late one night in 2018, when I sent several Maci stories I had written to my longtime friend and now book agent, Rob McQuilkin. Rob loved them and responded by sending me a contract, which is when our work began. As a professor at Columbia University's Teachers College and an international expert in education, I wanted to ensure my story transcended the moment and would remain a powerful lesson for generations to come. I wanted it to sensitize young adults to those who are other-ed and discriminated against. I wanted to bring the world together by changing youths' mind-sets. Thanks to Madeleine Morel and Jason Anthony, I was introduced to Laura Sullivan, who has published extensively for young adult audiences. After we spoke for the first time, I felt as if we could have been the best of friends had we grown up together. Laura and I have not yet met in person, but she is another soul whose love and support I have felt throughout this process. She understood and connected to my stories, and she has helped me formulate an authentic literary voice. Many tears have traveled virtually into her in-box, and Laura has sent equally as many virtual hugs, which have helped me maneuver the deepest and darkest of the war whirlpools with ease and strength. I am deeply grateful for the gift of Laura.

While a number of publishers had expressed their interest in sharing this book with the world, Susan Dobinick, a senior editor at Bloomsbury, was the first to recognize the educational power of Maci and my story. We started our collaboration in December 2018, and Susan is the masterful editor who has helped produce *The Cat I Never Named*. Susan has shown respect for my voice as the author. Her warm welcome into the Bloomsbury family has empowered me to share some of the more painful experiences in my book. Production editor Diane Aronson, copyeditor Jill Amack, and proofreader Regina Castillo ensured the details of the text were just right. Bloomsbury's amazing Beth Eller, Jasmine Miranda, Faye Bi, and Erica Barmash have worked hard, from speaking to teachers and librarians to creating marketing content, to ensure my story reaches the widest audience possible.

With the design guidance of Jeanette Levy and Donna Mark and the visual creativity of illustrator Shazleen Khan, my dream for the book's jacket, largely influenced by Jannah and Dinah's input, came to life. The blown-up mosque was inspired by a one destroyed in the village of Ahmići during a massacre against Bosniaks, Bosnian Muslims, on April 16, 1993. The goal was to counter a prevalent narrative that nearly two billion Muslims are a monolithic group of people. Instead, the book's jacket presents my authentic self, a liberal Muslim teen, yet a Muslim who was still so profoundly hated. The jacket illustration serves as a reminder that the hate is a product of its perpetrators rather a reflection of its victims. To those who spent years trying to kill me, it never mattered who I was. What mattered was how they saw me. There is nothing that victims can do to ameliorate that hate except to educate by telling our stories in hope of evoking collective empathy among those open to hearing our stories. The jacket also demonstrates a dichotomy between the love Maci and I felt for each other and destruction around us that the hatred produced.

After my first meeting at Bloomsbury, I remember traveling back home in a New York City yellow cab, thinking about those I had loved and some whom I had lost. They all would come to life in *The Cat I Never Named*. While I was growing up, Tata was a charismatic, handsome, and eloquent storyteller. I would watch him garner respect from our friends and family, who regularly gathered in our happy home. Mama, similarly, always adorned with her bright red hair and colorful jewelry, told stories that would take us to different historical periods or countries. She made us feel that we were there, as if we visited those places in person. Now it was my turn to tell their stories: Maci's story, our story, all in hope that our suffering, which we never once anticipated before the war, would become a global lesson on hate.

My tata is no longer here, but he taught me to be intellectually curious and gifted me with the ability to understand even those who hate me. Thanks to him, I was able to write this story and thanks to him, I now study different forms of radicalization around the globe and work on educating young people to help thwart their radicalization. Tata taught me to accept those seeking refuge, like we accepted Maci, when he didn't know that one day I would end up seeking the same kind of refuge in America. As I was thinking about writing these acknowledgments, I had a dream about Tata and Maci. We were back in the war, yet I was happy to feel their love and hugs one more time before bringing the book to a close.

I am immensely grateful to still have my mama and my brother, Dino, with me. They are the treasured remnants of our once-happy family. Dino still lives in Bosnia, but we talk every day. My mom lives with my family and tells her stories about other places and countries to my daughters, whose lives have been deeply enriched by having their articulate and stoic grandmother close by. For me, Dino and Mama have been a source of continued love and strength during the entire writing process, as have been Jannah, Dinah, and my husband, Tamer. Tamer in particular has lived with my stories for many years now, always showing his love, understanding, and desire to protect me from the pain I felt during the war. In the early years of our life together, I would regularly wake up in the middle of the night scared by a vivid war nightmare, and Tamer was always there to catch me before I fell. He is the love of my life, and he, Jannah, and Dinah have healed me. With their love, laughter, and our happiness, I was able to set all my nightmares free. I wouldn't have been me nor would my story be what it is without their collective love and support for all I do in life.

While Alzheimer's disease has taken Tetka Fatma away from me, her kindness, love, and elegance have helped enrich my life and *The Cat I Never Named*, as did Tetak Ale, who still resides in their home in Bihać.

I write this only days ahead of July 11, 2020, the twenty-fifth commemoration of the Srebrenica Genocide. Like Bihać, Srebrenica was proclaimed a UN safe area, but those proclamations, as you now know, were meaningless. The UN failed to protect Srebrenica's Muslims once Serbs (from Bosnia and Serbia) marched into the city. Serbs executed thousands of Bosnian Muslims.

The fear that Bihać would be next was what changed my fate. With the Herculean efforts of those Bosnians who were defending us at the front lines (and perhaps along with a few of my office markers), our freedom was finally possible. They broke the Serb siege around Bihać, and we were free. So, I want to acknowledge and thank the unsung heroes in *The Cat I Never Named*, those who died and those who risked their lives to save mine and who kept Bosnia alive. No lecture I ever taught and no story I ever told would have been possible without their sacrifices. For those heroes who did not survive, as we say in Bosnian, "Rahmet njihovim dušama" or "Mercy upon their souls." I remain grateful to them and to all those who brought love, laughter, and life to my days during the Bosnian war.

BOSNIA AND HERZEGOVINA TODAY

The Dayton Peace Agreement ended the war in late 1995, and Bosnia and Herzegovina (Bosnia for short) was split into two ethnic units: Federation of Bosnia and Herzegovina (where mostly Bosniaks and Croats live today) and Republika Srpska (Serb Republic, where Serbs live). Serbs who left my hometown at the onset of the war never came back. They sold their homes in Bihać, and many of them now live in Serb Republic. Muslims who escaped the ethnic cleansing by Serbs during the war either left Bosnia or have moved into the Federation entity.

For example, in Srebrenica, where Muhamed (the young soldier my parents tried to save when he escaped from Yugoslav National Army) lived, Serbs committed genocide against Bosniaks, killing about 8,000 boys and men and persecuting 25,000 to 30,000 women. Srebrenica is now in the Serb Republic, so the majority of people living in that town are Serbs even though the majority of its residents prior to the war were Bosniaks. I do not know if Muhamed survived.

Today, Bosnia is dealing with young people leaving due to difficult economic circumstances, corrupt education, and continued ethnic tensions. A top Serb leader, Milorad Dodik, is trying to escalate ethnic tensions to break up Bosnia. The US government has asked that he stop blocking progress in Bosnia. Because of people like Dodik, I worry about the future of peace in Bosnia. But Bosnia's problems don't stop there. Today, Bosnia is home to many migrants escaping wars and persecutions in other parts of the world. Bihać, in particular, because of its proximity to more prosperous countries in Europe, has thousands of refugee and migrant families living in the city's outskirts.

Despite its troubles, Bosnia remains a beautiful country, and tourism has been growing as one of its more important sectors.

ABOUT THE WRITING OF THIS BOOK

The Cat I Never Named is a true tale of my life during the war. In this book, I wanted to tell *my* story, but I also wanted to tell *a* story. So in a few places I've changed events just a little bit to make the book more readable. Some things I compressed, for example taking details of several different bombings and using them all in one scene. Other things I combined to make the emotion more immediately understandable, such as my first meeting with Maci. Those events in the city happened to me, and I met Maci shortly afterward when my father found her, lost and alone, with the refugees, but I put the two events together to show the power of Maci's comfort and love in the worst times.

I didn't keep a perfect diary during the war and even the one I had was lost, so sometimes timelines blur in my mind. Today, I can't always remember if one person was killed before or after another person, or what month it was when I ate cow udder. So the exact order of events might be a little different than how they actually happened.

Sava, the Russian teacher, taught me when I was younger, before the war began, but her actions and attitudes so perfectly exemplified the treatment of Muslim students that I included anecdotes from her class.

Some names remain unchanged. Some I changed, though, either to protect those I love, or, as with the character called Ilma, when I believe but cannot absolutely prove that they committed a crime. Only a few characters are composites, such as the criminal brothers Bakir and Irfan, who are inspired by several young men of that type.

Maci, the cat I never named, was the most incredible and intelligent cat, one who found her way home multiple times. She was all I say she was and more, but not all stories and moments with Maci or other characters could fit into one book. I hope to tell the rest of their remarkable stories one day.

A NOTE FROM THE AUTHOR

There are so many parallels between my experience of surviving the war in Bosnia and what many are going through right now, in the United States and all over the world.

I write this as COVID-19 overtakes the world, and what we are experiencing now reminds me of many moments I describe in this book. For instance, how difficult it was to be isolated in a neighbor's basement or in my home at the onset of the war . . . or how much I missed being with my friends or how sad I was that my schooling was interrupted. Schools are not only about learning. They are also rare physical spaces where young people still come together and need to learn how to engage in real time, with real people and with complex issues. During the war, we all risked our lives to gain an education and to see our peers because both kept us in a routine, engaged and happy to the extent we could be. When we all protected our friend Dani, we built a stronger sense of community, which helped us get through the worst times in war.

I hope that my story shows you how important education, teachers, and schools are. Maci saved my life. Education gave me a new life.

I also wrote this book to illustrate how deeply damaging hatred is. Hatred is the most powerful emotion, more powerful than love. Love compels us to do selfless things, like Maci traveling for miles to get back to me. But hate can make people commit horrific violence, such as Serbs raping my relative in a rape camp. Only hate is that powerful, and I see hate on the rise in the United States and around the world. I hope my story compels you to act and end hate, in whatever ways you can.

The prevalent stereotype of a Muslim as a terrorist is something I face almost every day. Islamophobia is another reason that motivated me to share my experience. I was a good student and a nice kid, but even I stereotyped Maci at first because of my uncle Ejub's dog, who attacked me when I was little. I simply hated everything with claws.

But then Maci came into my life and changed it for better. She taught me to open my mind and heart to making connections with others.

I am a mom, a good friend, a complete nerd, an academic, a researcher, a proud Bosnian American, a teacher, and a woman who learned from her Tetka Fatma to love food, fashion, lipstick, and hair dyes with a gusto! We can be many different things, and this is what makes us diverse and interesting. If you ever felt out of place or excluded for being different like I did for being six feet tall in fifth grade or for being a Muslim, then I want you to find yourself in my story. Those idiosyncrasies are what make you special and why you should feel proud. As I said to my parents when they urged me to leave Bosnia at the onset of the war: I want to be Amra Šabić, no one else, even if pretending to be someone else can at times seem easier.

Attacks on immigrants, on racial or religious groups, on people of different sexual orientations are happening all over the world and particularly in the United States. In recent weeks, we have witnessed widespread protests in support of the Black Lives Matter movement and in reaction to the merciless killings of Black people in our country. These protests have spread around the world and symbolize a broad rejection of racism and related violence, irrespective of their manifest form.

When violence against certain groups becomes normalized, stories like mine happen. It became normal for Serb soldiers to try to kill me every day. Doesn't that sound horrific? A teen being a target every day for who she is? No child, no teen, no adult should ever live under such threat, here or there or anywhere.

Over the last several years, the Me Too movement brought the issue of sexual violence against women to the forefront. In Bosnia, rape was a tool of war. That moment when I came close to being raped by the drunken Serb soldier while my mother and I tried to buy food for our family is the ultimate example of how life's circumstances can put young women in vulnerable positions. Would I ever willingly subject myself to that kind of risk? Under ordinary circumstances, no young woman would, but I wanted to help my family survive.

Many young women today find themselves in professional settings where they face choices of losing their livelihoods or allowing sexual harassment and abuse to go unchecked. I hope that sharing my story brings to light how harmful such experiences are, which is why it often takes victims decades to share them.

As you can imagine, writing this book has been very emotional, but I am grateful to have survived and to share my experiences with you.

RESOURCES

FOR FURTHER READING

Professor Amra Sabic-El-Rayess's research on Bosnia: https://www
.sabicelrayess.org/

Innovative Lessons on Bosnia: https://cmes.arizona.edu/innovative
-lessons-bosnia

Srebrenica Web Genocide Museum: http://www.srebrenica360.com/
Remembering Srebrenica Genocide: https://www.srebrenica.org.uk/

Educational Resources from Remembering Srebrenica: https://global
dimension.org.uk/resource/remembering-srebrenica-primary/

Educate Against Hate: https://educateagainsthate.com/resources
/remembering-srebrenica-pshe-resources/

United Nations International Criminal Tribunal for the former
Yugoslavia: https://www.icty.org/

United States Holocaust Memorial Museum's Bosnia and Herzegovina
Case Study: https://www.ushmm.org/genocide-prevention
/countries/bosnia-herzegovina/case-study/background/1992-1995

World Without Genocide—Bosnia Case Study: http://worldwithout
genocide.org/wp-content/uploads/2012/06/Bosnia-case-study
-materials-SI-EL-2012.pdf

Permanent Exhibition "Srebrenica": https://galerija110795.ba
/exhibitions/permanent-exhibition-srebrenica/

International Coalition of Sites of Conscience: https://www.sitesof
conscience.org/en/membership/srebrenica-potocari-memorial
-center-cemetery-bosnia-i-herzegovina/

Human Rights Watch World Report 1996: Bosnia and Herzegovina
https://www.refworld.org/docid/3ae6a8ad18.html

MOVIES ABOUT THE BOSNIAN WAR

No Man's Land (Oscar winner in 2002)
https://www.imdb.com/title/tt0283509/?ref_=kw_li_tt
In the Land of Blood and Honey (addresses sexual violence against
 women)
https://www.imdb.com/title/tt1714209/?ref_=kw_li_tt
The Whistleblower (addresses human trafficking and sexual violence
 against women)
https://www.imdb.com/title/tt0896872/
As if I Am Not There (addresses sexual violence against women)
https://www.imdb.com/title/tt1456477/plotsummary?ref_=kw_pl
Esma's Secret (original title: *Grbavica*)
https://www.imdb.com/title/tt0464029/?ref_=kw_li_tt
Scream for Me Sarajevo (documentary)
https://www.imdb.com/title/tt6481232/plotsummary?ref_=tt_ov_pl
In the Name of the Son (short film): https://www.imdb.com/title/tt09
 99895/?ref_=kw_li_tt
Srebrenica: A Cry from the Grave (documentary)
https://www.imdb.com/title/tt0225448/?ref_=kw_li_tt
Bosnia 1992: Omarska Camp (documentary)
https://www.imdb.com/title/tt8499302/?ref_=kw_li_tt
The Bosnian-Herzegovinian Film Festival
https://www.bhffnyc.org/?gclid=Cj0KCQjwx7zzBRCcARIsABPRsc
 MtIgWVE0wFy6WYY6p4RfLs7v4aw3F0Ezj_HSXuZlS5rM5
 Y9PToRRQaApx7EALw_wcB